FIRST EDITION

*The Collectors Encyclopedia of*

# WELLER POTTERY

by
SHARON AND BOB HUXFORD

Collector Books
P.O. Box 3009
Paducah, Kentucky   42001

# To All
# Who Cherish The Beauty
# of Weller Pottery ...

# and
# to Betty, with Love

*The artist may catch an idea of form from a flower, leaf or cluster, and turning to his clay express in a vase all the rhythm of line and beauty of form which he saw there...and when he has blended form and color, and endowed them with his own individuality, he has added materially to the world's happiness.*

—*William Day Gates*

*Book Design by Joyce Cherry*

The current values in this book should be used only as a guide. They are not intended to set prices, which vary from one section of the country to another. Auction prices as well as dealer prices vary greatly and are affected by condition as well as demand. Neither the Author nor the Publisher assumes responsibility for any losses that might be incurred as a result of consulting this guide.

Additional copies of this book may be ordered from:

Collector Books
P.O. Box 3009
Paducah, Kentucky 42002-3009
or
Mr. and Mrs. Bob Huxford
1202 7th Street
Covington, IN 47932

@ $29.95. Add $2.00 for postage and handling.

Printed by IMAGE GRAPHICS, INC., Paducah, Kentucky

# ACKNOWLEDGMENTS

We respectfully acknowledge the early research done in this field by such pioneers as Norris Schneider, Lucile Henzke, and Ralph and Terry Kovel. We only claim to add to their foundation with bits of new material it has been our delight to unearth. Much to the chagrin of researchers, very few records of these old potteries remain in existence . . . fires that were a plague to the industry destroyed them periodically. Original Weller material is practically nonexistent, except for a few privately owned catalogues and those on deposit with the Ohio Historical Society in Columbus. The Weller Company advertised very little in the journals of the trade until the 1920's and 30's, and then the occasional ad we found rarely named a specific product. And so a completely accurate account of the years of Weller's productivity may never be fully realized. But it has been our goal to report with open minds all authentic information available—from our own studies of original material, trade journals, histories, city directories, published works, interviews with former Weller employees and their families; and from that supplied by so many people whose personal interest in Weller Pottery spurred them into their own search for knowledge.

To thank everyone properly who have helped us with our book would require a second volume—we've been overwhelmed by the generosity, support and encouragement of many fine people. Not only do we wish to acknowledge the more tangible contributions of pottery, original photographs and material, but also the invaluable personal aid given in the form of time spent for research, inconveniences graciously endured, long distance phone calls to Indiana, fine meals—and above all, the spirit of friendship in which it was offered. From the bottom of our hearts, we thank you all:

Alice and Lewis Bettinger, Susan and Lewis Bettinger, Jr., Kathy and Robert Bettinger—for loaning us a large amount of pottery, gracious hospitality, and for sharing the benefit of their experience and general knowledge of art pottery . . .

Si Lambert; Connie and Mike Nickel; Faydell and Sam Schott; Rose and Ervin Sowards; Maxine Ferguson, Wayside Antiques, Zanesville, Ohio; Tenna and Larry Seyler; Thelma and Ed Newman; Debbie and Bill Reese; Carol and Jr. Kinnen; Bill Clark; Eva and Ray Thomas; Bunny Walker; Mark Finlaw; Juanita and Glenn Wilkins; Elaine and Wes Hart; Virginia and John Pearson; Keith Knight, General Store, Zanesville, Ohio; Richard Lyles Antiques, Ardmore, California; Madeline and William Beck; John Ketcham; Donna and Max Hazzard; Mary and Mark Mulder; Roz and Jeff Abrams; Francis Hall; Alice and William Truszkowski; and Harold Nickel—for contributing fine examples of quality art pottery . . . in many instances driving a long distance to bring it to be photographed . . .

Mr. and Mrs. Merrill B. Weller, Roland B. Weller; Robert J. Weller and Carol and Roger Weller—for loaning pottery and providing genealogical information . . .

Dorothy England Laughead, Mr. and Mrs. Charles Staley, and Ethel and William Curphey—for contributing personal knowledge of the industry . . .

Lucile Henzke—for graciously sharing with us her own research . . . and our daughter, Marka, for helping us with ours . . .

Arlene Peterson, Reference Librarian; and the entire staff of the Ohio Historical Society Archives—for the courteous assistance they've provided many times . . .

Ted Wright—for his expert photography and help "beyond the call of duty" . . .

and last, but certainly not least, Betty Blair, Catalba Antiques, Zanesville, Ohio, our right hand "person"—a special "Thanks" for pottery loaned, hospitality, numerous and lengthy long distance calls, "leg-work," and for being our very special friend.

## About The Authors

*As pottery editors and authors for Collector Books, the Huxfords have written several books on the Zanesville art potteries:* The Collectors Encyclopedias of Roseville; McCoy; *and* Brush McCoy; The Collectors Catalogues of Early Roseville; Brush-McCoy *and on the popular dinnerware lines of* Homer Laughlin China The Collectors Encyclopedia of Fiesta, *now in its third edition.*

# TABLE OF CONTENTS

# INTRODUCTION

Early in the nineteenth century, such men as Samuel Sullivan, Solomon Purdy, Joseph Rosier and Burley were producing stoneware and redware in quantities sufficient to fill the needs of both the local settlers of Muskingum County and those pressing westward. Rich veins of clay that often erupted through the topsoil of their fields coupled with a market that grew with the population turned farmers into potters during winter months. In crude sheds with the most primitive tools they turned and fired their wares. From this nucleus grew an industry that by 1840 consisted of 99 potteries in the state of Ohio, employing 199 men with Muskingum County accounting for 22 of these potteries and 66 workers.

These farmers-turned-potters not only stocked the local merchants, but produced enough stoneware to export huge shipments by flatboat to New Orleans. By 1880 the output of these Ohio potteries had increased to the extent of completely squelching their competitors in the South and East.

But with all this productivity, it was only during the last quadrant of the 19th century that men began to recognize the truly superior quality of the Ohio clays. Testing revealed them to be among the purest in the entire country. Karl Langenbeck made this statement concerning the local clays:

"Few of the busy men of Zanesville realize that right in the heart of this city is a huge monument covered with inscriptions. These describe with great accuracy where there lies buried an immense treasure sufficient to support for long years thousands in luxury and millions of toilers in comfort and well being."

This monument, which is known to all men who can read its inscriptions and which has advertised Zanesville among such men from the Atlantic to the Pacific is Putnam Hill. While from its summit many busy manufactories can be seen that work clays, the existence of which it tells, they produce but a small fraction of the kinds of products that the world today makes of just such clays as Putnam Hill shows are about us." (From Zanesville and Muskingum Co. History)

As men become more aware of its potential for wealth, the clay industry began to boom on a larger scale. Those with savings began to pour their money into some phase of the trade. Those with none nevertheless invested from their earnings all they could possibly spare.

In 1872, in a small settlement seven miles southwest of Zanesville, Ohio, one such perspicacious young man embarked on a career with such sagacity and tenacity of purpose, that he became the monarch of a manufactory that by 1906 was reported to be "the largest pottery in the world." That man would become a legend in the industry. His name: Sam Weller.

# THE WELLER POTTERY COMPANY
## ITS INCEPTION, GROWTH AND DECLINE

Throughout the rural districts around Zanesville, Ohio, it was common practice after their crops were laid by for farmers of the mid-19th century to turn to working the clay they found in abundance in their fields. They made stone canning jars, depending on the local fruit crop for a market; and the helpless, disparaging groups who gathered to watch the devastating effects of the killer frosts on the blooming fruit trees were made up of both fruit growers and potters.[1]* In small sheds constructed of unhewn logs, equipped with only the most basic tools of the trade they turned out jugs, crocks and other domestic wares as was needed for use on their farms. From fire clay dug in the hills of the area they produced sewer tile which they fired in simple outside ovens.

One of these early craftsmen was Samuel A. Weller. For several seasons he had been content to produce this common ware. But as he became more adept at his task, he began to display the ingenuity that would become his stock in trade. Utilizing sections of common sewer tile, he designed a milk pan for which he found a ready market.[2] Fortified with this initial success, Sam Weller established his own pottery in Fultonham, near Zanesville, in 1872.

*Weller's original pottery, from a drawing by Sumner Fauley*

His "factory" consisted of a small log cabin and one kiln. A necessary and familiar fixture of these early potteries—and Weller's was no exception—was the old white horse who pulled wagon loads of the crude red clay to the shop, propelled the grinding machine that broke and processed the clay and then hauled the finished product—and the potter—to town.

As his friends were to fondly recall in later years, both Sam's horse and wagon were equally dilapidated . . . but Sam and his assistant Sumner Fauley would hitch the old horse up to the wagon and head for the city. At the edge of town, Sam would leave his unpretentious conveyance with Fauley, directing him to wait at the livery stable until he returned. Then—ever mindful that a prosperous image was conducive to a prosperous business—he would assume a suave, confident bearing, board a streetcar and make his entrance into Zanesville. Although this arrangement became a matter of routine, it was never discussed between them.[2]

Weller was not only an able potter, but a born salesman. He turned out flower pots, crocks, cuspidors and vases for which he recruited a growing number of buyers. Weller's small pottery prospered to the extent that the original building and equipment were no longer efficient. By 1882, the business moved to Zanesville to a small frame pottery located along the river at the foot of Pierce Street.[3, 4, 5] (An article from the Zanesville and Muskingum Co. History, "Local, Potters Stood at the Wheel as Early as the Year 1808," states that this location was used as a storeroom only, manufacture in Zanesville did not begin until 1888, however other sources indicate that the pottery was in operation.) In addition to his established product, he began to experiment with a more decorative ware. Weller was a man with vision, and his dream was to produce an artistic, refined type of pottery.

*Numbers indicate source of information. *See* Bibliography

# PUTNAM PLANT # 1 IS ERECTED

In 1888, Weller acquired a wareroom on South 2nd Street conveniently situated along the Cincinnati and Muskingum Railway. By 1890 the demand for his product necessitated further expansion. Weller purchased a tract of ground along the same railway in the Putnam section of the city, between Pierce Street and Cemetery Drive, and there erected a pottery that was large for its time, employing 68 men.[3] With the construction of this plant, both the factory on the river and the South 2nd Street wareroom were abandoned.

In these improved facilities he began to experiment with glazes, intent upon developing a more finished product. He soon added ornamental flower baskets, umbrella stands and jardinieres to his line. The public response was instantly favorable. Business expanded at such a rate that by 1892 Weller found it necessary to build an addition, followed by a second in 1894.[4] The combined area of these additions was 300 x 90 feet, erected at a cost of $30,000. One hundred seventy-five potters were employed.[8] In these well equipped, modern facilities, progress toward the higher forms of art pottery was swiftly and efficiently accomplished.

At the Rookwood Pottery of Cincinnati, Ohio, in 1884, Laura A. Fry introduced a revolutionary process involving the use of an airbrush to apply background glazes. Her method allowed a controlled, even application, and a subtle degree of shading not before possible. In 1886, she applied for and was granted a patent, #399,029, issued March 5, 1889. Rookwood's Standard glaze was perfected through the use of this method, and soon became the pace setter in the race for artistic achievement. Fry left Rookwood and from 1891 until mid-1892 held the position of Professor of Industrial Art at Purdue University, La Fayette, Indiana. In 1892, she joined the Lonhuda Pottery of Steubenville, Ohio.[6]

# THE LONHUDA POTTERY OF STEUBENVILLE

William A. Long was born July 18, 1884, in Harrison County, Ohio. After serving a term of enlistment during the war, he became a druggist in Steubenville. In 1875, he attended the Philadelphia Exposition, where he viewed the pottery exhibit with growing fascination.[7] In addition to his knowledge of chemistry, Long was an accomplished artist in oils. He began to experiment with ceramics and glazes in a back room of his drugstore. After years of long and dedicated study, he achieved his goal in 1889, when he at last succeeded in producing a successful piece of brown glaze slip decorated ware, worthy of competing with Rookwood's "Standard."

Along with his partners, W.H. Hunter, editor of the *Steubenville Daily Gazette*, and Alfred Day, secretary of the United States Potters Association, he continued his experiments determined to perfect both clay and glaze. Finally, by 1892, all was in readiness for production on a regular, continuing basis. The firm became known as the Lonhuda Pottery Company, a name coined from the first two letters of the last name of each partner: Lon-Hu-Da.

Laura Fry joined the firm in 1892. With her, she brought a license for Long to use her blending process. Other Lonhuda decorators were Sarah McLaughlin, Helen Harper and Jessie Spaulding. Painting with thin, colored slip (liquid clay) they used the dark blended backgrounds as an artist does his canvas—executing a variety of nature studies, florals, animals and portraits . . . often signing their finished work with their initials. Their monograms were listed by Edwin AtLee Barber in *Marks of American Potters*, published in 1904.

Miss Laura A. Fry.

Mr. W.A. Long.

Miss Sarah R. McLaughlin.

Miss Jessie R. Spaulding.

Miss Helen M. Harper. **HMH**

Three types of marks were used on the Steubenville Lonhuda ware. The first was a linear composite of the letters LPCO with the name "Lonhuda" impressed above it.

The second, adopted in 1893, was a die stamp representing the solid profile of an Indian (used on ware patterned after pottery made by the American Indians). This mark was later replaced with an impressed outline of the Indian head, with "Lonhuda" arched above it.[7]

At the Chicago Exposition in 1893, Weller saw an exhibition of both the Lonhuda ware and the Fry process of decorating. He immediately recognized the commercial potential of this highly developed artware, and at once began negotiations with Long to move his organization to Weller's new Zanesville factory. Lacking any real sales organization, the Lonhuda Company—although able to successfully develop their product—had failed to show much profit.[6]

# WELLER AND LONG BECAME PARTNERS

By the following year, Weller had convinced Long to accept him into the firm, and early in 1895, the Lonhuda Faience Company was moved to Zanesville. The Fry process was used at Weller in the continued production of Lonhuda.* The mark adopted for use in Zanesville was an impressed shield containing the monogram L F and the name "Lonhuda" above it.

On the morning of May 10, 1895, only three months after the first Lonhuda was produced, "fire consumed one of the new buildings in Putnam. The gold kiln had overheated, igniting the timbers above it. The night watchman noticed a small fire while on his midnight round, but in the short time it took for the firemen to respond, the whole south end went up in flames. In spite of the gallant efforts of the firemen, the flames kept ahead of the water and continued to make way for the south end where the office, Lonhuda department, and power plant were located. Bystanders broke in and rescued valuable books and papers, even carrying a large safe outside. By two o'clock many walls were down, but the paint and oil rooms were finally saved by desperate work and a solid brick fire wall."[8]

Weller, exhibiting his determination and drive, rebuilt immediately on an even larger scale. The new building covered 300,000 square feet, was equipped with 23 kilns and employed 500–600 people.[19] By October of the same year, production of the Lonhuda ware had resumed.

During this time, Sam and his brother William Weller formed a partnership . . . Sam was to be in charge of production and marketing; William would mine the coal to fire the kilns and cut the timber needed for packing cartons and construction. But William was soon convinced there was more money to be made in mining independently, and the brothers terminated the merger—with the stipulation that William's sons, Harry** and Frank, would have lifetime jobs in their uncle's pottery. Until 1922, when stocks were finally sold, the Weller Pottery remained a sole proprietorship.[9]

Just less than a year after Long went to Zanesville, his partnership with Weller came to a bitter halt. Whatever the reason—personality conflict . . . financial disagreements . . . or as some feel, Long may have simply outgrown his usefulness to Weller—he left to work for a short time at the J.B. Owens Pottery, also in Zanesville. Leaving Owens in 1900, he organized The Denver China and Pottery Company, in Denver, Colorado. From 1905 to 1908 he was employed at the Clifton, New Jersey Pottery. But by 1909, he had returned to Zanesville, and badly needing work, made peace with Weller where he remained for some time. He is listed in the 1912 Zanesville Directory as being employed by the Roseville Pottery, and by 1914 he was associated with the American Encaustic Tiling Company. Long died on October 14, 1918.[7]

---

*In 1893 Fry had filed a suit against Rookwood, charging patent infringement, and would later bring the same charges against J. B. Owens and Sam Weller. In 1897, Judge William Howard Taft of the Circuit Court of the Southern District of Ohio, ruled strongly in favor of the defendants. [10]

**Leaving his uncle's employment from 1908 to 1909, Harry A. Weller operated his own pottery in the old Neilson plant in Zanesville, producing jardinieres, umbrella stands, fern dishes, and cuspidors, as well as a line of artware none of which has been found marked. [6]

# ART LINES INTRODUCED

Weller continued to produce Lonhuda under the name Louwelsa (L-o-u, from the first three letters of his daughter's name, Louise; W-e-l, from his last name; and S.A., his initials). Louwelsa sold in 500 different shapes until after 1924,[12] and in addition to the typical brown glaze was also made in blue. Very rarely, a piece is found in a matt glaze marked with the Louwelsa seal, and a hand incised "Matt." Early attempts at these matt glazes were often unsuccessful, and the ware came from the kilns plagued with fissures and holes in the surface.

*Sam Weller with daughter Louise*

Long was replaced as art director by Charles Babcock Upjohn, who retained that position from 1885 to 1904. Upjohn studied art in France, and Italy, and upon returning to America served as an apprentice under the master Viennese sculptor, Karl Bitter. His grandfather, Richard Upjohn, was the architect who had designed the Trinity Church in New York where Bitter was engaged in sculpting a door frame in bronze. Because of his relationship to the architect, Upjohn was used as a model for one of the figures in Bitter's bas-relief.[9]

The first line attributed to Upjohn's tenure was Dickens Ware. It was described in a letter written years later by the company: "decorated with painting on the clay, executed in broad touches, but withal, very effective."[12] In the late 1800's Dulton of England had very successfully produced and marketed, both in England and in America, a line of figurines and accessory items portraying characters from Charles Dickens stories. Sam Weller, perhaps as much impressed with Dulton's sales volume as he was amused that his name was also the name of a Dickens character (Pickwick Papers), declared that he must reciprocate and name a line for Dickens.[11]

Other fine prestige lines developed during this period were Turada—designed by Weller himself—featuring applied bands of openwork, unbelievably delicate, on solid dark or blended backgrounds; Aurelian and Corleone — both similar to Louwelsa but with brushed on streaking rather than sprayed, solid backgrounds; and Samantha—an example of which has yet to be found.[6] (According to Paul Evans in *Art Pottery of the United States* pg. 32, Samantha had a solid brushed background; the line disappeared after the Fry litigation was resolved.)

Auroral may also have been produced during the time this case was pending, since it, too, has a brushed on background, of splotchy, yet delicate strokes. Soft pinks and blues over white were popular, although pale greens and yellows may also be found. While usually decorated with simple floral studies, one fine example in the color plates is decorated with goldfish by artist Hattie Mitchell. Any example is very rare; Auroro and Auroso are alternate spellings.

Eocean was introduced in 1898. In contrast to the dark browns of Louwelsa, soft shades of gray, ivory and pink were used as backgrounds for high quality artwork executed under the glaze in muted colors. Examples characterized by a deeper rose-shading toward the base of the ware are sometimes marked "Eocean Rose." Eocean was produced as late as 1918, although toward the end of its production the artwork had evolved from the delicate and refined to a heavier, more vivid style of decoration. (See catalogue reprints)

In 1900, Upjohn created the line that would bring him his greatest recognition as an artist and craftsman —"2nd Line" Dickens Ware. Although a few pieces of high gloss 2nd Line have been found, the line is characteristically soft matt, with tan or golden caramel melting into peacock blue or turquoise the most common colors. Other combinations were also used; examples of these may be seen in the color plates. A variety of subjects were used: animals, golfers, monks, and Indians to name but a few; but among the most popular were scenes taken from Dickens novels. An appropriate quotation from the novel being featured was incised on the reverse side. The method of decoration was sgraffito, an ancient process discovered in the catacombs of Rome. Upjohn drew the original patterns, which were cut out and the inner lines perforated. The paper patterns were dipped in water, so that they adhered to the surface being decorated. The perforated lines were traced with black ink and the background color sprayed on before the paper was removed. The figures were filled in with colored slip, and the clay allowed to cure to a "leather-like" hardness. Using a thin cutting instrument much like a needle with a small loop on the end, the design was "engraved" by removing a tiny strip of the surface, and exposing the clay beneath.[13] The procedure was slow and great care had to be exercised to avoid making an error in the carving.

Upjohn left the Weller Pottery for a short time late in 1901 to work at the Cambridge Art Pottery in Cambridge, Ohio, as its designer and modeler. But by 1902 he had returned to his position at Weller. When he left again in 1904, it was to establish his own pottery, in Zanesville, Ohio. But the ill fated C.B. Upjohn Pottery ran into financial problems, and by June of 1905 had been sold. Upjohn relocated in Trenton, New Jersey, where he was associated with the Trent Tile Company, until 1916 when he left to accept the post as art instructor at Teachers College, Columbia University. He remained at the university until 1940.[6]

*A. Radford modeling at the Weller Pottery*

With the art pottery movement gaining momentum, many great craftsmen migrated into the area. They did their work carefully and with great pride, and consequently their product was art— unique beauty of the highest caliber. Weller made every effort to recruit the most talented, renowned artists available. Albert Radford, master potter, modeled at the Weller plant from 1898 until he went to the Zanesville Art Pottery about 1900.[14] Many authorities feel that the line marked simply "Weller Matt Ware" may have been created by Radford.

While fine artware gained recognition for the company, commercial lines were the most profitable. Shortly after the turn of the century, Weller acquired his second plant—the property formerly belonging to the American Encaustic Tiling Company on Marietta Street.[3,4,15] The building was remodeled and equipped to Weller's specifications. An addition was built to Plant #1 in Putnam; the artware stock and sales rooms were relocated on the second floor, the art department occupied the third, and the main floor was used for office buildings. H.A. Weller, son of Sam's brother William, was placed in charge of manufacturing at Plant #2. Utility ware—crocks, cookingware and bean pots—were produced at Plant #2; artware continued to be made at the Putnam Plant #1.

## SICARDO LINE CREATED

Perhaps the most colorful figure in the Weller saga was Jacques Sicard—a Frenchman who had studied ceramics at the studio of Clement Massier of Golfe Juan, France. He came to the United States accompanied by his assistant Henri Gellie, and began his association with Weller in 1901, where he continued to experiment with the metallic lustre glazes as he had in France. The line he developed for Weller was called Sicardo.[16] The following is an excerpt from an article by a contemporary writer, May Elizabeth Cook, published in *The Sketch Book*, May, 1906.

"M. Sicard, after coming to the Weller Pottery, experimented in the metallic lusters for two years, aided in every way by Mr. Weller, until he achieved the beautiful luster known as Sicardo. The forms which he uses are those thrown on the potter's wheel, and this method, or modeling by hand, gives a character and purity of line to a vase thus made, which can never be obtained by the commercial method of moulding.

The metallic lusters require, not only the fine color sense of the artist, but the skill and knowledge of the chemist; these gifts M. Sicard happily possesses. Accustomed to the use of peat or dead brushwood to fire the kilns in France, M. Sicard could with difficulty be persuaded to use the natural gas in the kilns in which the luster ware was to be fired. In his first experiments, he insisted on firing the kilns with the wild growths found along the roadsides around Zanesville. Was it not a pretty thought that the wild blossoms, having caught all the glow and richness of the summer, in rainbow tints, should through sacrificial fires transfer their glory to the molded clay? The large showroom devoted to the Sicardo ware would indicate most satisfactory results from the complicated experiments requiring such care in decoration and firing. Beautiful forms with exquisite tones of flame, rose, blue, green, bronze, purple and crimson, melting into one another like colors in an opal, or in the great arch of the rainbow, are most harmonious and restful. To obtain this beautiful luster, the vases are first treated all over with a metallic preparation, and then decorated in conventional designs, in long flowing lines and curves, with chemically prepared pigments. This glaze is fired at a very high temperature, resulting in a texture and lustrous, changing color much like the Tiffany glass."

Sicard and Gellie kept the processes of the manufacture of their luster ware a closely guarded secret, perhaps fearing that once Weller learned their methods, they—like Long—would be dismissed. Working together behind locked doors, they spoke only in a French-Swiss dialect not likely to be understood by an eavesdropper.[11] Each morning they checked the walls to make sure no "peep holes" had been drilled during the night. Their air of secrecy only heightened the aura of mystery that continues even now to intrigue.

Sicard's metallic luster ware resulted in accelerated, wide-spread acclaim for the Weller Pottery, and some of the finer pieces sold through exclusive stores—Tiffany's and Wanamaker's in particular—for $300 and upwards. But because there was no way to properly control the firing process, much of the finished ware was imperfect; only 30% was considered marketable.

The steps in the making of the luster ware were these: first the piece was biscuit fired and covered with a clear copper glaze. Then Sicard would place the item to be decorated on a platform which he could turn with one hand, while brushing on the design with the other.[18] Metallic pigments such as gold or silver salts when fired in a reducing atmosphere (that is, lacking in oxygen) would produce reds and rose shades, while copper oxides with oxygen would produce blues and greens. The oxygen was reduced by burning common sawdust in the kiln; but because the results were impossible to predict, the kiln was always in danger of exploding. To diminish damage, a special type of kiln was designed with a top section that would separate under extreme pressure.

Although Roseville succeeded in making a comparable line which they called Mara, most companies were reluctant to face the problems and expenses of manufacturing such a line. Even though with modern techniques the "secret" methods of Sicard could be easily duplicated, his own artistic flair and expertise will remain forever inimitable.[9]

Sicardo ware was nearly always signed. Often the name Sicard or Sicardo Weller was an integral part of the design and can be found on the face of the ware near the bottom. Occasionally you may find the name simply scratched into the clay.

Sicard and Gellie left Weller in 1907. Both soon returned to France. Sicard operated a small pottery in Amiens until the German occupation; finally returning to Golfe Juan, he continued with the work he loved. Gellie served in the Battle of Verdun in WWI. He was wounded and recovered only to die of pneumonia shortly after the war was over.[7]

Weller estimated that the cost of the materials that were used to make Sicardo, plus the two Frenchmen's salaries amounted to about $50,000. He was left with a huge amount of overstock which it is said he regarded as an asset, due to the fact that prices on the ware only continued to increase.

## THE WELLER THEATRE

Sam Weller had an interest in many business ventures other than his pottery. Almost weekly, Sam and Bill Adams, a local contractor, enjoyed a game of checkers or billiards. During the course of one of these games they discussed the erection of a fine theatre for Zanesville. Construction began immediately, and progress reports became a casual yet confidential part of each week's meeting. The theatre Adams completed in 1903 became one of the most renowned in the country. Performers looked forward to appearing there; the acoustics were excellent. George M. Cohan sent contractors to Zanesville to measure the stage in the hopes of learning the secret of the construction.[9]

The following is an excerpt from the Zanesville and Muskingum County History:

"When S.A. Weller, manufacturer of art pottery, decided to build in Zanesville a new theatre worthy of the city —one larger and more costly even than the Schultz—he chose a site on North Third Street, West side, between Main Street and Fountain Alley, which had been occupied by the residence of Z. Clements. The Architects were Harry C. Meyer of Zanesville and Frederick Elliott of Columbus, and the contractors were Adams Bros. and C.O. Vinsel of Zanesville. Hugo Herbt (sic) of the decorative department of the Weller Pottery, designed and executed the building's interior stucco work and he produced the auditorium's mural decorations.

John Rettig of Cincinnati painted the drop curtain, taking an ancient triumphal procession as his subject, and producing a strong, bold and highly dramatic scene. As construction progressed, the public manifested deep interest in the enterprise and opening days were looked forward to with corresponding zest and curiosity. The initial event was set for Monday, April 27, 1903, with "When Johnny Comes Marching Home" as the attraction. The sale of seats took place at Schultz's Opera House, beginning at 7:30 A.M. on Thursday, April 23. As early as the evening of Tuesday, the 21st, twenty-one boys established themselves in Fountain Alley at the rear of the Schultz, to await Thursday morning's opening sale.

They worked in pairs for purposes of periodical relief and held their positions until ticket sale time came, when they could purchase the six tickets allotted to each. Although rain fell during all of Wednesday, these and other "early birds" to the total number of 200 were in line on Thursday morning at 7 o'clock. The sale went on until 5 in the evening and was resumed on Friday.

When ticket holders entered the auditorium they found it all that had been promised in beauty and proportions. They looked upon a theatre altogether modern in architecture and appliances, and when the curtain rose they saw a stage 42 by 70 with a height of 69 feet from floor to gridiron. All of the 1,700 first, second and third floor seats were occupied on opening night, as were those in the six boxes."

Weller pottery decorated the theatre. For many years several large Sicardo vases graced the lobby; even the box offices were adorned with beautiful examples of Dickensware. Small ceramic mementos of the opening were given to theatre goers by the thousands. Some of these trinkets survived, and are today prized highly by collectors. The Zanesville City Directories list a long succession of theatre managers. The Weller Theatre closed in 1958.

# RHEAD'S TENURE WITH WELLER

Fredrick Hurten Rhead came from a long line of English Stoke-on-Trent potters and must without doubt be considered one of the most productive artisans in the history of the industry. After leaving his home in Staffordshire, England, in 1902, he worked at the Vance/Avon Faience Company, in Tiltonville, Ohio, for a short term of about six months before going to the Weller Pottery in mid-1903.

During his brief but prolific tenure with Weller (mid-1903–04) Rhead created several new prestige lines, perhaps the most famous of which was the Jap Birdimal line. Reminiscent of a line he developed at Vance/Avon, Jap Birdimal was decorated with various types of original designs executed in colored slip, with the outlines emphasized by fine ribbons of heavy slip forced through the tiny nozzle of a squeeze bag. The motif varied from the more commonly used Geisha girl, landscapes, and a stylized peacock feather design, to include even fish, birds, and a type of stylized tree effect that Rhead favored throughout his career. Although collectors sometimes refer to the Geisha girl pieces as "Oriental" and the more unusual patterns mentioned above as "Birdimal-type" the 1905 catalogue shows them all under the Jap Birdimal line name.

A similar line, possibly Rhead's initial work after arriving at Weller, can be found only rarely. It is marked Rhead, Weller Faience.

Rhead's L'Art Nouveau was first produced in a rich brown high gloss glaze, and then in a matt pastel green typically accented with soft pink. The idea for this high relief Art Nouveau style of decoration was also carried over from his Vance/Avon association.[6]

While 2nd Dickens Ware was always a highly esteemed art line, Weller realized the need for one less time consuming and therefore less expensive to produce. He assigned the task to Rhead. Without altering the popular theme, Rhead designed 3rd Line Dickens Ware, which was actually a variation of Eocean. The characters from Cruikshank's illustrations, rather than executed by the slow painstaking sgraffito technique, were simply molded into the ware, and painted with colored slip over pale background colors. Often a black disk on the reverse identified the particular Dickens novel featured on the front; occasionally a similar disk with Dickens in profile was also added.[13] Although it seems unlikely, of the last two Dickens Ware variations, 3rd Line is much the rarer.

Rhead left Weller in 1904 to accept a position with the Roseville Pottery where he remained as art director until 1908. From there he went to the William Jervis Pottery on Long Island.[6] In 1909, he accepted the post of instructor in pottery at the University City Pottery in St. Louis. From 1911–1913 he was associated with the Arequipa Pottery in Fairfax, California. Leaving Arequipa he organized the Pottery of the Camarata in Santa Barbara, later to be incorporated as The Rhead Pottery. In December, 1916, Rhead published *The Potter,* a monthly magazine dealing with the progress of the industry. The editor of the historical department was Edwin A. Barber—whose death was reported in the 3rd issue (February, 1917), and with that the paper was abandoned.[6]

Rhead's pottery ran into financial difficulties, and by 1917 he had returned to Zanesville, where he joined the American Encaustic Tiling Company, serving as director of research until 1927, when he moved to the Homer Laughlin China Company of Newell, West Virginia. His best known design for the china company was the popular Fiesta dinnerware line which was introduced in 1936. He remained there until his death in 1942.

# OTHER ART LINES ADDED

Weller artists continued to experiment in glazes and techniques, and other fine art lines were introduced in rapid succession.

Floretta was decorated with fruits or flowers in relief—suggesting a "blown-out" effect. Rich brown high gloss glazing is typical of the line, but gray and green were also used. Completely atypical is a variation achieved through the use of the same glaze technique and coloration of 2nd Line Dickens Ware. Rather than molded, fruits and flowers are incised into the ware, more commonly on pitchers, ewers, or mugs. The contrast of these two Floretta types are a very good example of the ambiguous nature of some Weller lines—made even more complicated since many early pieces were flagrantly mismarked.

Hunter is a brown glaze artware, decorated with birds or animals; it is marked on the base with the incised line name.

Perfecto is a unique art line—decorated with very heavy matt slip on a plain or lightly blended matt body. Although examples of this elusive line are rarely marked at all, of the two that are (to our knowledge) one is marked with the Louwelsa seal and the other with the Perfecto double circle die. Our theory—and you may develop your own—is that due to the problems encountered in trying to produce a "matt" Louwelsa (see color plates for example of piece marked "Matt" Louwelsa) this "unglazed" finish, as the company referred to it in an old catalogue, was utilized—and the very satisfying results soon rechristened "Perfecto." Experimentation would account for the slight variations within the line.

Etched Matt is characterized by incised work and the matt body. Marked examples of this line are decorated with the profile of a girl with flowing hair. (While pieces with branches and berries or simple flower studies are often accepted as belonging to this line, none have been reported marked with the line name, and many collectors prefer to term the latter "Modeled Etched Matt".)

Dresden is a semi matt glazed line decorated with windmills and Dutch children in native dress, in shades of blue.

Before being employed by Roseville in 1905 where he designed a similar ware called Woodland, Gazo Fudji (also written Foudji, Fudjiyama) worked for Weller, where he developed a line referred to in Weller catalogues as "Fudzi." Fudzi featured slip painted naturalistic flowers and leaves outlined in sgraffito, on unglazed backgrounds decorated by stippling (simply pricking the soft clay with needles). The interior of the ware was glazed to hold water.

Since neither pottery was consistent about marking their ware, it is often difficult to credit a piece of Fudji's work to one or the other, although some believe that examples of his work that bear the monogram "Fudzi" were produced at Weller, while "Fudji" or "Fudjiyama" were the Roseville spellings.

Oriental, Monochrome and Golbrogreen were other early lines, and although examples appearing in the color plates may qualify for Monochrome and Golbrogreen, we can offer no positive identification. (Oriental may have simply been another name for Fudji's artware.)

The Etna line was made in the soft gray and rose combination of Eocean and gray Floretta, and was usually decorated with flowers—a full blown rose was a popular motif. "Weller" was sometimes marked by hand on the face of the ware. Etna, introduced in 1906, was the last notable art line produced for several years. and reflected the changes that were being made in the pottery industry. Art Nouveau, 3rd Dickens, Floretta, and Etna were designed with inmold decoration to which color needed only be added. So, in the strictest sense, the only true "art" involved was from the hands of the designer who created the various shapes for each line. Less prestige, but more profit!

# MODEL POTTERY ERECTED AT ST. LOUIS

Weller was rightfully proud of his product; in 1904 he elected a model pottery, fully equipped and manned with his best workers, on the grounds of the St. Louis Exposition to demonstrate the processes involved in the manufacturing of art pottery.[3] Erected at a cost of $20,000.00 the model covered 30,000 feet of floor space, and under Weller's personal supervision, small vases and souvenir plaques commemorating the Louisiana Purchase were distributed to their visitors. Examples of these are shown in the color plates. (The plaques were created by Hugo Herb, a noted sculptor from Berlin, who left Weller's employ in 1905 to work for the J.B. Owens Pottery Company, of Zanesville.) The June 1904 issue of *Brick* magazine described the clayworkers' contributions to the Exposition. Weller's exhibition was especially noted:

"The Weller Pottery, of Zanesville, Ohio, has made several displays. It has quite a large building in the "Gulch" just outside of the mining building, in which is shown a model pottery plant in operation and a large- and tastefully arranged display of many varieties of the Weller product. This pottery was originated by Samuel Weller many years ago, and starting in a small way the business was built by the sheer merit of his products, until now the pottery is one of the greatest in Ohio. The vase shown stands over seven feet in height.

The display of the Weller Pottery in the clayworkers' industrial exhibit is between the Ohio mineral ehibit exhibit and the "Brick" booth. In this display are shown samples of the ware to be purchased in the pottery previously mentioned. The company's French or Sicardo artware is worthy of special attention. Excellent luster effects are produced and the blue, green and gold coloring are so delicate and rich that they have created for themselves a special class of artware. The Weller Pottery has also two exhibits in the Jerusalem concession."

The spectacular entry in the exhibit mentioned above was an Aurelian vase standing 7½ feet tall (including the 6" display platform) and weighing over 400 lbs. Against the fiery orange and gold highlights in the dark brown Aurelian glaze, the large yet graceful vase was decorated with realistic apple tree boughs heavily laden with lush fruit and foliage.

Many problems were encountered in its production, and eight attempts were made before the vase was successfully molded and fired. The upper portion was molded in two parts (not including the flared foot) and joined together in a special firing before it was decorated by Frank Ferrell. (It is signed and dated 1897.) A special kiln was constructed to accommodate the huge vase; and including labor, materials and expenditures from the seven previous failures, the manufacturing cost was estimated at $2,000.

Weller's perseverance was rewarded; his magnificent entry was selected by the International Jury of Awards to receive the Gold Medal in the Arts Category.

After the exhibit closed, the trophy vase was returned to Zanesville and for several years was stored in the stock room of the Putnam plant.[21] Dorothy England Laughead, who worked for Weller from about 1913, recalls that as a child she and her father (who was the first manager of the Weller theatre) went to see the big vase . . . Sam jokingly promised that "when she grew big enough to carry it home, it would be hers."

In later years, the vase was displayed in a Weller showroom in Mentor, Ohio. In 1932, Johnson's Pottery Manufacturers Exhibits, Indiana, purchased the chain of Weller stores and acquired the vase and all the museum pieces contained in the stores. The Aurelian vase alone was valued at $10,000, and because it was difficult to locate a moving company willing to assume the responsibility of transporting the vase, it remained in the Mentor store until 1954, when the Pottery Manufacturers' Exhibit corporation decided to take it to their New Market, Virginia, store to be displayed at the Apple Blossom Festival.

The difficult job of transportation was accomplished in a most unconventional manner. A local New Market undertaker drove to Mentor in his new Cadillac hearse, packed the vase in the space usually occupied by the casket, and returned safely to New Market without mishap. In 1967, the vase finally returned to Zanesville, where it remained for over a decade before it was sold to an out of state collector. Its value today is estimated at $250,000.

# COMMERCIAL ARTWARE DEPARTMENT EMPHASIZED

By the end of the first decade very little "art pottery" was being marketed. "Commercial artwares" were being mass produced—originality and creativity yielded to volume business. However, it must be stated, that even in conforming to these modifications, Weller's early commercial production remained of superior quality . . . his dedication to his craft and his drive to excel provided a stimulus that resulted in the limited production of artware for several years longer than many of his contemporaries.

Through the first several years of the second decade, reports in the trade papers of that era indicate that business overall was booming— the potteries became very prosperous. They reported "a refinement and delicacy of treatment such as have never before been seen." In mid-1913, pressure was exerted by the jobbers on the manufacturers:

"We jobbers don't want new shapes—those of today are good and selling fine . . . we do want a greater variety of high class treatments . . . (we) prefer to do business with those (shapes) we now have in stock."

As a result, new shapes were modeled infrequently; modelers were not kept busy through the year.[20] This is no doubt one of the reasons that several different glaze treatments can be found on the same shapes . . . and it is the glaze, not the shape, that determines its identification.

This entry is from Crockery and Glass Journal, July 30, 1914:

"The S.A. Weller line of pottery has been considerably augmented by the arrival of a lot of new samples which are now being shown by the concern's local manager, C.H. Taylor. Usually praise worthy are some odd designs, rather oriental in treatment, in jards and pedestals, vases and fern dishes, etc. (This may be the unnamed line we refer to as Camelot; see color photos and catalogue reprints.) There are also several additions to the "Ivory" ware line as well as an entirely new creation which shows a striking combination of coloring very effectively blended in a fascinating striped pattern." (Marbleized ?)

The principal modeler of the second decade was Rudolph Lorber. He was born and educated in Austria.[9] His association with Weller began in 1905; Weller soon recognized his abilities, and placed him in charge of designing new lines— a position he maintained until the 1930's. Some of his most important works were "Roma" (listed in the trade papers in 1914), Flemish, Zona, Forest, Muskota, Ivory, Knifewood, and Ting . . . there were of course many, many others.[20]

*Lorber Modeling at Weller*

Copra ware was described in a 1915 journal: "of rich colors with a matt finish." By 1915, decorated gardenware was coming into vogue, and the Weller Pottery manufactured a wide variety of yard ornaments. In July, 1916, the journals mention "sunflowers on a stick" (to be used as "birdbaths or flower bowls for cut flowers in the garden"); "small flying birds and perch birds"; and flower holders "in the shape of lobsters, crab, fish, toadstools, star fish, etc." Several new additions had been made to the "Dunton" line, said to be "exceptionally attractive (with) floral and bird designs on a glazed black background."[20] (Possibly this was the same line later called Rosemont.)

In 1920, Weller purchased the old Zanesville Art Pottery on Ceramic Avenue which was referred to as Plant #3— adding more credibility to Weller's claim that his was the largest pottery in the country. In 1924, a new addition enlarged the plant to a three story building, 50 x 300 feet. The Harrop tunnel kiln was installed—a long structure of brick with an iron track inside on which 90 flat cars carrying ware to be fired moved slowly and continuously. Total cost of the renovation of the plant neared $150,000. With three factories operating at three locations, the Weller pottery spread over 400,000 square feet of floor space! [12]

# LESSELL BECOMES ART DIRECTOR AT PLANT # 3

In the new plant "artware" enjoyed a revival. John Lessell was hired as art director in 1920. A native of Mettlach, Germany, Lessell was a well-known pottery and glass decorator, specializing in the use of metallic luster glazes. In 1903 he was one of the founders of the Arc-En-Ciel Pottery in Zanesville, but soon left that company to work for Owens until 1905.[6] From 1911 until 1913, he operated his own pottery (Lessell Art Ware Company) in Parkersburg, West Virginia. During the next few years he experimented with glass decorating; in 1916 he applied for a patent for a method of decorating . . . "which produce(d) results unlike anything so far seen."[20]

While at Weller, Lessell created several art lines—the most familiar among them are LaSa, Lamar, Marengo, and Chengtu.

Working as his assistant was Art Wagner, a native of Ohio, whose natural abilities as an artist won him much acclaim throughout his lifetime. Wagner worked in the steelmills before becoming a potter, and during the course of his career was associated with American Encaustic Tiling Company, Weller, Mosaic Tile, and finally the Fraunfelter China Company. Before his death in 1977, he became friends with Mrs. Lucile Henzke and their conversations concerning his career at Weller provided much fascinating information, which she has graciously passed on to us.

Wagner recalled that the LaSa line required many steps in its production. First, a white glaze was applied to a white body and fired; then a grounding oil was applied with a brush. The entire surface was dusted with a mixture of overglaze enamel powder and lampblack, and designs were scratched on through the powder with a pointed wooden stick. The piece was fired a second time at 1250° to 1310°F. Next, it was covered with a thin coat of liquid bright gold, and a third firing was required. A fourth followed the luster application for background colors; the inside of the ware was glazed, and it was fired a fifth time. Before the sixth and final firing the trees and ground were painted on by hand in black luster. The ware is marked "LaSa Weller" within the luster glaze on the decorated surface near the base.

Lamar, too, demanded a very exacting mode of decorating. Mr. Wagner explained that a layer of carmine was applied first by a brush followed by the initial firing; a second application of carmine was sprayed on and the piece was fired again. The landscape, usually of various kinds of trees, water and shoreline, was added by hand with black luster and the ware fired for the third and last time.

Marengo was a simple yet striking line, decorated with basic drawings of trees, water and shoreline, narrowly outlined with white and filled in with color a shade darker than the background.

In one of his letters, Mr. Wagner made this statement: (speaking of artists monograms)

"We seldom signed the smaller pieces in production, only now and then the larger, and only LaSa and Lamar . . . of the several artists who worked on LaSa and Lamar, only Dunlavy (Anthony) and I signed the larger pieces. Marengo was never signed."

Mrs. Jennie Lessell, Art Lawyer, Raymond Emmert, and Carl Weigelt also decorated the luster wares.[27]

Two other lines must be attributed to this period, and to Lessell's expertise with metallic luster. Besline, a gold luster ware with overall woodbine (Virginia Creeper) decoration was first attempted by acid-etching the design over a white englobe, and the gold luster added overall before the piece was fired. Later the process was reversed, so that the acid etching was done over the gold luster. The latter method produced a more pronounced pattern. Cloudburst, offered in 1921, was described in *The Crockery and Glass Journal*, October issue:

"The body is in an artistic crackled effect, in rich shades of green, blue, red, buff, etc. with a very lovely iridescent finish which seems to fairly radiate every color of the rainbow just as the sun when it breaks through the clouds floods everything with light and color."

Art Wagner recalled that in the early months of 1926, John Lessell and his wife went to Camden, Arkansas, to work in the newly organized Camden Art and Tile Company there. (Henry Fuchs replaced Lessell as head of the art department at Weller.) At Camden, Lessell developed several lines of art pottery reminiscent of those he created while at Owens and Weller. The Lessell line was almost an exact replica of Marengo, with the exception of a slightly wider white outline around the decoration. The name "Lessell" often appears on the decorated surface. He also reproduced the LaSa line, which was marketed under the name "Le-Camark." Perhaps the most outstanding ware he made there was the mirror black line, decorated in gold, similar to Ownes' Sudanese. John Lessell died in Newark, Ohio, in 1926, and was buried in Zanesville. Mrs. Lessel remained in Camden, where she continued to decorate the lines her husband had developed there.[22*]

In 1922, Weller incorporated his firm, which was capitalized at $750,000. Except for a few years in the 1890's, when the brothers were partners, the Weller Pottery had been a sole proprietorship.[9]

## THE HUDSON LINE INTRODUCED

Perhaps one of the most lovely artware lines—certainly one of the most popular with today's collectors was— surprisingly enough a relatively late line developed in the early 1920's, well toward the end of the era of hand decorated artware. The Hudson line was beautifully artist decorated under a semi-matt glaze in a soft, yet striking palette of lovely hues. The first Hudsons were characterized by a shaded background of strong pastels decorated in heavy slip with floral studies, landscapes, animals, and birds . . . and were often artist signed. Only a rare few were finished in a high gloss glaze; this type was called Glossy Hudsons. Other variations of the line were Delta, Rochelle, Blue and Decorated, White and Decorated, and Perfecto* *(see color plates for description). The Hudson line was originated in the Putnam Plant # 1. Edwin L. Pickens, one of the original Weller artists, and Mrs. Sam Weller's brother, was the supervisor of the art department.

*Decorating Room at the Putnam Plant during the 1920's. Walter Gitter in white, Ed Pickens in dark coat.*

Signed examples of Hudsons shown in the color plates bear the monograms of artists Hester Pillsbury, Mae and Sarah Timberlake, L. Morris, Eugene Roberts, Claude Leffler, Sarah Reid McLaughlin, Frank Dedonatis, Dorothy England (Laughead), Ruth Axline, Naomi Walch, Sam Celli . . . and there were others.

## METHODS OF MANUFACTURE

*The following is an excerpt from a company letter written about 1924 to buyers and clerks in china departments of retail stores. Its purpose was to acquaint them with the growth and development of the Weller product, and it describes in detail the progress that had been made in methods of manufacture.*

In the manufacture of pottery today a differentiation of the process formerly in use, to a certain extent, has been evolved. Some of the phases of the vogue since the inception of the art, centuries back. (sic) New ideas in the machinery used for washing, grinding and mixing the clays have lessened the labor of those details. Improvements in building the kilns to fire the raw ware—rendering possible the treatment of more pieces at one time—have been

*The Camden Art Tile & Pottery Company later adopted the name "Camark" for their company.

**It was not an uncommon practice for potteries to reuse an older line name in later years... Roseville used the names Ivory, Velmoss, and Imperial twice each to designate different lines. One of Weller's late floral lines was called Rosemont, as was an earlier line. To avoid confusion, we use the hyphenated term Hudson-Perfecto to distinguish one Perfecto line from the other.

attained. But withal, the same amount of heat must be used, the same time taken.

Use of plaster of paris moulds or casts may be, and often is substituted for the potter's wheel of former days in fashioning the desired article, but never will a complete discarding of the latter be possible. And the clever ideas of the designer, the skill and deft hand of the potter are required now, and forever will be, as at any time in the past. Few would suppose from a casual inspection of a finished piece of the finer grades of ware that during the course of its production it has passed through the hands of thirty-two skilled workmen, has been inspected time and time again, for several days and has been kept in a "damp" room, thence transferred to a "drying" room, and finally receives always two, and frequently three and four firings, lasting from six to fifty hours each, in order to produce the article free from defect and make it of permanent beauty.

To create and successfully complete a specimen of high grade pottery, unblemished and on artistic lines, is, as already intimated, a problem entailing much skill, time and craftsmanship, with all these factors present, failure oft-times ensues. The rule taught by repeated annoying experiences, is to expect one perfect piece from each twelve attempts. (!) Obviously, success in ceramics depends primarily upon the right selection of the proper qualities and quantities of the clays, which are the web and woof, the alpha and omega of the craft. No one grade of clay contains all the properties required for the production of high class pottery. A mixture must be made which will give a certain degree of pliability, reinforced by tenacity, necessary for the stage of the work when the article is to be fashioned by the potter. Then too, the compound must be such that the heat of the subsequent kilning will not burn or crack the ware. And, of equal importance the body must be capable of properly retaining the glazes which are afterward applied. The clays yielding the best results are found in England, certain sections of this country, notably Kentucky and Tennessee. The states mentioned are particularly prolific in the "Ball Clay," which best gives the desired plasticity. Kaolin, pica and quartz are the other constituents usually sought, and each of these elements can only be extracted from a certain grade of clay. The raw materials are obtained chiefly by mining, and the business of gathering them is one of no mean proportions.

Upon the arrival of the clays at the pottery, they are deposited in huge bins, each grade in separate compartments. Now comes the need of skilled chemists. The clays must be properly assayed and ascertainment made how much of one grade, how little of another to combine in the initial mixing. The proportions are, of course, kept secret, and the task of weighing the crude clay is not given public exhibition. Indeed, many details of the work are closely guarded; only the initiated are possessed of the mysteries. After the assemblage and weighing of the different grades of clay, the mass entire is placed in a large vat of circular shape, in which are four revolving blades, rapidly propelled by steam power. This contrivance is known as a "washing" machine. The apparatus is set in motion and the swiftly revolving blades rapidly induce the solution of the clays and water. The combined clays once in the washing machine, are covered with water. The heavier foreign substances fall to the bottom of the machine beneath the zone of the blades, and a thorough co-mixture of the desired elements is accomplished. Next, the solution, now of cream-like consistency, is transferred by means of pipes to the screening machine, its meshes of wire averaging one hundred and fifty to the square inch. Sifted through this, as nearly purified as is possible, the substance technically "slip" flows in a wide and shallow cistern placed beneath the floor of the screen. Thence by suction it is transferred to a contrivance called the "compressor," to expel the water still in the solution. The compressor is of iron frames, from which are suspended long, sack-shaped arrangements of canvas. These once filled with the "slip," are steadily forced together by a steel screw shaft, and the nearly dry sheets of clay are taken out by hand and laid away in large piles to ripen and dry. The last step in the preliminary preparation of the clay is to run it through a "plugger" machine. This is really a regrinding and renders doubly sure the complete co-mixture of the component clays.

The clay or "slip" is now ready for fashioning into the articles desired. To perform this work, two methods are extant—that of the potter's wheel, the original way, and the modern use of plaster of paris moulds, or casts, made from dies. The potter's wheel is simply a circular shaped piece of wood placed atop an upright shaft, the motive power being through a foot treadle attached beneath. A lump of moist clay is placed on the wheel and with deft hands, meantime rotating the disk, the artist fashions his vase or jar, adding raised decorations as fancy dictates. Of course, when the piece, be what it may—vase, bowl or cup—is "thrown," by hand on a potter's wheel exact reduplication of every curve and line is impossible. To obviate this difficulty when desiring to perpetuate a pleasing design, the potter has recourse to the making of a die, from which he will make a plaster cast and duplicate the model infinite times. These casts, or models, generally are of two sections, fastened by hoops or staves of iron. In jardinieres and umbrella stands, cuspidors and the like, moist clay is inserted by an expert craftsman in the mould, which has been placed on a standard rotated by foot or steam power. The clay is pressed firmly into place by a wooden forcer against the sides and bottom of the cast and then the whole is set away to dry prior to the first firing. In the case of articles where insertion of the hand or wooden instrument is impossible—for instance, a narrownecked vase or candlestick— the use of the mold is different. The clay, with the consistency of thick cream is poured into the cast until the entire interior is filled. The workman, wise by long experience, knows just when to invert the cast and pour from the center, leaving only enough clay to cover the bottom and sides. Next, it is placed in the drying room to further "set." This process is quickened by the use of coils of steam heated pipes placed beneath slatlike platforms on which the raw ware is arranged. When sufficiently dried, the impressions are removed from the casts and taken to the cleaning department, where the seams and blemishes are pared off. Afterward, the pieces requiring handles are fitted with them, these having previously been fashioned in separate molds. Now the ware is placed in rooms artificially damp-ened by means of water flowing constantly down the walls. Here the ware is left until the "blender" is ready for it. Most classes of the higher grades of pottery are decorated by hand-sprays or single blossoms of flowers, landscapes, portraits, anything in the realm of art. But before this is done, the ware must be treated to a blending of body which will assist in retaining the colors and prevent their spreading, while the process of firing is taking place.

Should the worker in oils or water colors attempt to decorate pottery so it would successfully pass the firing test his effort would meet with flat failure. The different colors must be mixed from mineral paints and knowledge must be had of the change in color which the application of heat will induce. The preparation of the preliminary blend is kept a secret and enormous sums have been spent in experimenting on causes and results. To the success of this research is due the fine ware produced today. The application of the mineral paints is done by the hand, and many well-known artists are engaged in the work. New tones are constantly being produced, and already the ware is famous for the nature tints—rich golden browns, greens and chromatic combinations.

The decoration having been completed, next comes the crucial test—the initial firing. On this depends every-thing, all is at stake, wrong combinations of the crude clays, an error in the percentage of a certain mineral paint, any carelessness in the earlier treatment of the ware will surely result in ruining the product.

"Kilning" the ware is one of the most interesting and difficult phases of pottery making. For the benefit of the uninitiated, let it be said that kilning, or firing, is the application of intense heat which will give a ripidity and perma-nency to the ware and render the applied decorative effects non-erasable.

The old style kilns, still used today in the less modern plants, were beehive in shape, built of brick.* They were large users of fuel and required many wasted hours in bringing up the heat and cooling. The kilns of today are known as tunnel kilns, long structures of brick with all iron track inside. On this track run cars with fireclay tops 5' x 8' and on these tops are placed the containers of the pottery to be fired. These cars are moving continuously thru the tunnel in the center of which is the "hot zone," a section kept at a uniform temperature by gas burners and controlled by elec-tric thermostats. While these kilns are very expensive they save from 60% to 80% of the fuel costs and all progressive clay industries have adopted them.

Each piece of ware is placed in a jar shaped casting of previously fired clay called a "sagger." No piece of the ware not even one-sixteenth of an inch of it must touch the "sagger." If so placed, it will burn and ruin the article. To avoid this each piece is placed on a small tripod of verified clay called a stilt. Similar pieces are placed along the sides of each "sagger."

For the first firing about 2,100 degrees are needed. The heat is gradually applied until the maximum temperature reached. The time required for kilning varies from thirty-six to fifty hours, and during this period the heat must be maintained uninterruptedly. The graduations in temperature must he carefully made, else the ware will crack from the resultant sudden contraction or expansion. To ascertain the temperature and know generally how the firing is progressing, the cone system of testing is generally in use. That is to say, tiny cones of clay, each susceptible of fusion at a different degree of heat, are placed in small openings in the kiln walls. In this way when a cone fuses at a temper-ature of 1,200 degrees, it indicates the heat within is of that temperature, and so on with the cones of various fusion.

After the firing is completed, the ware, some of it cracked and burned is termed "Biscuit." It is now ready for the glazing preparation, which is applied prior to the second firing, and by that rendered transparent "Mat" or opaque, as desired. The Matt Glaze is the connecting link between the others mentioned, and was discovered by accident. To make the glaze is an intricate process of grinding chemicals which are later fused by heat. The compound, in fluid form, is applied to the biscuit ware, either by dipping or spraying. Then comes the second firing and the completed ware.

---

*These periodic kilns at Putnam were 40 feet wide with a rounded crown—firing time was about five days. The kilns were loaded, doors bricked up, and fired with coal or gas. Saggers made of reprocessed, previously fired scrap material protected the ware from the fire and loose dirt.

# WELLER MOURNED, ADMINISTRATION CHANGES

After an illness of about three weeks, Sam A. Weller died in Washington, D.C. on October 4, 1925. He was 76. The pottery he began in such humble surroundings had grown to a great manufactory that was largely responsible for Zanesville's recognition as a great art center. He had been a man unrelenting in his pursuit to produce the best, and then to improve upon it. His innate ingenuity coupled with a keen sense of business acumen fortified with diligence resulted in a career both extremely profitable and productive.

After his death, Harry Weller, his nephew, became president; Frederick J. Grant, Sam's son-in-law, vice president and treasurer; and Edgar Bagley was named secretary. Walter Gitter was sales manager. Members of the Board of Directors were: Fred Gitter, C.H. Taylor, Mrs. S.A. Weller, Frank Weller, Wm. Hughes and Paul Philips—veteran salesman for Weller from 1898 to 1948. The company maintained offices in New York (5th Avenue Building), Boston (111 Summer St.), and Chicago (29 E. Madison.)[20]

On August 4, 1927, a fire originating in the third floor decorating room caused damage estimated at $250,000 to Plant #3 on Ceramic Avenue. Reconstruction began immediately.

# INNOVATIONS OF THE THIRTIES

Still standing on old Rt. 40 east of Zanesville—though now vacant and neglected—is the building that once housed the Weller Showrooms. From 1930–1942 tourists could select their purchases from lovely displays of the locally produced ware. Weller tiles spelled out the pottery's name over the front entrance—on either side of the doors were a matched pair of tall urns of red clay. Inside, alcoves in the walls held two huge handled vases in Coppertone glaze, turned especially for use in the showroom. Fred Gitter was the manager. A second salesroom at Willoughby, Ohio, was under the supervision of Laurence Stien.

In later years, Art Wagner used part of the building as a studio, where he continued to decorate pottery with the luster glazes, and occasionally in oils.[11]

During the 1930's, Graystone Garden ware became popular and a line of naturalistic, life sized dogs, cats, swans, geese, and playful gnomes provided colorful and decorative accents to yards and gardens. The Weller Company produced decorated tiles of many types, several of which are shown in the color plates. Their "Inca Tiles" reproduced carvings found on monolithic doorways discovered in Tiahuanaco, Bolivia.[23]

*Inca Tiles*

Bonito was artist decorated creamware, lined in soft green. Artist Naomi Walch (Truitt) recalled that the designs were sketched onto the ware with India ink (which burned out in the firing), before the colors were applied and blended. Colored stains, rather than slip, were used to execute original renderings of suggested designs.[24]

Other artist decorated lines of the thirties were: Stellar—blue, black, or white backgrounds alit with white or blue stars; Geode—the same stellar theme with comet trails added; Raceme—described in the 1934 journals as "a light bright blue and white raceme (?) in slip with raised cluster, on upper background of blue gray with lower background black"; and Cretone—either yellow with brown or white with a black stylized gazelle, leaves, and flowers.

Dorothy England recalls that as early as 1913 she worked for Weller at the Putnam plant. In the 1920's she began to learn the art of slip decorating. Because the artists sometimes would set up cardboard around their tables to correct the lighting, it was impossible to learn their techniques by observation, so Claude Leffler taught her the fundamentals of the art. Both she and Lorber moved to the Ceramic Avenue Plant about 1925, and although she was a talented decorator, she was also a gifted modeler, and was soon assigned to work with Lorber in designing new lines. Since "line names" were chosen after the modeling was finished, Mrs. Laughead was often unaware of the name given to her creations or the type of decoration used on them. But she recalled that she modeled the Neiska, Cornish, and Cameo lines, many of the floral patterns, Chelsea utility ware, and the Ollas Water Bottle. No doubt her most popular designs were the frogs, cats, the cocker spaniel and a rabbit with long, erect ears.

Carl Weigelt was a Bohemian, who before coming to the United States was a glass worker—one of many who moved from place to place as wood became available to fire the furnaces for their trade. A long time employee at the Weller Company, he was adept at operating the gold kiln. He assisted Art Wagner on the luster ware of the 1920's, and later decorated teapots with gold work. He was eventually promoted from decorator to modeler.[21, 27]

Naomi Truitt remembered Harry Weller as a man that "everybody loved—he was just wonderful to work for, and often strolled through the plant greeting everyone. The pottery was his life; he seemed to love every inch of it." When he was fatally injured in an automobile accident in 1932, "he was sorely missed, and everyone grieved for him."[24]

Frederick Grant was the next president of the company, followed in 1935 by Irvin H. Smith who was president and treasurer. Walter M. Hughes was vice president and H.C. Pugh was secretary.

In the mid-1930's Plant # I in Putnam and Plant #2 on Marietta Street were closed, and all operations moved to the Ceramic Avenue plant. The depression had brought a steady decline in sales, especially of non-essentials—consequently much of the production was limited to cooking utensils, beer mugs and cheap ornamental ware.

Walter Hughes became president in 1937; Paul Phillips, first vice president; Walter Gitter, Jr. vice president; and H.C. Pugh, secretary.

In 1939, the company increased the original capital of $750,000; Hughes continued as president; Wm. Curphey, Sam's son-in-law, became vice president; H.C. Pugh remained the secretary. A.W. Smith was appointed assistant secretary and assistant treasurer.

A second blow to sales came after WWII, when cheap foreign imports flooded the American market. In 1945, part of the Weller plant was leased to the Essex Wire Company of Detroit, Michigan. Two years later, the Essex Company bought the controlling stock, but announced that no changes would be made in operations. However, contrary to their expectations, the market for domestic pottery continued its downward trend, and early in 1948 the Weller Pottery closed.

"... the potter has the opportunity to combine those two most important producers of happiness, form and color; and when he uses them with enthusiasm and individuality he has indeed fulfilled a mission and has created. He has made something that makes him happier in the making of it, and that will go out carrying joy and enthusiasm to all who use it or see it ... And when he has blended form and color, and endowed them with his own individuality, he has added materially to the world's happiness."

William Day Gates

# WELLER ARTISTS AND THEIR MONOGRAMS

The lines after each indicate known examples of that artist's work. The asterisk indentifies those listed by Barber, before 1904; and numbers correspond with the pargraphs that follow.

**Abel**

*A BEL*

Aurelian

**Virginia Adams***

*VA.*

Louwelsa

**M. Ansel**

*M AnSEL*

2nd Dickens

**Ruth Axline**

*R*

Aurelian, Bonito, Hudson

**Elizabeth Ayers***

*EA*    *EA*

Aurelian, Louwelsa, Dickens

**Elizabeth Blake**

*E B*

Eocean, Louwelsa

**Lizabeth Blake***

*L·B.*    *LB*

Eocean, Louwelsa

**Levi J. Burgess*** (1)

*L. J. B.*

Portraits, Indians, Louwelsa, Dresden, Eocean, 2nd Dickens

**John Butterworth**

*B*    *B*

Louwelsa, Dickens; Indians

**Charles C. Chilcote**

*c.c.chilcoTe*    *C.C.*

Worked with Upjohn on 2nd Dickens

**Laura Cline**

*L C*

1st Dickens

**N. C. (Unknown)**

*η C*

Bonito

**A. C. (Unknown)**

*A C*

Louwelsa

**Anna Dautherty***

*A.D.*

Portraits, Indians; Dickens, Louwelsa

**Frank Dedonatis**

*E*    *FOOTIS*

Bonito, Hudson

**Charles John Dibowski**

*C.J.D.*

Louwelsa; former Rookwood artist

**Anthony Dunlavy*** (3)

*AD*

Aurelian, 2nd Dickens, Louwelsa Indians

**C. A. Dusenbery**

*C. A.DUSENBERY*    *C.D.*

Dickens, Perfecto

**Dorothy England (Laughead)**

*DE.*    *D*

(see text); Hudson, Chase

**Frank Ferrell*** (4)

*F F*

Aurelian, Dickens, Louwelsa, Perfecto

**Charles Fouts**

*F*

Aurelian

**Henry Fuchs (5)**

*H. FUCHS*

Luster lines, 1920's

**Gazo Fudjiyama (6)**

Fudzi; (see text)

**I.F. (unknown)**

*IF*

Hudson

**T. F. (unknown)**

*T.F.*

Dickens

**M. Gibson**

*M. Gibson*

Dickens

**W. Gibson**

*W. GIBSON*

Dickens

**Mary Gillie***

*MG mg.*

Jap Birdimal, Aurelian

**Charles Gray**

*C. G*

Dickens

**William F. Hall**

*W. H.    WH*

Louwelsa

**Delores Harvey**

*D. H.*

Louwelsa, Aurelian

**Albert Haubrich* (7)**

*A.H.    AH*

Louwelsa, Lonhuda, Eocean,
Perfecto

**John Herold (8)**

*JH    JH*

Dickens

**Hugo Herb**

*H H*

(see text)

**Hood**

*Hood*

Hudsons

**Madge Hurst***

*MH*

Perfecto, Brighton,
Louwelsa, Aurelian

**VMH (unknown)**

*VM H*

Jap Birdimal

**TTH (unknown)**

*F F H*

Louwelsa

**Josephine Imlay***

*J.I.    JI*

**Karl Kappes***

*K. K.*

Louwelsa; Indian

**L. Knaus**

*K    LK.*

2nd Dickens

**Claude L. Leffler**

*C.L.    ¢*

Hudson, Perfecto, Louwelsa,
Eocean

24

John Lessell

*J L*

Luster lines of 20's

Sarah Reid McLaughlin*

Dresden, Lonhuda, Hudson, Glendale, Eocean

L.B.M. (unknown)

Hudson

J. L. (unknown)

*J L*

Louwelsa

Hattie Mitchell*

*H. M.*

Louwelsa, Aurelian, Dickens

KE or EK  M (unknown)

Louwelsa

JBL (unknown)

*JBL*

Dresden

Lillie Mitchell*

*L M   ɭ M*

Dickens, Louwelsa

Lizzie Perone

*L P*

Jap Birdimal, Turada

W.A. Long*

Lonhuda

Minnie Mitchell*

*M     m m*

Louwelsa, 1st Dickens

Mary Pierce

*AP    MP*

Aurelian, Louwelsa

M. Lybarger

*M. LyBArg*

Louwelsa

L. Morris

*Morris*

Hudsons

Edwin L. Pickens*

*E L P*

Dickens, Perfecto, Eocean

H.L. (unknown)

*H. L.*

Copra, Louwelsa

Gordon Mull*

*GM   GM*

2nd Dickens

Hester Pillsbury* (10)

*HP*

Louwelsa, Rochelle, Perfecto, Bonito, Corleone, Glendale, Hudsons, Stellar

S.L. (unknown)

*S. L*

Louwelsa

M. Myers

*M-M*

Former Rookwood artist

Albert Radford

*A R*

(see text)

Marie Rauchfuss

*MR*

Louwelsa, Aurelian,
Eocean; Former Rock-
wood artist

Eugene Roberts*

*ER*    *Er*

Hudson, Aurelian, Louwelsa

Fredrick Hurten Rhead

*FR*

(see text); Jap Birdimal

Hattie M. Ross

*HMR*

Jap Birdimal

Schnieder

Aurelian

Jacques Sicard

*SICARD*

Sicardo; (see text)

Helen Smith

*HS*

2nd Dickens, Louwelsa

Jessie R. Spaulding

*JRS*

Lonhuda

Tot Steel*

*TS*

William H. Stemm

*WS    WHS*

Eocean

E. Sulcer

*E SuLCER*

Louwelsa

M.S. (unknown)

*M.S.*

Louwelsa

H.S. (unknown)

2nd Dickens

C. Minnie Terry*

*CT*

Louwelsa

Madeline Thompson

*M. T.*

Lonhuda, Floretta

Mae Timberlake (11)

*M.T.    Timberlake*

Aurelian, Eocean, Hudsons,
Louwelsa

Sarah Timberlake (11)

*S*

Hudsons

Naomi Truitt Walch

*WALCH*

Hudson, Bonito; (see text)

R.G. Turner

*R G TURNER*

Louwelsa, Dickens; Portraits

Charles B. Upjohn

*U*

Dickens, Louwelsa, Hunter; (see
text)

Arthur Wagner

LaSa, LaMar, Marengo; (see text)

Carl Weigelt

*C W*

Luster lines of the 20's

T.J. Wheatly (2)

Aurelian

Carrie Wilbur

*C W*

Dickens, Perfecto

Edna Wilbur

*E W*

2nd Dickens

Albert Wilson

*A WILSON*

Louwelsa, Dickens

Helen B. Windle*

*H . W.*

Etna

Clotilda Marie Zanetta

*cZ   C.3.   M.Z.*

Louwelsa

Other recognized Weller artists:
W. Alsop
A.F. Best
Florence Bowers
E. Brown
O.B.
M.B.
Sam Celi
L.T.
Norman Scotthorn
Irvin Smith
Amelia B. Sprague
Anna Jewett
Kennedy
Joe Knott
Rose Langstaff
Cora McCandless
Margaret McGinnis
L. McGrath
L. McLain
E. Fox
Kathryn de Golter
Roy Hook

1. Levi J. Burgess was Sam Weller's nephew; he was well traveled and cultured—his wife was a Stansberry of the A. E. Tile family. He was a most capable artist, perhaps most famous for his portraits and Indians for which he is said to have been paid $1.00 each.

2. Charles Chilcote served as an apprentice to Upjohn in 1904, working with him on 2nd Dickens. He also worked for Roseville, Owens, Zane, and J.W. McCoy. He still resides in Zanesville, Ohio.

3. Anthony (Tony) Dunlavy worked for Weller as decorator over a period of at least 20 years—his excellent artwork appears as early as Aurelian… his Indians, on 2nd Dickens as well as Louwelsa, are highly prized. During the 20's, he moved to Plant #3 where he assisted John Lessell on the luster art lines. At one time, he also worked for Roseville.

4. Frank Ferrell was a noted Zanesville artist who worked for Weller prior to 1905. After leaving Weller, he worked for Owens until that firm discontinued the production of art pottery. We find no record of his where-abouts from 1906 until 1912 when he is credited with designing Moss Aztec for Peters and Reed. But J.W. McCoy lines Pompeian, Oriental, and Chromart which nearly duplicate others modeled by Ferrell for Peters and Reed suggest an association at one time or another—even though these McCoy lines were not popularly marketed until the 1920's. It is possible as some sources indicate, that Ferrell did some "free lancing" during this time, and so may not have been associated with one pottery exclusively. (City directories list him simply as "artist" and later as "modeler" from 1906 to 1910). He must have continued to build his reputation as an artist and a crafts-man, for in 1918 he became art director for the Roseville Pottery Company—a position he held until 1954.

5. Henry Fuchs worked with Lessell in the decorating department of Plant #3 in the 1920's. After Lessell's departure, Fuchs served for a time as head of the department until he was succeeded by Ed Pickens.

6. Gazo Fujiyama was a Japanese artist who designed a line called "Fudzi" while at Weller, before becoming employed by the Roseville Pottery in 1905. The oriental art style of decoration has remained popular since work of this type had been displayed in this country for the first time at the Centennial Exposition in Philadelphia in 1876.

7. Albert Haubrich is listed by Barber in his *Marks of American Potters,* published in 1904. His signed work has been found on examples of Perfecto, which establishes that this line was made prior to 1904, at which time Haubrich left Weller to work for the Radford Pottery Company of Clarksburg, West Virginia.

8. John J. Herold was a noted decorator who served from 1900 to 1908 as superintendent of the Art Department at the Roseville Pottery Company. From 1897 until his association with Roseville began, he worked for both Owens and Weller—exact dates are not known.

9. Ed Pickens was Mrs. Sam Weller's brother. He worked from the very early years of the pottery through the 1920's when he became director of the Art Department at Plant #1, and later at Plant #3. He was a charming and well-liked man, and his ability as an artist was outstanding as evidenced by many fine examples bearing his monogram.

10. Hester Pillsbury was described as "tiny, dainty, and with a zest for living." Her tenure with Weller extended over many years, and her work is among the finest and most sought after.

11. Mae and Sarah Timberlake were sisters, and most devoted. Besides Weller, they also worked at Owens and Roseville. Mae was regarded as very fine artist and found ready employment wherever she went—but one condition of her employment was that sister Sarah come with her. The most difficult assignments of the day were often given to Mae, but she was never too busy to help Sarah when she was needed. Artwork signed M.T. or Timberlake is very desirable.

12. Thomas Jerome Wheatly began his career in the production of art pottery in 1879, and after a short and tumultuous association with the Coultry Works of Cincinnati, Ohio, he opened his own pottery in 1880. He was involved in a legal dispute with M. Louise McLaughlin over the patent rights for the method of under glaze decorating. Like Miss McLaughlin, Wheatly claimed the "Limoges" process of decorating the green, or unbaked ware with slip mixed with appropriate mineral colors, which when subjected to the fire, united with the body of the ware. Although his claim was not upheld by the courts, his business prospered and continued until 1884 when fire destroyed his pottery. In 1897, he joined the Weller firm, an association lasting until 1900, when he again returned to Cincinnati.

Russell Wright once attempted to design some pottery for Weller—but the merger was never successful. It is said that Mr. Wright arrived in Zanesvile with his pet frog (about whose health he was concerned) and plans for a casserole with a lid which had a hinge made of pottery. Although the modeler whom they consulted insisted that anything made of metal could be reproduced in pottery; he promptly declined to model the hinge.

# TRADEMARKS OF THE WELLER POTTERY

By evaluating the marks found on well over 2,000 pieces of Weller pottery, and correlating them to known dates relating to the production period of various lines, it became obvious that each mark could be attributed to a specific time span.

Some of the dates used in our evaluation were indicative of the introduction of new lines—these were usually from trade journals; and from old company price listings, we could follow some lines through several years of production...the dates of a few lines are general knowledge...old photographs contained clues...and dated pieces established some dates of manufacture. Except for those of the early art lines, the dates of the marks shown on these pages represent *time spans*, not specific years, so allow for a slight margin of fluctuation, even though they remained consistently accurate as we studied each line. By no means are all trademarks shown here—there are many others.

LONHUDA
1895 – 96

*Aurelian*
WELLER
1898 – 1910

*Eosian*
WELLER
1898 – 1918

LOUWELSA WELLER     TURADA WELLER     DICKENS WARE WELLER     SICARDO WELLER

These half circle seals were used from 1896 until sometime near the end of the first decade of the 1900s.

LOUWELSA WELLER

The circle seal is the least common Louwelsa mark.

# WELLER

Both this size and a smaller die stamp was in general use from the late 1900's until just before 1925.

LOUWELSA WELLER    ART NOUVEAU WELLER    FLORETTA WELLER    PERFECTO WELLER    ETNA WELLER

These double circle seals designated artware lines after the turn of the century.

Weller
Faience
Incised, 1903 3rd Dickens

Weller
Ahead
Faience

| 7 |
| WELLER |

Embossed on 3rd Dickens

ETNA
WELLER
Die stamp Etna sometimes incised by hand

974
WELLER
Incised on Etched Matt

*SAWeller*
Incised on Greenaways

SA WELLER
ZANESVILLE
OHIO
Early Utility Ware

Paper label

Black and silver foil label

Ink stamp or
paper label

Ink Stamp

These marks and labels were used during the 20's.

Die stamp

**WELLER WARE**

Die impressed on
Creamware

Ink Stamp on Barcelona

"Full-kiln" ink stamp,
middle 20's

"Half-kiln" ink stamps, late 20's

*Weller Hand Made*

Incised on Ansonia, Fleron, Velvetone,
and Coppertone.

*Weller*

Incised by hand from
about 1927 to the early
30's.

*Weller Pottery*

Incised by hand from about 1927 to the
early 30's; same mark, in-mold script, in
continuous use from around 1933.

# Weller Pottery
## Since 1872

In-mold script after 1935

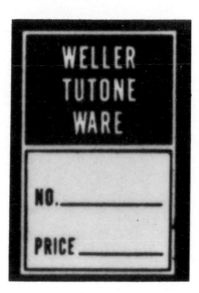

*Lines of the teens through the early 30's often carried paper labels printed with the name of the line with spaces left for the stock number and price. These lines have been found with labels of this type, you may find others: Pumila, Marvo, Coppertone, Silvertone, Chengtu, Zona, Greora, Muskota, Malvern, Ardsley, Woodcraft, Nile, Hudson, Flemish, Sydonia, Forest, Tutone, Elberta, Roma, Turkis, Chase, Barcelona, Florenzo, Lorbeek, Glendale, Warwick, Sabrinian, Blo'Red, Greenbier, Velvetone, Softone, Clarmont, Bonito, Florala, Classic, Cornish, Manhattan, Klyro, Velvo, Besline.*

*Collectors report that the Barcelona line is sometimes marked with the line name in black ink; and Orris may be found marked with crayon-like underglaze lettering.*

*The hand incised script mark was the work of finisher Maud Wagstaff—at least for sometime; Dorothy England later "marked the die" so that it was incorporated within the mold.*

*The vase on the opposite page earned S.A. Weller Pottery the "Gold Medal" award at the St. Louis Louisiana Purchase Exposition in 1904.*

*This Aurelian vase measures 7½' from the top to the floor. The display platform is 6" high, and the vase itself is in 2 sections—the top portion is 6' tall, and the flared foot adds another 12". It is signed Frank Ferrell and dated 1897.*

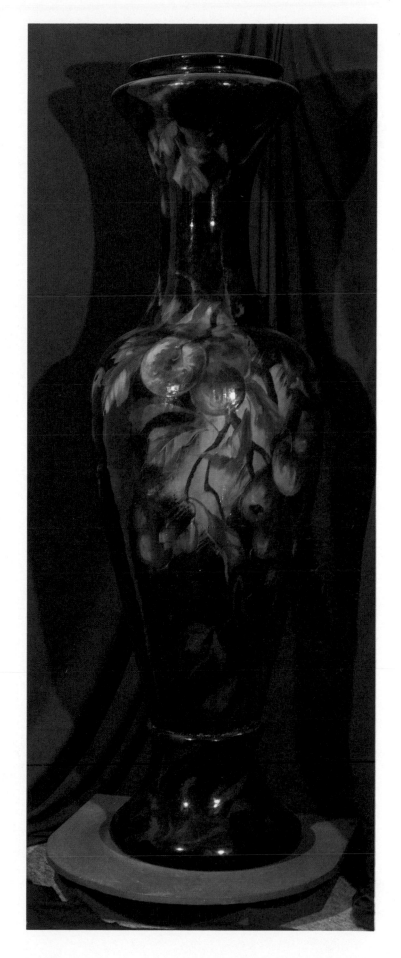

## Louwelsa

*Row 1:*
    *1. Vase, 17"; Marked with the Louwelsa half circle seal; Artist signed: Lybarger; $1150.00 – $1450.00*

*Row 2:*
    *1. Vase, 23½"; Same mark; Artist signed: A. Haubrich; $1275.00 – $1550.00*
    *2. Vase, 25"; Same mark; Artist signed: C J. Dibowsky; $1750.00 – $2250.00*

*Louwelsa Mug, 6½"; Marked with the Louwelsa half circle seal, #432; Artist signed: Ferrell; $800.00 – $1000.00*

# Louwelsa

**Row 1:**
  Clock, 10½" x 12½"; Marked with the Louwelsa half circle seal ; $800.00 – $1000.00

**Row 2:**
  1. Vase, 14"; Marked Louwelsa Weller (by hand); Artist signed: H. Pillsbury; $1250.00 – $1550.00
  2. Vase, 7"; same mark as clock; Artist signed: L. Blake; $850.00 – $1150.00
  3. Ewer, 12½"; Marked with the Louwelsa circle seal; Artist signed: L.J. Burgess, F.M. on base; $1450.00 – $1800.00

**Row 3:**
  1. Vase, 10½"; Marked with the Louwelsa circle seal; Artist signed: A. Wilson;  $1400.00 – $1700.00
  2. Vase, 16"; same mark as #1; Artist signed: L.J. Burgess; $2500.00 – $3000.00
  3. Vase, 11"; Marked with the half circle seal; Artist signed: R.G.T. ; $1300.00 – $1600.00

*Artwork such as this defies commentary! The dogs are by Albert Wilson and Elizabeth Blake—Wilson, especially is noted for his preference toward painting "man's best friend"…and he does it particularly well. "The Monk" by Burgess is one of our favorites—exquisite shadings and detail  make him come alive. Hester Pillsbury's goldfish are most unusual; and of course, Burgess' "Rubens" (middle of bottom row) is magnificent.*

# Louwelsa

*Row 1:*
1. Vase, 5"; Marked with the Louwelsa half circle seal; $125.00 – $150.00
2. Pitcher, 5"; same mark; Artist signed: M.T.; $165.00 – $195.00
3. Pillow Vase, 4"; No mark; Artist signed: M; $125.00 – $150.00
4. Ewer, 6½"; Louwelsa half circle seal; Artist signed: J.B. ; $150.00 – $190.00
5. Mug, 4½"; same mark; $80.00 – $100.00

*Row 2:*
1. Pitcher Vase, 3"; same mark; Artist signed: A.C.; $125.00 – $150.00
2. Vase, 6½"; same mark; Artist signed: V.A.; $150.00 – $200.00
3. Vase, 5"; same mark; Artist signed: M H; $165.00 – $200.00
4. Mug, 6"; same mark; Artist signed: E.A.; $235.00 – $275.00
5. Vase, 3½"; same mark; $115.00 – $140.00

*Row 3:*
1. Vase 5½"; same mark; Artist: E.A.; $145.00 – $195.00
2. Vase, 7"; same mark; Artist signed: L.B.; $150.00 – $175.00
3. Tobacco Jar, 5½"; same mark; Artist signed: C.A.; $450.00 – $550.00
4. Ewer, 7"; same mark; Artist signature obscured; $150.00 – $195.00
5. Jug Vase, 6½", same mark; Artist initialed: D.; No stopper; $150.00 – $175.00

*Row 4:*
1. Vase, 6"; same mark; Artist initialed: H ; $125.00 – $150.00
2. Vase, 3½"; same mark; $110.00 – $125.00
3. Vase, 7"; same mark; Artist signed J.B.; $200.00 – $250.00
4. Vase, 4"; same mark; Artist signature obscured; $110.00 – $125.00
5. Vase, 6½"; same mark; $185.00 – $235.00

*Row 5:*
1. Vase, 10"; same mark; Artist signed: V. Adams; $250.00 – $300.00
2. Vase, 11"; same mark; Artist signed: M.M.; $275.00 – $325.00
3. Vase, 10"; same mark; Artist unknown; $250.00 – $300.00
4. Vase, 9½"; Weller (die impressed); $225.00 – $275.00
5. Ewer, 10"; Marked with the Louwelsa double circle seal; $275.00 – $325.00

## Louwelsa

*Row 1:*
1. Vase, 2"; Marked with the Louwelsa half circle seal; $80.00 – $100.00
2. Vase, 3"; same mark; $90.00 – $120.00
3. Mug, 5½"; same mark; Artist signed: M. M.; $185.00 – $220.00
4. Jug Vase, 3½"; same mark; $140.00 – $170.00
5. Vase, 2"; same mark; $115.00 – $145.00

*Row 2:*
1. Vase, 4"; same mark; $120.00 – $150.00
2. Mug, 6½"; Marked with the Louwelsa double circle seal; Artist signed: M.M.; $210.00 – $250.00
3. Ewer, 4"; Half circle seal; Artist signed: Ferrell; $140.00 – $170.00
4. Mug, 5"; same mark; Artist signed: L.J B; $230.00 – $275.00
5. Bowl, 2½"; same mark; $80.00 – $115.00

*Row 3:*
1. Mug, 8½"; same mark; Artist signed: H.M.; $275.00 – $325.00
2. Vase, 4½"; Louwelsa double circle seal ; $110.00 – $135.00
3. Pillow vase, 7½"; Half circle seal; Artist signed: TTH, unknown; $1350.00 – $1650.00
4. Vase 8½"; same mark as #3; Artist signed: U J ; $130.00 – $170.00
5. Vase, 11"; same mark; Artist signed: J.L.; $275.00 – $325.00

*Row 4:*
1. Vase, 12"; same mark; Artist signed: C.J. Dibowski; $600.00 – $800.00
2. Vase, 15"; same mark; Artist signature obscured; $500.00 – $700.00
3. Ewer, 17"; same mark; Artist signed: Ferrell; $650.00 – $850.00
4. Ewer, 12"; same mark: Artist signed: KK; $450.00 – $550.00

# Louwelsa

*Row 1:*
    1. Vase, 6½"; Pansies with silver overlay; Marked with the Louwelsa half circle seal; $2500.00 – $3000.00
    2. Ewer, 9"; Floral with silver overlay; same mark; $1750.00 – $2250.00
    3. Mug, 6"; Indian portrait by artist E. Sulcer, same mark; $1100.00 – $1500.00

*Row 2:*
    1. Mug, 7"; Portrait of a Black Man by artist Turner; same mark; $1350.00 – $1600.00
    2. Vase, 10"; Portrait of Young Indian Girl; same mark; $1750.00 – $2250.00
    3. Mug, 7"; Portrait of Monk; same mark; $750.00 – $1000.00

*Row 3:*
    1. Vase, 11½"; "Chicks" by artist Minnie Mitchell, same mark; $1750.00 – $2250.00
    2. Vase, 14"; "Young Spotted Eagle"; Artist signed: Marie Rauchfuss; $2250.00 – $2700.00
    3. Vase, 11½"; Indian in Full Headdress by artist Burgess; Marked with the Louwelsa full circle seal; $2350.00 – $2750.00

Portrait pieces are very rare and difficult to find, and in the finely attuned network of art pottery news, it is unusual for one to appear on the market without attracting several immediate and eager bidders. It goes without saying that the Indian pieces rank at the top, and these by Levi J. Burgess, E. Sulcer and Marie Rauchfuss are of the best. But the portrait mug with the Black Man by R.G. Turner, and the most unusual and endearing "Chicks" by Minnie Mitchell are also quite rare, and very desirable . . . and of course, the silver overlay pieces are lovely—the contrast of the silver over the deep brown of the Louwelsa glaze provides a striking, yet complimentary effect.

## Louwelsa

*Row 1:*

    *1. Ewer, 6½"; Marked with the Louwelsa circle seal; $150.00 – $200.00*

    *2. Ewer, 6"; Marked with the Louwelsa half circle seal; Artist signed: Burgess; $150.00 – $200.00*

    *3. Vase, 5" x 8"; same mark as #2; Artist signature obscure; $150.00 – $175.00*

    *4. Double Jug, 6"; same mark as #2; $165.00 – $195.00*

    *5. Candleholder, 4½"; same mark; Artist signed: M.H.; $120.00 – $145.00*

*Row 2:*

    *1. Ewer, 5"; same mark; $125.00 – $160.00*

    *2. Vase, 9½"; No mark; Artist signed; $150.00 – $200.00*

    *3. Vase, 10½"; same mark as #2, Row 1; $175.00 – $225.00*

    *4. Vase, 10½"; Marked Weller (die impressed); $175.00 – $225.00*

    *5. Tankard, 11"; Marked with the Louwelsa half circle seal; Artist signed; $175.00 – $250.00*

    *6. Ewer, 5"; same mark as #5; $125.00 – $160.00*

*Row 3:*

    *1. Vase, 11"; same mark as #6, Row 2; Artist signed: H.M.; $300.00 – $450.00*

    *2. Vase, 16"; same mark; Artist signed: L.M.; $450.00 – $700.00*

    *3. Vase, 14½"; Marked with the Louwelsa circle seal; Artist signed: W.H.; $500.00 – $650.00*

    *4. Vase, 10½"; same mark as #3; $250.00 – $350.00*

    *5. Candleholder, 9"; Marked with the half circle seal; Artist signed: H.L.; $175.00 – $225.00*

*Louwelsa was made in 500 shapes! And often it is the shape of an unmarked piece that reveals its manufacturer. Some of the more frequently used shapes are as distinctively Weller as any trademark.*

*Literally hundreds of artists decorated Zanesville art pottery—only a few remained dedicated to one particular company; by far the majority migrated from one to another. The monograms of most of these artists translate easily into a name now well-known in pottery books—but several remain yet to be decoded. Such is the monogram on the second vase in Row 2:* ▆▙ *The candleholder, last in Row 3, is also by an unknown, H.L.*

*Top,*
*Left to Right:*
   *1. Louwelsa Vase, 16"; Marked with the Louwelsa half circle seal; Artist signed: C.L.; $950.00 – $1150.00*
   *2. Aurelian Lamp, 29"; Marked Aurelian Weller (by hand); Artist signed: E. Roberts; $1500.00 – $1900.00*
   *3. Louwelsa Ewer, 22½;" Marked with the half circle seal; Artist signed; $1400.00 – $1600.00*

*Bottom,*
*Left to Right:*
   *1. Louwelsa Vase, 25"; Marked with the Louwelsa half circle seal; Artist signed: E. Roberts; $2000.00 – $2500.00*
   *2. Louwelsa Vase, 24½"; No mark; Artist signed: H. Pillsbury; $2000.00 – $2500.00*

*The thought that such an ornate, fragile handle could have survived for so many years tends to precede the viewer's appreciation of the extraordinary beauty of the ewer, top right. Here, the modeling, rather than the slip work, is featured—and the delicate blossoms and leaves around the base serve only to accent. The large surface areas of the other pieces provide artists Claude Leffler, Roberts and Miss Pillsbury with an opportunity to demonstrate their talents at their best.*
*Aurelian Silver Overlay Mug, 6"; Marked Aurelian Wells, H, 435/6; (by hand); on handle, 1874 WBW 1899. How delighted the recipient of this 25-year presentation piece must have been! $3000.00 – $3500.00*

*Top,*
*Left to Right:*

    *1. Glossy Art Nouveau Umbrella Stand, 26"; No mark; $800.00 – $1000.00*

    *2. Ivory Jardiniere and Pedestal, 36"; Marked Weller (die impressed); $1200.00 – $1500.00*

    *3. Aurelian Jardiniere and Pedestal, 26½"; Molded in only one piece; No mark; $1275.00 – $1550.00*

*Bottom,*
*Left to Right:*

    *1. Louwelsa Jardiniere and Pedestal, 33"; Marked with the Louwelsa half circle seal; Artist signed; $1150.00 – $1450.00*

    *2. Aurelian Jardiniere and Pedestal, 38"; No mark; $3000.00 – $3500.00*

49

*Row 1:*
 *1. Dickens Ware, 1st Line: 3-handled Loving Cup, 5½"; Marked with the Dickens Weller seal; Artist signed; $300.00 – $400.00*

*Row 2:*
 *1. Aurelian Pillow Vase, 7½" x 8"; Marked Aurelian (by hand); $1250.00 – $1500.00*
 *2. Louwelsa Vase, 11"; Marked with the Louwelsa half circle seal ; Artist signed: A.H.; $800.00 – $1000.00*
 *3. Aurelian Mug with Silver Lid, 7"; Marked Aurelian Weller (by hand); Artist signed: K ; $1250.00 – $1550.00*

*Row 3:*
 *1. Louwelsa  Ewer, 14"; Marked with the Louwelsa half circle seal; Artist signed: R.G.T.; $950.00 – $1250.00*
 *2. Aurelian Vase, 18"; Marked Aurelian Weller; Artist signed: Fouts; $2500.00 – $3250.00*
 *3. Corleone Vase, 17"; Marked Corleone (by hand); Artist signed: H.P.; $1050.00 – $1350.00*
 *4. Silver overlay Aurelian Vase, 11½"; Marked Aurelian Weller (by hand); Artist signed: H.M.; $1250.00 – $1500.00*

*Two beautiful Aurelian pieces with silver accents stand out on this page—the vase by artist Hattie Mitchell, and the mug by Kappes (who also signed the pillow vase with the bird dog). The Louwelsa vase by Albert Haubrich has ring handles, an unusual feature. Corleone, decorated by Hester Pillsbury, is streaked with green brush strokes rather than golds and orange.*

*Row 1:*
    *1. Lonhuda Vase, 4½"; Marked with the Lonhuda shield, #820; Artist signed: A H ; $170.00 – $200.00*
    *2. Louwelsa Vase, 7"; Marked with the Louwelsa half circle seal; Artist signed: L.M.; $125.00 – $175.00*
    *3. Lonhuda Ewer, 6"; Marked with the Lonhuda shield; $225.00 – $250.00*

*Row 2:*
    *1. Louwelsa Lamp, 6½"; Marked with the Louwelsa  half circle seal; Artist signed: M.M.; $750.00 – $1000.00*

*Row 3:*
    *1. Aurelian Oil Banquet Lamp, 27"; Marked Aurelian (by hand), Weller (die impressed); Artist signed: Schnieder; $1400.00 – $1900.00*
    *2. Louwelsa Lamp, 10"; Marked with the Louwelsa half circle seal; Artist signed;  $800.00 – $1100.00*

*Lonhuda Pillow Vase, 11½"; Marked with the Lonhuda shield, #275; $3400.00 – $4400.00*

## Aurelian

*Row 1:*
  1. Ewer, 6"; Marked with the Aurelian Weller double circle seal; Artist signed: M.P.; $150.00 – $200.00

*Row 2:*
  1. Vase, 9"; No mark; $225.00 – $275.00
  2. Vase, 13"; Marked with the circle seal; Artist signed: R.A.; $650.00 – $900.00
  3. Vase, 7"; Marked Aurelian Weller (by hand), K on base; Artist signed: E.A.; $225.00 – $275.00

## Turada

*Row 3:*
  1. Mug, 6"; Marked with the Turada half circle seal; 562/7 on base; $250.00 – $325.00
  2. Jardiniere, 8½"; No mark; NPA
  3. Tobacco Jar, 5½"; shown without lid; same mark as #1; $250.00 – $350.00

*Row 4:*
  1. Lamp Base, 8"; same mark; $800.00 – $1000.00
  2. Jardiniere, 9½"; No mark; NPA

The large Aurelian vase with Ruth Axline's monogram poses a question! Was she a much earlier artist than was originally assumed?? or could Aurelian have been in production (perhaps limited) for nearly as long as Louwelsa? In a company letter written in 1924, the statement was made: "Louwelsa...is still produced in large quantities."

## Blue Louwelsa

*Row 1:*
  1. *Vase, 3"; Marked with the Louwelsa half circle seal; $350.00 – $500.00*

## Auroro

  2. *Vase, 9"; Marked Auroro Weller (by hand); Goldfish by artist Hattie Mitchell; $1100.00 – $1300.00*

## Dickens Ware, 3rd Line

  3. *Mug, 4"; No mark; $425.00 – $500.00*
  4. *Vase, 6"; Marked Weller (die impressed); $350.00 – $450.00*
  5. *Mug, 5"; "Master Belling"; Marked Weller, #7, in embossed rectangles; $350.00 – $400.00*

## Dickens Ware, 1st Line

*Row 2:*
  1. *Mug, 7"; Artist's initials obscured; Marked with the Dickens Ware half circle seal; $175.00 – $225.00*
  2. *Mug, 4½"; Artist's initials obscured; same mark; $125.00 – $150.00*
  3. *Mug, 4½"; Artist signed M.M.; $125.00 – $150.00*
  4. *Mug, 5"; Portrait of the Admiral; same mark; $750.00 – $1000.00*
  5. *Mug, 6"; same mark; $135.00 – $175.00*

*Row 3:*
  1. *Vase, 11"; same mark; $350.00 – $450.00*
  2. *Lamp, 11"; variation of same; $900.00 – $1100.00*
  3. *Jug, 6½"; same mark; $275.00 – $350.00*

*Row 4:*
  1. *Jardiniere, 8½"; same mark; $300.00 – $400.00*
  2. *Jardiniere, 8"; same mark; $300.00 – $400.00*

*Blue Louwelsa is a very rare line, and we were fortunate to be allowed to photograph several nice examples of it for you. Auroro is extremely rare—especially decorated with anything other than simple floral studies. It is interesting to note that in the photo of the decorating room of the 1920's, four pieces of Auroro occupy the top of a cabinet on the right with a stuffed crane! It seems unlikely that these should have remained there more than a few years at the most after the line was dropped from production.*

## Louwelsa

*Row 1:*

    *1. Green Vase, 6½"; Marked with the Louwelsa half circle seal; x/516/xxx on base; $550.00 – $750.00*

    *2. Blue Vase, 10½"; same mark as #1; $900.00 – $1100.00*

    *3. Blue vase, 6½"; same mark; 525 on base; $500.00 – $750.00*

    *4. Blue Mug, 5½" same mark; 562 on base; Artist signature obscured; $520.00 – $600.00*

## Dickens Ware

*1ST LINE*
*Row 2:*

    *1. Pillow vase, 7"; Marked with the Dickens Ware seal;  $1800.00 – $2200.00*

*2ND LINE*

    *2. Vase, 12½", Rare hi-gloss glaze; same mark; Artist signed: R.G.T.;  $2000.00 – $2500.00*

    *3. Vase, 10½"; "Dombey and Son"; same mark; Artist signed: W. Gibson; $950.00 – $1500.00*

*Row 3:*

    *1. Vase, 13"; "Chief Hollowhorn Bear"; same mark; Artist signed: A.D. (Dautherty); $2000.00 – $2500.00*

    *2. Vase, 15"; same mark; $1500.00 – $2000.00*

    *3. Vase, 11½"; same mark; $900.00 – $1200.00*

*Anna Dautherty displays her expertise with "Chief Hollowhorn Bear"... and even rarer than Blue Louwelsa, here is a Green piece—possibly experimental.*

# Dickens Ware, 2nd Line

*Row 1:*
>     *1. Vase, 9"; Marked Dickensware Weller; Artist signed E.L. Pickens; $1400.00 – $1700.00*
>     *2. Mug, 5½"; Rare hi-gloss glaze; "Prost" in the shield; $700.00 – $900.00*
>     *3. Vase, 9"; "Bald Eagle"; artist signed Anna Dautherty; $1550.00 – $2050.00*

*Row 2:*
>     *1. Vase, 12"; Artist signed Dusenbery; $2500.00 – $3000.00*
>     *2. Vase, 14"; Hi-gloss glaze; Artist signed Upjohn; $2250.00 – $2750.00*
>     *3. Vase, 10"; "Black Bear"; Artist signed Anna Dautherty; $1575.00 – $2075.00*

*Row 3:*
>     *1. Vase, 16"; Artist signed Dunlavy; $1750.00 – $2250.00*
>     *2. Vase, 13"; Artist signature indecipherable; This vase once decoarted the Weller theatre! $1250.00 – $1750.00*
>     *3. Vase, 17"; Artist signature indecipherable; $1400.00 – $1900.00*

*These prime examples of 2nd Dickens are among the finest to be found. The Indian portraits by Anna Dautherty, the Girl on the Lily Pad by Dusenbery, John Herold's Inn Scene, the rare hi-gloss Maid Marion by Upjohn, E.L. Pickens' Dog, and Dunlavy's Hunter are all immortal attestations of the calibre of these artists.*

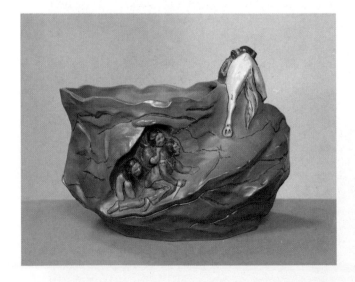 

*The Jardiniere, 11" x 14½", (both sides shown), displays a tableau of drama and suspense! Marked with the half circle seal; Artist signed by both Anthony Dunlavy and C.B. Upjohn; and dated 1903. $4500.00 – $5500.00*

# Dickens Ware, 2nd Line

*Row 1:*
   1. Vase, 8"; No mark; Artist signed: D.S.; $800.00 – $1000.00
   2. Vase, 11"; Marked with the Dickens Ware seal; Artist signed: H.S.; $900.00 – $1100.00
   3. Vase, 9"; Marked Dickens Weller (by hand); $1500.00 – $2000.00

*Row 2:*
   1. Vase, 13"; same mark as #2, Row 1; $2000.00 – $2500.00
   2. Vase, 9½"; Weller (die impressed); $1600.00 – $1800.00
   3. White Vase, 12"; Marked with the Dickens Ware seal; Artist signed: Uj and H(erold); $900.00 – $1200.00

*Row 3:*
   1. Vase, 16"; "Don Quixote and Sancho Setting Out"; Artist signed: E.L. Pickens; $2750.00 – $3250.00
   2. Advertising Plate, 12½"; $2000.00 – $2500.00
   3. White Vase, 16"; Marked Dickens Weller (by hand); "Sam Weller Despilling The Feverish Remains of the Previous Evening's Conviviality"; Artist signed: E.L. Pickens; $2000.00 – $2500.00

These 2nd Dickens pieces are most unusual: The rare hi-gloss Indian by Helen Smith; the two very unique "white" examples; the advertising plate . . . neither the cat nor the fish are typical Dickens Ware "characters." And the pair of magnificent vases on Row 3 leaves no doubt concerning the expertise of E.L. Pickens.

## Dickens Ware, 2nd Line

*Row 1:*
> 1. Ewer, 10½"; No mark; $950.00 – $1250.00
> 2. Ewer, 8½"; Marked with the Dickens Ware half circle seal; $500.00 – $750.00
> 3. Jug, 5½"; "The Mt Vernon Bridge Co, Mt Vernon, O"; same mark; Artist signed: U J; $600.00 – $900.00

*Row 2:*
> 1. Mug, 6"; "Black Bird"; same mark; Artist signed: UJ; $700.00 – $900.00
> 2. Vase, 1¼"; "Apr.27-28-29, 1903. Weller Theatre"; same mark; $300.00 – $350.00
> 3. Ewer, 12"; "Chief Blackbear"; same mark; Artist signed: A.D(unlavy) and Anna Dautherty ; $1750.00 – $2250.00
> 4. Mug, 5"; Marked Dickens Weller (by hand);  $150.00 – $200.00

*Row 3:*
> 1. Vase, 15½"; Marked Weller Dickensware (by hand); $1600.00 – $1900.00
> 2. Vase, 17½"; Marked with the Dickens Ware seal; Artist signed: C.B. Upjohn; $2250.00 – $2750.00
> 3. Vase, 15½"; Marked Dickens Weller (by hand); Artist signed: E.L. Pickens; $1200.00 – $1500.00

*Here are some very fine examples of 2nd Dickens by some of the top artists: Indians by Upjohn . . . the ewer for some obscure reason was signed by both Anthony Dunlavy and Anna Dautherty—one may have been responsible for the sgraffito work and the other for the slip decorating. Those little Weller Theatre souvenir pieces are very rare; so are the Mt. Vernon Bridge items!*

## Etched Matt

Row 1:
   1. Vase, 11"; Marked Weller Etched Matt; $750.00 – $1250.00

## Dickens Ware, 2nd Line

   2. White Pillow Vase, 7" x 8"; "Old North Church, Boston, Mass"; Marked with the Dickens Ware half circle seal; $1750.00 – $2250.00

Row 2:
   1. Vase, 11"; Marked Weller (by hand); Artist signed: C.A. Dusenbery; $1750.00 – $2250.00
   2. Tankard, 12½", very rare semi-gloss glaze; Marked Weller Dickens (by hand); Artist signed both F.F. and Ferrell; $2000.00 – $2400.00
   3. Tankard with Nude, 12"; No mark; Artist signed and dated E L. Pickens, 1902; $2500.00 – $3000.00

Row 3:
   1. Vase, 14"; "A danger forseen is half avoided"; Marked Dickens Weller (by hand); Artist signed: A. Wilson; $2000.00 – $2400.00
   2. Vase, 13½"; Hi-gloss; Marked with the Dickens Ware half circle seal; $3000.00 – $4000.00
   4. Vase, 13½"; Hi-gloss; No mark; Artist signed: J.H.; $1000.00 – $1250.00

Two very rare pieces of Weller Pottery are shown on Row 1—Etched Matt and "white" Dickens ware. The tankard in the middle of Row 2 has an unusual semi-matt englobe; and on its right, "The Nude" by E.L. Pickens is one of the most intricately executed examples of this type we've seen. High gloss 2nd Dickens is very rare, and both the large vase in the bottom row and the unusual blue-on-blue Cavalier by artist John Herold are magnificent examples of this line.

## Dickens Ware, 2nd Line

*Row 1:*
1. Pitcher, 4"; Marked with the Dickensware seal; Artist: C.W.; $400.00 – $500.00
2. Mug, 5½"; same mark; Artist signed: L.J.B.; $500.00 – $600.00
3. Vase, 6½"; same mark; Artist signed: A.D.; $800.00 – $1000.00
4. Mug, 6"; same mark; Artist signed: E.W.; $400.00 – $450.00
5. Mug, 5"; same mark; Artist signed: H.S.; $300.00 – $350.00

*Row 2:*
1. Vase, 5½"; same mark; Artist signed: L.J.B.; $750.00 – $1000.00
2. Vase, 6½"; same mark; Artist signed: U J ; $350.00 – $500.00
3. Vase, 9½"; hi-gloss glaze; same mark; $550.00 – $700.00
4. Pitcher, 7"; same mark; $350.00 – $500.00
5. Vase, 6½"; "The Mt. Vernon Bridge Co., Mt. Vernon Ohio"; same mark; $550.00 – $650.00

*Row 3:*
Tobacco Jars
1. The Captain, 7"; Marked inside: Dickens Weller (by hand); $1200.00 – $1700.00
2. The Irishman, 6½"; Artist signed: R. D.; No mark; $1100.00 – $1500.00
3. The Skull, 5½"; Marked Dickens Weller inside the lid, (by hand); $1350.00 – $1650.00
4. The Chinaman, 6"; same mark; $1000.00 – $1400.00
5. The Turk, 7"; same mark; $1000.00 – $1500.00

*Row 4:*
1. Ewer, 11"; Marked with the Dickensware seal; Artist signed: M.A.; $550.00 – $750.00
2. Vase, 11"; same mark as ewer; $800.00 – $1000.00
3. Vase, 13"; "Mr. Micawber impressing the names of streets upon me that I might find my way back again early in the morning. David Copperfield"; same mark; $1250.00 – $1750.00
4. Ewer, 11½"; Marked Dickens Weller (by hand); Artist signed: E.L. Pickens, full signature; $800.00 – $1200.00

No doubt the most exciting piece on this entire page of outstanding 2nd Dickens (and maybe the most unattractive) is not the rare "Mt. Vernon Bridge" vase… or Dunlavy's Indian …or even the most unusual high gloss piece in Row 2! It's the smiling one staring out at the world from the center of the page—but can one smile with no teeth or stare with no eyes??? To our knowledge, this is one of three in existence—and this one is especially unique since the finial is also a skull.

*Row 1:*
  1. *Vase with Dog, 5" x 5½"; No mark; Artist signed: CMM; $500.00 – $700.00*
  2. *Auroro Candleholders, pr., 9"; Marked Weller (by hand); Artist initialed: W. ; $500.00 – $800.00*
  3. *Vase, 7"; No mark; $200.00 – $250.00*

*Row 2:*
  1. *Fudzi Vase, 7"; #525; No mark; $700.00 – $900.00*

# Matt Floretta

  2. *Tankard, 13½"; No mark; Artist signed: C.D.; $450.00 – $550.00*
  3. *Tankard, 10½"; Marked Floretta Weller (by hand); $300.00 – $400.00*

# Eocean

*Row 3:*
  1. *Vase, 10½"; Marked Eocean Rose Weller (by hand); Artist signed: E.B.; $1200.00 – $1500.00*
  2. *Vase 10½"; #9613, WELLER in embossed rectangles; Artist signed: E.P.; $500.00 – $700.00*
  3. *Vase, 11½"; Marked Eocean Weller; Artist signed: L.J.B.; $450.00 – $650.00*
  4. *Vase, 7½"; Marked Weller (die impressed); $400.00 – $500.00*

*Even though it seems a most unlikely identification, ewers and mugs in the matt finish and typical colors of 2nd Dickens, decorated with fruit design in sgraffito, are nonetheless designated Floretta by the hand incised mark on the base! The Auroro and Fudzi lines are extremely rare.*

## Eocean, Late Line

Row 1:
   1. Bud Vase, 6½"; No mark; $80.00 – $110.00
   2. Vase, 10½"; Artist signed: M.T.; $350.00 – $450.00
   3. Vase, 8½"; No mark; $300.00 – $400.00
   4. Bud Vase, 5"; Weller (small die impressed); $70.00 – $90.00

## Louwelsa

Row 2:
   1. Jardiniere, 9½"; Marked with the Louwelsa half circle seal; $275.00 – $325.00
   2. Jardiniere, 6½"; Weller (die impressed); $135.00 – $165.00

Row 3:
   1. Jardiniere, 12½"; No mark; $300.00 – $400.00

There were several pages of Eocean in the old Weller Catalogues, some of which we have reproduced for your study and all displayed the change that evolution had wrought. These were decorated with bolder brush strokes, brighter colors—perhaps less finesse—than the Eocean made approximately two decades earlier; even so, the ware is beautiful.

Row 1:
    1. *Vase, 8"; Very high glassy glaze; Artist signed: D.E.; $350.00 – $450.00*
    2. *Jap Birdimal Vase, 7"; No mark; $350.00 – $450.00*
    3. *Auroro Vase, 6"; Marked Auroro Weller (by hand); Artist signed; $400.00 – $500.00*
    4. *DRESDEN Vase, 8½"; Marked Weller (die impressed); $600.00 – $700.00*

## Eocean

Row 2:
    1. *Basket, 6½"; No mark; $250.00 – $350.00*
    2. *Vase, 7"; Marked Eocean Weller (by hand); $300.00 – $450.00*
    3. *Candlestick, 9"; same mark as #2; Artist signed: L.J.B.; $250.00 – $300.00*
    4. *Candlestick, 9"; same mark; Artist signed F.F.; $250.00 – $300.00*
    5. *Vase, 8"; Marked Weller (die impressed); $250.00 – $350.00*

Row 3:
    1. *Vase, 13"; Eocean Weller (by hand); Artist signed: L.J.B.; $650.00 – $850.00*
    2. *Vase, 16"; Marked Weller (by hand); $500.00 – $600.00*
    3. *Vase, 13½"; same mark as #1, Row 1; Artist signed: A.H.; $500.00 – $700.00*
    4. *Vase, 12½"; same mark as #3; Artist signed: M. Rauchfuss; $450.00 – $600.00*

*The work of some of Weller's finest artists is displayed here on the Eocean line: Levi J. Burgess, Frank Ferrell, Albert Haubrich, and Marie Rauchfuss. The tall candlesticks are very rare!*

*Row 1:*

    *1. St. Louis Fair, LPE,1904 Souvenir Vase, 4"; rare; $175.00 – $225.00*

    *2. McKinley Plaque, 5"; Souvenir of St. Louis Fair; $650.00 – $750.00*

    *3. Vase with Seahorses, 5½"; Marked Weller (small die impressed); $400.00 – $500.00*

*Row 2:*

    *1. Vase, 8"; Marked Weller (by hand); Artist signed: Pillsbury; $275.00 – $325.00*

    *2. Vase, 5"; Marked WELLER WARE (die impressed); $135.00 – $165.00*

    *3. Vase, 7"; One of the circle seals only partially visible; $125.00 – $150.00*

*Row 3:*

    *1. DICKENS WARE, 2ND LINE Vase, 10"; "God Bless Me, What's the Matter. Pickwick Papers, (BILST UM PSHI S.M. . ARK)"[sic]; Characters are finished in a glossy glaze; Marked with the Dickens Ware die; Artist signe C.W.; $1000.00– $1250.00*

    *2. Turk Tobacco Jar, 7½"; Very unusual in Green Matt glaze; No mark; $650.00– $950.00*

    *3. DICKENS WARE, 2ND LINE Vase, 9½"; "Withers Meeting Him on the Stairs Stood Amazed at the Beauty of His Teeth and His Brilliant Smile. Dombey & Sons"; Marked with the Dickens Ware die; Artist signed: E.L.P.; $700.00 – $900.00*

*Row 4:*

    *1. DICKENS WARE, 2ND LINE Vase, 9½"; Marked with the Dickens Ware die; Incising around the pattern; $400.00 – $500.00*

    *2. TURADA Lamp, 10"; Marked Turada Weller (die impressed); $800.00 – $1000.00*

    *3. LOUWELSA Vase, 12"; Marked with the Louwelsa circle seal; $450.00 – $550.00*

*Row 1:*

    *1. DICKENS WARE, 3RD LINE Teapot, 7"; "Captain Cuttle, Florence Dombey; #5055, WELLER in embossed rectangles; $670.00 – $810.00*

    *2. Vase with Owls, 8"; No mark; Artist signed: L.P.; $600.00 – $850.00*

    *3. JAP BIRDIMAL Vase, 4½"; No mark; $400.00 – $500.00*

    *4. JAP BIRDIMAL Pitcher, 4"; #7034, WELLER in embossed rectangles; Artist signed: L.P. and Rhead; $400.00 – $450.00*

*Row 2:*

    *2. LONHUDA Vase, 5½"; Marked with the Lonhuda shield; Artist Signed: S. Reid McLaughlin; $300.00 – $350.00*

    *2. LONHUDA Ewer, 7"; same mark as 31, #215; Artist signed: J.R.S.; $375.00 – $475.00*

    *3. HUNTER Ewer, 11"; x357 on base; $625.00 – $825.00*

    *4. HUNTER Pillow Vase, 5" x 3½"; Marked Hunter (by hand); Artist signed: U.J.; $375.00 – $425.00*

*Row 3:*

    *1. DICKENS WARE, 2ND LINE Vase, 15½"; Hi-gloss; Peepy was Sufficiently Decorated to Walk Hand in Hand with the Professor of Deportment. Bleak Mouse"; Marked with the Dickens Weller die; Artist signed: H.S.; $2000.00 – $2400.00*

    *2. DICKENS WARE, 1ST LINE Lamp with Owl, 14"; Marked with the Dickens Weller die; Artist signed: E A.; $1250.00 – $1500.00*

    *3. BLUE LOUWELSA Vase, 10½"; Marked with the circle seal; $900.00 – $1200.00*

    *4. BLUE LOUWELSA Vase, 10"; Marked with the Louwelsa half circle seal; Artist signed: L.M.; $700.00 – $900.00*

*All lovely, and all very rare! A fact that should not discourage, but rather serve to enhance our appreciation of these very fine artware lines.*

*Row 1:*

    *1. HUNTER Vase, 7"; Marked Hunter (by hand); $475.00 – $575.00*

    *2. LA SA Vase, 9"; Bi-plane decoration; $1500.00 – $1800.00*

    *3. BLUE LOUWELSA Vase, 6½" Marked Weller (by hand); $450.00 – $600.00*

*Row 2:*

    *1. EOCEAN Vase, 11½"; Marked Eocean Weller (by hand) Artist signed: K.K.; $400.00 – $500.00*

    *2. LAMAR Vase, 14½"; Marked with the round WELLER WARE Ink stamp; $450.00 – $550.00*

    *3. ETNA "Beethoven" Vase, 12"; Marked with the Etna Weller circle seal; $500.00 – $750.00*

    *4. BLUE LOUWELSA Vase, 10"; Marked with the Louwelsa circle seal; $900.00 – $1200.00*

*Row 3:*

    *1. AURELIAN Vase, 16"; Marked Aurelian (by hand); Artist signed: T.J.W.; $1400.00 – $1800.00*

    *2. AURELIAN Tankard, 12½"; Marked Aurelian Weller (by hand); $900.00 – $1200.00*

    *3. LOUWELSA Tankard, 16½"; Marked with the Louwelsa circle seal; Artist signed: E. Roberts; $500.00 – $700.00*

*Many pieces of the rare Hunter line differ from 2nd Dickens in glaze treatment only—shapes and decorations are often identical.*

## L'art Nouveau

*Row 1:*
   *1. Corn bank, 8"; No mark; $400.00 – $550.00*
   *2. Vase, 4½"; Marked with the Art Nouveau Weller double circle seal; $200.00 – $300.00*
   *3. Vase, 8"; Weller (small die impressed); $175.00 – $225.00*
   *4. Vase, 8"; Weller (small die impressed); $425.00 – $525.00*
   *5. Bud vase, 7½"; no mark; $475.00 – $575.00*
   *6. Mug, 5"; Weller (small die impressed); $200.00 – $250.00*

*Row 2:*
   *1. Ewer, 14½"; Marked with the Art Nouveau Weller seal; $500.00 – $600.00*
   *2. Vase, 12"; Weller (small die impressed); $225.00 – $300.00*
   *3. Vase, 12"; Marked WELLER MATT WARE (by hand); $500.00 – $650.00*
   *4. Ewer, 12½"; Marked with the Art Nouveau Weller seal; $375.00 – $475.00*
   *5. Vase, 13½"; same mark as #4; $375.00 – $475.00*

*Row 3:*
   *1. Vase, 13"; same mark; $1700.00 – $2100.00*
   *2. Vase, 9"; Weller (small die impressed); $175.00 – $225.00*
   *3. Vase, 17½"; No mark; $650.00 – $850.00*
   *4. Ewer, 8"; Weller (small die impressed); $150.00 – $200.00*
   *5. Vase, 16"; Marked with the Art Nouveau Weller seal; $450.00 – $600.00*

*The double circle seal used on the pastel Art Nouveau ware sometimes contains the word "Matt" within the inner circle. In addition to the two ewers shown, at least seven more sizes are known to exist—there are probably even more. They measure: 22½ , $450.00 – $650.00; 13", $250.00 – $300.00, 11" , $225.00 – $275.00, 10¼", $200.00 – $250.00; 9½", $175.00 – $225.00; 8¾", $150.00 – $200.00, and 7½", $125.00 – $175.00. The darker vase in the center of Row 2 is from a line nearly always marked "Weller Matt Ware," and is believed by some authorities to have been modeled by Albert Radford.*

*Row 1:*
   *1. Vase, 8½"; Marked WELLER MATT WARE (by hand); $400.00 – $500.00*
   *2. ART NOUVEAU Vase, 14½"; Marked Weller (by hand); $900.00 – $1200.00*
   *3. ART NOUVEAU Vase, 7½"; Marked Weller (small die impressed); $750.00 – $1000.00*

## Perfecto (Matt Louwelsa)

*Row 2:*
   *1. Ewer, 12"; No mark, #580/2 on base; $450.00 – $550.00*
   *2. Ewer, 17"; No mark, #436 on base; Artist signed: H.P; $650.00 – $750.00*
   *3. Ewer, 12"; No mark, #580/4 on base; Artist signed: A Haubrich; $650.00 – $750.00*

Very slight differences are apparent between some pieces of Art Nouveau and (marked) Weller Matt Ware; this is a good example. Here the coloration of both lines are basically the same, while other Weller Matt Ware tends to a deeper teal with more distinct differences in pattern. It may well be that Art Nouveau evolved from the earlier Matt Ware concept.

Perfecto! One of the most quietly elegant art lines made by Weller. Very rare—with marked examples even rarer, this line, we believe, developed over a period of time, through experiments aimed toward the development of a matt glaze. The only marked piece we can locate (below) carries the double circle "Perfecto" seal —but at least one exists with the Louwelsa die stamp. To distinguish between this type of ware and the vase on pg.87 marked Matt Louwelsa, we prefer the use of the Perfecto name—either would be proper.

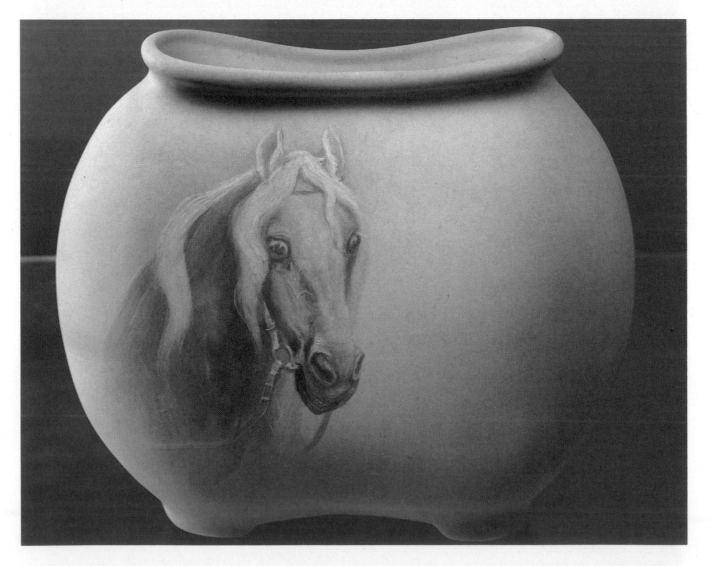

*PERFECTO Pillow Vase, 10½"; Marked with the Perfecto Double circle seal, x220 1; Artist signed: Hester Pillsbury; $3250.00 – $3750.00*

*Row 1:*

1. *JAP BIRDIMAL Oil Pitcher, 10½"; Artist signed: HMR; $800.00 – $1000.00*
2. *JAP BIRDIMAL Vase, 4"; No mark; $500.00 – $650.00*
3. *EOCEAN Flask Vase, 7½"; Artist signed: L. Blake; $900.00 – $1100.00*
4. *LOUWELSA Mug, 3"; Marked with the Louwelsa half circle seal; $75.00 – $125.00*
5. *LOUWELSA Mug, 6"; same mark as #4; Artist signed: M.R.; $450.00 – $500.00*

*Row 2:*

1. *JAP BIRDIMAL Vase, 13"; Artist signed: V.M.H.; $1600.00 – $2000.00*
2. *PERFECTO Vase, 14"; Artist signed: M.H.; $500.00 – $700.00*
3. *HUDSON-PERFECTO Vase, 13"; Weller (die impressed); $3250.00 – $3750.00*

*Row 3:*

1. *AURELIAN Ewer, 12"; Marked Aurelian (by hand), Weller (small die impressed); Stag by artist Abel; $800.00 – $975.00*
2. *AURELIAN Ewer, 16½"; same mark as #1; Cavalier by artist Fouts; $1400.00 – $1800.00*
3. *LOUWELSA Vase, 16½"; Marked with the Louwelsa half circle seal; Artist signed: A. Dunlavy; $2000.00 – $2500.00*
4. *LOUWELSA Vase, 13½"; same mark as #3, Horse by artist M.T.; $1250.00 – $1650.00*

Whether you prefer to call the line Matt Louwelsa or Perfecto, either is probably correct as both the Louwelsa and Perfecto seals have been found on examples of this line. The technique differs from other artware lines in that while the "englobe" effect (that is, the sprayed or brushed on background slip uniting as one layer with the slip artwork) is common to most, Perfecto slip work is applied over a bisque-like background—the old catalogues referred to it as "unglazed ware." On its right is a magnificent example of a Hudson-Perfecto—probably 15 to 20 years later, and its technique of painting with flat mineral stains over the "englobe" (no heavy slip work here) qualify it for the Hudson-Perfecto line. (Albert Haubrich's signature on the earlier Perfecto indicates the date of manufacture was before 1904, when he left Weller to work for Radford.)

# Sicardo

*Row 1:*

    *1. Mug, 3½"; No mark; $450.00 – $500.00*
    *2. Vase, 4½"; No mark; $300.00 – $400.00*
    *3. Vase, 6"; Signed Weller Sicard on surface of ware; $400.00 – $600.00*
    *4. Vase, 5½"; Signed Sicard; $400.00 – $550.00*
    *5. Vase, 4½"; Signed Sicard; $300.00 – $400.00*
    *6. Vase, 3½"; Signed Sicard; $300.00 – $400.00*

*Row 2:*

    *1. Vase, 5"; No mark; $350.00 – $450.00*
    *2. Vase, 5"; Signed Weller Sicard; $350.00 – $450.00*
    *3. Vase, 6"; Signed Weller Sicard; $650.00 – $850.00*
    *4. Vase, 4"; No mark; $300.00 – $400.00*
    *5. Vase, 4½"; No mark; $300.00 – $375.00*

*Row 3:*

    *1. Pillow Vase, 6½" X 10"; Marked Weller (small die impressed); $900.00 – $1200.00*
    *2. Vase, 2"; No mark; $200.00 – $250.00*
    *3. Plate, 9"; A gift to Sicard when he left France for America; Inscribed on back:"24 December 1901, 10 o'clock in the evening. The unknown awaits us. Go! And be happy J. Sicard." The French crest appears in the center and it is signed by an unknown artist, possibly "Lapir." One of a kind.*
    *4. Vase, 2½"; Signed Weller Sicardo; $250.00 – $300.00*
    *5. Bow, 5"; No mark; $525.00 – $625.00*

*Row 4:*

    *1. Vase, 9"; Signed Sicard; $800.00 – $950.00*
    *2. Vase, 6"; No mark; $400.00 – $500.00*
    *3. Vase, 12½"; Signed Weller Sicard on the bottom; $2000.00 – $2500.00*
    *4. Vase, 15½"; Signed Weller Sicard; $1400.00 – $1700.00*
    *5. Vase, 6"; No mark; $400.00 – $450.00*
    *6. Vase, 9"; Signed Weller Sicard; $900.00 – $1050.00*

## Sicardo

Row 1:
1. Tambourine Boy, 9½"; no mark; $4000.00 – $5000.00
2. Vase with Locust, 3"; Signed: Sicard, Marseille; $125.00 – $150.00
3. Plaque, 10½"; No mark; $2250.00 – $2750.00

Row 2:
1. Vase, 12½"; Three sides show progressively: closed dandelion, blooming flower, and dispersing seeds; Signed: Sicard Weller; $2250.00 – $2750.00
2. Vase, 15½"; This vase was shown in a Tiffany catalogue; #10 on base; $1500.00 – $2000.00
3. Vase, 12"; Marked Sicard Weller; $1250.00 – $1750.00

*Plaque, 18" x 12¼"; Extremely rare; $7000.00 – $9000.00*

## Hunter

*Top,*
*Left to right:*

1. Vase, 6½"; Marked Hunter, #343 (by hand); $650.00 – $750.00
2. Vase, 7½"; Marked Hunter, #413 (by hand) Artist signed: UJ; $750.00 – $950.00
3. Pillow vase, 4¾"; No mark; $550.00 – $650.00

## Cabinet Pieces

*Bottom,*
*Row 1:*

1. Ewer, 3½"; Decorated with Gremlin in relief in the manner of 3rd Line Dickens; Marked Weller (by hand); $175.00 – $225.00
2. Vase, 3½"; Marked Louwelsa Weller (by hand); $145.00 – $165.00
3. Vase, 4"; Louwelsa half circle seal; $155.00 – $175.00
4. Vase, 4"; Signed Weller LaSa; $225.00 – $275.00
5. Ewer, 4"; no mark; Artist signed: V. Adams; (Although Virginia Adams was an early Weller artist, she decorated this piece for Roseville! ); $195.00 – $220.00
6. Vase, 4"; Birdimal-type, no mark; $175.00 – $225.00
7. Jug, 3"; Marked with the Louwelsa half circle seal; $175.00 – $200.00
8. Vase, 2½"; Marked Sicard Weller; $250.00 – $350.00

*Row 2:*

1. Bowl, 2"; Claywood; no mark; $100.00 – $150.00
2. Jug, 3½"; Marked with the Louwelsa half circle seal; Artist signature obscured; $135.00 – $165.00
3. Vase, 4"; Eocean; Marked with the small Weller die stamp; $125.00 – $175.00
4. Ewer, 5"; Marked with the Dickens ware half circle seal; this is 2nd Line; $250.00 – $300.00
5. Vase, 4½"; Marked with the Louwelsa half circle seal; $140.00 – $170.00
6. Vase, 4½"; Eocean; Marked with small Weller die stamp; $125.00 – $150.00
7. Vase, 2"; Marked with the Louwelsa half circle seal; $140.00 – $160.00

*Row 3:*

1. Star with lid, 2½"; Marked with the Louwelsa circle seal; $275.00 – $350.00
2. Vase, 5"; Marked with the Louwelsa half circle seal; Artist signed: C T.; $200.00 – $225.00
3. Vase, 5½"; Marked with the Floretta circle seal; $175.00 – $200.00
4. Vase, 5½"; Marked with the Louwelsa circle seal, Matt (by hand); $200.00 – $250.00
5. Vase, 4½"; Louwelsa; no mark; $150.00 – $175.00
6. Vase, 4½"; Eocean: Marked with the small Weller die stamp; $125.00 – $175.00
7. Vase, 2"; marked with the Louwelsa half circle seal; Artist monogram unknown; $160.00 – $180.00

# Dickens Ware, 3rd Line

*Top,*
*Row 1:*

    *1. Vase, 10½"; Marked Weller, Artist signed: L.S.; "Wilkins Micawber, David Copperfield" ; $700.00 – $800.00*

    *2. Vase, 8"; Shape #15 impressed on base, no mark; "Mr. Weller, Sr., Pickwick Papers"; $900.00 – $1100.00*

    *3. Vase, 9½"; Marked Dickens Weller incised by hand; Inscription on base, "Bailey" ; $600.00 – $850.00*

*Row 2:*

    *1. Ink well, 2½"; Marked Weller (by hand), #0038, Artist signed: R; "Income twenty pounds, expenditure nineteen-six, result happiness. Income twenty pounds, expenditures twenty pounds and six, result misery. Remain of a Fallen Tower, Wilkins Micawber"; $350.00 – $500.00*

    *2. Flask vase, 7½"; Marked Weller, #0021 (embossed in rectangles), Artist initial P; "Dombey and son" on disk; $450.00 – $550.00*

    *3. Creamer, 4"; Marked Weller (die impressed), #0034; "Charles Dickens" on disk; $150.00 – $200.00*

*Bottom,*
*Left to right:*

    *1. Vase, 13"; Marked Weller, #12; "Carker, Dombey and son" on disk; $650.00 – $800.00*

    *2. Carafe with Cup, 14½"; Marked Weller, #0002, Artist initial: R; "David Copperfield" ; $1200.00 – $1500.00*

    *3. Ewer, 12½"; Marked Dickens Weller (by hand), Artist signed: L.M.; "Squeers"; $550.00 – $750.00*

95

## Floretta

*Row 1:*
    *1. Vase, 7½"; Marked with the Floretta Weller double circle seal; $110.00 – $135.00*
    *2. Vase, 5½"; same mark; $60.00 – $80.00*
    *3. Vase, 5½"; same mark; $95.00 – $110.00*
    *4. Ewer, 6"; same mark; $60.00 – $90.00*
    *5. Vase, 6½"; same mark; $90.00 – $125.00*

*Row 2:*
    *1. Ewer, 10½"; same mark; $100.00 – $135.00*
    *2. Vase, 9"; same mark; $160.00 – $185.00*
    *3. Vase, 7½"; same mark; $60.00 – $85.00*
    *4. Vase, 12"; No mark; $300.00 – $350.00*

*Row 3:*
    *1. Vase, 17"; same mark;   $250.00 – $300.00*
    *2. Vase, 19"; same mark; $500.00 – $650.00*
    *3. Vase, 13½"; same mark; $275.00 – $325.00*

*Unless you are familiar with typical Floretta molds, it is sometimes difficult to distinguish between unmarked Etna and gray Floretta!!*

## Floretta

*Row 1:*
1. Vase, 5½"; No mark; $100.00 – $125.00
2. Vase, 5½"; Marked with the Floretta double circle seal; $150.00 – $200.00

*Row 2:*
1. Vase, 7"; same mark as #2, Row 1; $400.00 – $600.00

## Etna

2. Vase with Lizard, 4½"; Marked Weller (small die impressed); $400.00 – $500.00
3. Vase with Frog and Snake, 6½"; same mark; $500.00 – $600.00
4. Bowl with Mouse, 2½"; same mark; $300.00 – $400.00
5. Vase, 5½"; Marked Weller Etna (die impressed); $100.00  – $125.00

*Row 3:*
1. Vase, 11"; Marked Weller in slip on side of ware; $275.00 – $325.00
2. Vase,15"; Marked Weller in slip on side of ware, and Weller Etna die on base; $300.00 – $375.00

## Floretta, cont.

3. Vase, 13½"; No mark; $325.00 – $425.00
4. Vase, 11½"; Marked Floretta with the double circle seal; $275.00 – $350.00

Etna is sometimes marked "Weller" on the side of the ware, near the base; this may help you to identify unmarked examples of this line. The Etna trio in Row 2 are very difficult to find.

## Floretta

*Row 1:*
1. Vase, 4½"; Marked with the Floretta double circle seal; $90.00 – $125.00
2. Vase, 6"; same mark; $100.00 – $125.00
3. Vase, 6"; No mark; B/15 incised on base; $100.00 – $150.00
4. Mug, 5"; same mark; $75.00 – $95.00
5. Ewer, 4½"; same mark; $60.00 – $75.00

## Eocean

*Row 2:*
1. Vase, 6"; Artist signed: M.S.; $150.00 – $210.00
2. Vase, 9"; No mark; $175.00 – $225.00
3. Vase, 10½"; Marked EOCEAN ROSE WELLER; Artist signed: L.J.B.; $350.00 – $400.00

## Dresden

4. Vase, 10½"; Marked Weller (by hand); Artist signed: L.J.B.; $500.00 – $650.00
5. Mug, 5½"; Marked Weller Matt (by hand); Artist signed: L.J.B.; $400.00 – $500.00

## Jap Birdimal

*Row 3:*
1. Vase, 4"; Weller (small die impressed); $400.00 – $500.00
2. Mug, 5"; Marked Weller Rhead Faience; $800.00 – $1000.00
3. Vase, 7"; No mark; $375.00 – $450.00
4. Pitcher, 4"; Weller (small die impressed); $350.00 – $400.00
5. Mug, 5"; 2nd Dickens type; Weller (small die impressed); $325.00 – $400.00
6. Vase, 4½"; Marked Weller (by hand); $200.00 – $225.00

## Jap Birdimal

*Row 4:*
1. Vase, 14"; Weller (small die impressed); $800.00 – $1200.00
2. Urn, 9"; Weller (die impressed); $375.00 – $475.00
3. Vase, 11"; No mark; $600.00 – $800.00

*Row 1:*

1. DICKENS WARE Jug, 4½"; Marked with the Dickensware seal; $175.00 – $250.00
2. LOUWELSA Clock, 9½"; Marked with the half circle seal; $500.00 – $700.00
3. Red Vase with Burgundy Slip Decoration, 8"; Marked Weller (by hand); $375.00 – $425.00

*Row 2:*

1. SICARD Vase, 5"; Marked Weller Sicard on side of ware; $400.00 – $500.00
2. SICARD Vase, 9"; Marked Weller Sicard on side of ware; $800.00 – $1000.00
3. LA SA-type in black and white; Vase, 13½"; No mark; $900.00 – $1100.00
4. LA SA Vase, 13½" No mark; $750.00 – $1000.00
5. LA SA Vase, 7"; No mark; $400.00 – $500.00
6. LA SA Bud Vase, 5½"; Marked Weller La Sa; $200.00 – $300.00

## Glossy L'Art Nouveau

*Row 3:*

1. Vase, 12"; Marked with the Art Nouveau double circle seal; $350.00 – $400.00
2. Console Bowl, 6" x 12"; same mark; $200.00 – $300.00
3. Vase, 12½"; No mark; $300.00 – $450.00

The red vase on Row 1 would suggest "Red Louwelsa"!!! Whatever its proper genus, it is extremely rare. Almost every Weller collection will contain at least one "mystery" vase or urn—many are no doubt one-of-a-kind items that were never provided with a proper name. The black and white "La Sa type" is another one of these. And on the bottom row, the rich brown glossy Art Nouveau ware is harder to find than the matt pastel line.

# Etna

*Row 1:*

    *1. Vase, 6½"; Marked with the Weller Etna die stamp; $125.00 – $150.00*

    *2. Vase, 9"; same mark; $350.00 – $450.00*

    *3. Vase, 5½" same mark; $100.00 – $120.00*

*Row 2:*

    *1. Vase, 6"; No mark; $100.00 – $125.00*

    *2. Pitcher, 6"; Weller Etna die stamp; $125.00 – $150.00*

    *3. Pitcher, 6½"; same mark, and Etna (by hand); $140.00 – $160.00*

    *4. Mug, 5½"; same mark; $100.00 – $125.00*

    *5. Mug, 5"; Marked with the Weller Ware die stamp, #9005; both Etna and Eocean are incised into the base by hand!; $100.00 – $125.00*

*Row 3:*

    *1. Vase, 7"; Marked with Weller Etna die stamp; $125.00 – $150.00*

    *2. Vase, 10"; same mark; Artist signed: Windle; $200.00 – $250.00*

    *3. Vase, 10"; same mark; $175.00 – $225.00*

    *4. Vase, 11"; same mark; $250.00 – $300.00*

    *5. Vase, 10½"; No mark; $225.00 – $275.00*

    *6. Vase, 10"; Marked Weller (die impressed); $350.00 – $475.00*

*Row 4:*

    *1. Vase, 9"; JEWELL; Marked Weller (die impressed); $400.00 – $500.00*

    *2. Vase, 9½"; JEWELL; same mark as #1; $450.00 – $550.00*

    *3. Vase, 10½"; JEWELL; same mark; $400.00 – $500.00*

    *4. Jardiniere, 7½"; CAMEO JEWELL; Marked Weller (die impressed); identified from catalogue page; $350.00 – $450.00*

    *5. Mug, 6½"; JEWELL; Weller (die impressed); $375.00 – $475.00*

*Weller marks being as unpredictable as they are inconsistent often evoke skepticism when perhaps none is due—and not only that, but very often decorative tactics overlap from one line to another making proper identification difficult, or at least controversial! Etna and Eocean often seem mismarked—one with the name of the other . . . line names evidently weren't nearly as important to Weller craftsmen as they are with us! The mug in Row 2, #5, is marked with both line names!! Purists may accept questionable marks as "Gospel"— and that's well and good—but so many pieces are not marked with a line name; then the general rule of thumb with collectors is: Eocean is slip decorated artwork; Etna is the embossed line. The "jewells" and the "cameos" evidently don't always add up to "Cameo Jewell"! The vase with the Pope, Row 3, #6—though not marked here, is often found marked "Etna"—so is the "Beethoven" vase. The jardiniere on Row 4, although sans "cameo," is found on the Cameo Jewell catalogue page! The other four items on Row 4 are no doubt from another line; the glaze is a soft semi-matt, and although "Jewell" is not official, it is suggested for reasons of communication.*

# Cameo Jewel

Top,
Left to Right:
1. Umbrella Stand, 22"; Marked Weller (die impressed); $600.00 – $700.00
2. Jardiniere and Pedestal, 34"; No mark; $900.00 – $1200.00
3. Umbrella Stand, 20½"; Weller (small die impressed); $550.00 – $650.00

Bottom,
Left to Right:
1. Colored Glaze Umbrella Stand, 22½";Weller (die impressed); $350.00 – $450.00
2. Colored Glaze Jardiniere and Pedestal, 33½"; No mark; $900.00 – $1200.00
3. DUNTON Umbrella Stand, 23"; No mark; $1250.00 – $1750.00

*Courtesy Ohio Historical Society*

107

*Top,*
*Left to Right:*
   1. TURADA Umbrella Stand, 21"; Marked with the Turada Weller die stamp; $1000.00 – $1250.00
   2. EOCEAN Umbrella Stand, 22½"; No mark; $800.00 – $1000.00
   3. LOUWELSA Umbrella Stand, 21"; Marked Weller (die impressed); $800.00 – $900.00

*Bottom,*
*Left to Right:*
   1. FLEMISH Umbrella Stand, 22"; Marked with the round Weller Ware ink stamp; $700.00 – $900.00
   2. Garden Ware Urn, 18½"; Marked with the full kiln ink stamp; $500.00 – $600.00
   3. TEAKWOOD Umbrella Stand, 21"; Weller (die impressed); $550.00 – $750.00

*Teakwood*

## Souvenirs

*Top,*
*Row 1:*

1. "St. Louis, 1904" Vase, 3"; No mark; $200.00 – $250.00
2. "St. Louis, LPE, 1904", 3½"; No mark; $150.00 – $175.00

*Row 2:*

1. "St. Louis, LPE, Weller Pottery, 1904," 2"; No mark; $75.00 – $100.00
2. "Wellers Outing, Buckeye Lake, Aug 6, 1904"; $80.00 – $110.00
3. Pin Tray, 2½"; Marked Weller Pottery (by hand); Initialed: D.E.; $80.00 – $100.00

*Row 3:*

1. "St Louis, LPE, 1904,"3"; No mark; $90.00 – $120.00
2. "Weller Pottery, 1903," 3"; No mark; $125.00 – $150.00
3. "Weller Theatre, Apr. 27–28–29, 1903," 2"; Marked with the Dickens ware seal; $225.00 – $250.00

## Flasks

*Bottom,*
*Row 1:*

2. "Never Dry", 6"; No mark; $185.00  – $235.00
2. "P.A.P., Loyal Order of Moose," 4½"; No mark; $135.00 – $185.00
3. "Suffer-E-Get," 6"; No mark; $185.00 –235.00

*Row 2:*

1. "F.O.E.," 5½"; No mark; $110.00 – $150.00
2. "Take A Plunge," 6"; No mark; $110.00 – $135.00
3. "All's Well," 4", No mark; $150.00 – $200.00

*Row 3:*

1. "BPOE," 4½"; No mark; $125.00 – $150.00
2. "Dust Remover," 6"; No mark; $150.00 – $195.00
3. "Old Kentuc," 5"; No mark;   $150.00 – $200.00


At least five souvenir plaques were made at the 1904 St. Louis, Louisiana Purchase Exposition—no doubt there were others. (A) L.P.E. 1904, with Indian in profile, 4⅝"; (B) St. Louis L P (monogram), 1904 and axe superimposed over Maple Leaf, 5"; (C) Lincoln. 4⅝"; (D) L.P.E. 1904, Albert Cummins, 5"; (E) McKinley 4⅝". These were finished in a plain bisque-gray.

111

## Souvenirs of St. Louis Worlds Fair, 1904

*Row 1:*
   1. Vase, 4"; No mark; $175.00 – $225.00
   2. Vase, 6½"; No mark; $500.00 – $600.00
   3. Vase, 4"; No mark; $125.00 – $150.00
   4. Vase, 3"; No mark; $135.00 – $185.00

## Clewell Pottery

*Row 2:*
   1. Urn, 5½"; No mark; $500.00 – $600.00
   2. Vase, 10"; Marked Clewell, 328-2-6; $700.00 – $900.00
   3. Vase, 5½"; No mark; $300.00 – $400.00
   4. Powder Box, 4"; Clewell, Canton, Ohio; $500.00 – $600.00
\* \* \*
*Row 3:*
   1. BRONZE WARE Vase, 10½"; No mark; $250.00 – $350.00
   2. Plaque with Dogs, 7½" x 7½"; Weller (die impressed); $450.00 – $550.00
   3. GLOSSY BEDFORD Vase, 8"; No mark; $125.00 – $150.00

*Row 4:*
   1. Jardiniere, 10"; possibly MOROCCO; Weller (die impressed); $250.00 – $350.00
   2. Garden of Eden Plaque, 11½"; No mark; $800.00 – $900.00

Charles Walter Clewell operated a studio in Canton, Ohio, between 1910 and the mid-1950's. He made two types of ware—one a solid bronze, the other a pottery base covered with a thin coating of bronze, brass, copper or silver, sometimes in combination. The effect he achieved was that of corroded metal; the copper ore reverted to its original state producing beautiful blues and greens. "Seconds" from several Zanesville potteries were used as a basis for his work—Weller among them. The ware was never mass produced; each piece was made by Clewell himself, and is therefore very rare. [25]

## Brighton

*Top:*

    *Hanging Parrot with Spread Wings, 15"; No mark; $1500.00 – $2000.00*

*Row 1:*

    *1. Bluebird, 6"; #3 Made in Japan*
    *2. Bluebird, 5"; #6; Made in Japan*
    *3. Bluebird, 4½"; #2; Made in Japan*
    *4. Bluebird, 5½"; #5; Made in Japan*

*Row 2:*

    *1. Bluebird, 7½"; Marked Weller (die impressed); $500.00 – $700.00*
    *2. Woodpecker, 6½"; 3 x on base; No mark; $300.00 – $400.00*
    *3. Pheasant, 7" x 11½"; Weller die impressed); $550.00 – $750.00*
    *4. Crow, 6½"; No mark; $700.00 – $900.00*

*Row 3:*

    *1. Parrot, 7½"; Weller (die impressed); $600.00 – $700.00*
    *2. Parrot, 12½"; No mark; $1250.00 – $1750.00*
    *3. Parrot, 13½"; Weller (die impressed); $1400.00 – $2000.00*
    *4. Parakeets, 9"; same mark as #3; Rare; $1250.00 – $1500.00*

*These exquistely detailed, lifelike birds hold much appeal for all Weller collectors, and the prices they command are an accurate reflection of their popularity. They originated during the teens and all are quite rare today. The crow is the only known specimen of its kind, and is said to have been presented to the county winner of a crow shoot!*

# Brighton

## Row 1:
1. Penguins, 5"; No mark; $700.00 – $850.00
2. Flamingo, 6"; No mark; $400.00 – $500.00
3. Hanging Parrot, 12½"; No mark; $1800.00 – $2200.00
4, Kingfisher, 6½"; Marked Weller Ware within serrated circle (ink stamp); $450.00 – $550.00
5. Canaries, 4"; Weller (die impressed); $400.00 – $500.00

## Row 2:
1. Swan Flower Frog, 4½"; No mark; $300.00 – $400.00
2. Swan Flower Frog, 5"; Weller (die impressed); $275.00 – $375.00
3. Rooster, 9½"; No mark; $1100.00 – $1500.00
4. Chicks, 5"; No mark; $475.00 – $575.00

## Row 3:
1. Woodpecker, 5"; No mark; $175.00 – $250.00
2. Canary, 2½"; No mark; $150.00 – $200.00
3. Dove, 9"; No mark; $450.00 – $550.00
4. Blue Bird, 3½"; No mark; $175.00 – $225.00
5. Same As #1; $175.00 – $250.00

## Row 4:
1. Parrot, 10½"; Weller (die impressed); $1200.00 – $1500.00
2. Cardinal, 5½"; No mark; Initialed: M H.; $450.00 – $500.00
3. Kingfisher, 9"; Marked with the half kiln ink stamp; $300.00 – $400.00
4. Pheasant, 5"; No mark; $400.00 – $475.00
5. Parrot, 12½"; No mark; $1250.00 – $1750.00

*Top Plate:*
1. *Name Card with Black Bird, 2" x 3"; No mark; $100.00 – $125.00*
2. *Name Card with Bud Vase, Pink Birds, 3½" x 3"; No mark; $125.00 – $150.00*
3. *Large Butterfly, 3½"; No mark; $150.00 – $200.00*
4. *Brooch, 2½"; Earrings, 1"; No mark; $200.00 – $250.00*
5. *Small Pink Butterfly, 2½"; No mark; $125.00 – $175.00*

*Bottom:*
1. *Dragonfly, 3½"; No mark; $125.00 – $175.00*
2. *Blue and White Butterfly, 3¾"; No mark; $175.00 – $200.00*
3. *Same as #1, Color varies; $125.00 – $175.00*
4. *Bumble Bee, 2½" Wingspan; No mark; $125.00 – $175.00*
5. *Blue Butterfly, 2¼"; No mark; $125.00 – $175.00*
6. *Red Butterfly, 3"; No mark; $125.00 – $175.00*
7. *Navy Blue Butterfly, 3"; No mark; $125.00 – $175.00*
8. *Bumble Bee, same as #4, Color varies; $125.00 – $175.00*
9. *Pale Pink with Light Blue dots, Butterfly, 3"; No mark; $125.00 – $175.00*
10. *White with Black Edging, Butterfly, 3½"; No mark; $125.00 – $175.00*
11. *Pink with dark flecks, Butterfly, 2¼" No mark; $125.00 – $175.00*
12. *Blue Bird, 2¼"; No mark; $125.00 – $175.00*
13. *Red Bird, Bottom left-hand corner, 2½"; No mark; $150.00 – $200.00*
14. *Blue Butterfly, 2"; No mark; $125.00 – $175.00*
15. *Yellow Butterfly, 2"; No mark; $125.00 – $175.00*
16. *Red Bird, wings outspread, 2½"; No mark; $150.00 – $200.00*

*We have heard that the cameos from the Ethel line were used to make brooches, too! The name cards were once fashionable to use at dinner parties; and the butterflies and bees were decorative accents in flower arrangements or birdbaths.*

*Row 1:*

1. BURNTWOOD Vase, 5"; Marked Weller (small die impressed); $100.00 – $125.00
2. Vase, 7"; No mark; $150.00 – $200.00
3. BURNTWOOD Vase, 3½"; No mark; $90.00 – $120.00
4. CLAYWOOD Vase, 3½"; No mark; $50.00 – $75.00

*Row 2:*

1. BURNTWOOD Vase, 7"; No mark; $125.00 – $150.00
2. BURNTWOOD Vase, 8½"; No mark; $175.00 – $225.00
3. BURNTWOOD Vase, 8" No mark; $125.00 – $150.00
4. Vase, 7"; No mark; $150.00 – $200.00
5. BURNTWOOD Vase, 7"; No mark; $100.00 – $125.00

*Row 3:*

1. BURNTWOOD Plate, 7"; Wildey Picnic, Zanesville, 1910, Odd Fellows; $175.00 – $225.00
2. BURNTWOOD Plaque, 12"; No mark; $250.00 – $350.00
3. CLAYWOOD Plate, 7"; No mark; identified from catalogue; $125.00 – $150.00

*Row 4:*

1. Vase, 9"; No mark; $400.00 – $550.00
2. BURNTWOOD Vase, 7"; No mark; $100.00 – $125.00
3. BURNTWOOD Vase, 12"; No mark; $225.00 – $275.00
4. BURNTWOOD Vase, 5½"; No mark; $75.00 – $100.00
5. BURNTWOOD Urn, 6½"; No mark; $125.00 – $150.00

*Burntwood is distinguished from Claywood by the absence of the vertical ribs. Even though the ribs are not complete on the last vase in Row 1, the catalogues identify this one as Claywood. There is some doubt that the vases on Row 1, (#2) and Row 2, (#4) were made by Weller. A marked example would clarify the issue! If they were, we doubt they are Burntwood—the ancient Egyptian motif is completely out of character. The vase on Row 4 (#1) is very similar to a line usually marked Lorber (note smooth background) . . . but Burntwood may be the family name.*

## Claywood

Row 1:
1. Vase, 5½"; No mark; $75.00 – $85.00
2. Vase, 5½"; No mark; $75.00 – $85.00
3. Candleholder, 5"; No mark; $65.00 – $85.00
4. Vase, 5"; No mark; $65.00 – $80.00
5. Vase, 5"; No mark; $65.00 – $80.00

Row 2:
1. Mug, 5"; No mark; $75.00 – $100.00
2. Vase, 3"; No mark; $50.00 – $60.00
3. Vase, 3"; No mark; $50.00 – $60.00
4. Mug, 4½"; No mark; $75.00 – $100.00

Row 3:
1. Vase, 3½"; No mark; $45.00 – $65.00
2. Vase, 3½"; No mark; $45.00 – $65.00
3. Vase, 3½"; No mark; $45.00 – $65.00

Row 4:
1. Bowl, 2"; No mark; $45.00 – $65.00
2. Bowl, 2½"; No mark; $45.00 – $65.00
3. Bow, 2"; No mark; $45.00 – $65.00
4. Bowl, 2"; No mark; $45.00 – $65.00

Row 5:
1. Vase, 6½"; Marked Weller (die impressed); $65.00 – $85.00
2. Spitton, 4½"; No mark; $125.00 – $150.00
3. Vase, 8½"; No mark; $75.00 – $90.00

This is what a serene display of Claywood should look like—nothing out of character! Remember that Claywood differs from Burntwood with the addition of the characteristic vertical bars.

## Ivory (Clinton Ivory)

*Row 1:*
   *Window planter, 15½" x 6"; Marked with Weller die stamp; $160.00 – $210.00*

*Row 2:*
   *1. Planter Box, 5"; No mark; $110.00 – $130.00*
   *2. Square Planter, 4"; No mark; $85.00 – $110.00*
   *3. Jardiniere, 6½"; No mark; $125.00 – $150.00*

*Row 3:*
   *1. Jardiniere, 5"; No mark; $60.00 – $80.00*
   *2. Bottle Vase, 9"; No mark; $120.00 – $140.00*
   *3. Vase, 5; Marked with Weller die stamp; $90.00 – $110.00*
   *4. Vase, 8½"; No mark; $120.00 – $150.00*
   *5. Pillow Vase, 5"; No mark; $90.00 – $120.00*

*Row 4:*
   *1. Vase, 10"; Marked with Weller die stamp; $75.00 – $95.00*
   *2. Vase, 12"; No mark; $175.00 – $225.00*
   *3. Vase, 15"; No mark; $175.00 – $225.00*
   *4. Vase, 10"; Marked with Weller die stamp; $100.00 – $150.00*
   *5. Vase, 10½"; No mark; $225.00 – $275.00*

# Roma

*Row 1:*
1. *Double Bud Vase, 8½"; Marked Weller (die impressed); $90.00 – $110.00*
2. *Bud Vase, 6½"; No mark; $50.00 – $60.00*
3. *Tobacco Jar, 7½"; No mark; $250.00 – $350.00*
4. *Bud Vase, 6"; Marked Weller (die impressed); $50.00 – $75.00*
5. *Double Bud Vase, 8"; No mark; $100.00 – $120.00*

*Row 2:*
1. *Triple Bud Vase, 8"; Marked Weller (die impressed); $110.00 – $130.00*
2. *Vase, 2½"; No mark; $175.00 – $225.00*
3. *Triple Candlestick, 9"; No mark; $150.00 – $200.00*
4. *Bud Vase, 5"; No mark; $40.00 – $65.00*
5. *Candlelabrum, 8"; Marked Weller (die impressed); $175.00 – $225.00*

*Row 3:*
1. *Comport, 5"; No mark; $90.00 – $100.00*
2. *Candlestick or Lamp Base, 9½"; No mark; $95.00 – $120.00*
3. *Candlestick, 11½"; Weller (small die impressed); $100.00 – $130.00*
4. *Candlestick, 8½"; same mark; $95.00 – $120.00*
5. *Comport, 5"; same mark; $90.00 – $100.00*

*Row 4:*
1. *Comport, 5½"; Weller (die impressed); $85.00 – $95.00*
2. *Comport, 9½"; Weller (small die impressed); $125.00 – $175.00*
3. *Comport, 11"; No mark; $100.00 – $125.00*
4. *Comport, 9½"; Weller (small die impressed); $100.00 – $125.00*
5. *Comport, 8½"; same mark; $100.00 – $125.00*

*Roma is probably the most plentiful of the Weller commercial artware lines, and was made in hundreds of shapes. On an ivory background, details are tinted red or green and vary from dainty floral sprays and swags to bolder, more intricate designs. Zona shapes as well as those from other lines were borrowed and glazed in the matt colors of Roma. A beautiful jardiniere and pedestal decorated with a kingfisher and cattails was included in the line . . . both Roma and its woodsy counterpart, Flemish, were designed by Rudolph Lorber, about 1914.*

# Roma

Row 1:
  1. Pot, 3½"; Marked Weller (small die impressed); $50.00 – $75.00
  2. Vase, 6½"; No mark; $55.00 – $85.00
  3. Log Planter, 3" x 10½"; Weller (die impressed); $125.00 – $175.00
  4. Vase, 6"; same mark; $50.00 – $75.00
  5. Bowl, 3"; same mark; $60.00 – $80.00

Row 2:
  1. Planter, 3½"; No mark; $40.00 – $50.00
  2. Triple Bud Vase, 6½"; Weller (small die impressed); $70.00 – $90.00
  3. Comport, 4½" x 11"; No mark; $150.00 – $175.00
  4. Basket, 7½"; Weller (die impressed); $90.00 – $125.00
  5. Planter, 3½"; same mark; $40.00 – $50.00

Row 3:
  1. Wall Pocket, 7"; same mark; $225.00 – $275.00
  2. Ash Tray, 2½"; No mark; $45.00 – $60.00
  3. Console Bowl, 4½" x 10½"; No mark; $175.00 – $200.00
  4. Bowl, 2"; Weller (die impressed); $40.00 – $50.00
  5. Wall Pocket, 8"; No mark; $200.00 – $250.00

Row 4:
  1. Jardiniere, 5"; No mark; $60.00 – $70.00
  2. Console Bowl, 4½" x 16"; Weller (die impressed); $150.00 – $175.00
  3. Planter, 4½"; same mark; $50.00 – $65.00

Row 5:
  1. Candleholder, 10½"; No mark; $95.00 – $120.00
  2. Console with liner; 6½" x 18"; No mark; $150.00 – $200.00
  3. Vase, 9"; Weller (small die impressed); $75.00 – $125.00

Collectors report a "Roma-type" hanging lamp: the shape is a hemisphere, 21" in diameter; on an ivory background elongated petals in an antiqued effect of tan and dull green radiate from center bottom. The upper edge is banded in the same colors. Supported by three chains, the lamp hangs 34" from the ceiling. The ceiling cap is also made of pottery and measures 4½" deep by 9½" wide. Embossed in the clay is a rectangle containing the name "Rush Bros."; and the small die stamp "Weller" confirms the identity of the manufacturer.

*Row 1:*
1. KENOVA Vase 5½"; Marked Weller (die impressed); $225.00 – $275.00
2. KENOVA Vase, 6½"; same mark; $250.00 – $300.00
3. Vase, 6"; same mark; $225.00 – $275.00
4. Bowl, 3½"; same mark; $100.00 – $125.00

## Roma

*Row 2:*
1. Vase, 6"; No mark; $45.00 – $60.00
2. Vase, 8½"; Marked Weller (small die impressed); $65.00 – $75.00
3. Vase, 7"; No mark; $55.00 – $70.00

*Row 3:*
1. Vase, 9"; No mark; $60.00 – $75.00
2. Vase, 10"; No mark; $85.00 – $95.00
3. Vase, 10"; No mark; $85.00 – $95.00
4. Vase, 9"; Marked Weller (die impressed); $50.00 – $60.00

## Parian

*Row 4:*
1. Wall Pocket, 10"; No mark; $200.00 – $250.00
2. Vase, 13"; No mark; $175.00 – $225.00
3. Vase, 8½"; No mark; $120.00 – $180.00

The third example on Row 1 would seem to fit well into either the Woodcraft or Flemish lines, but the lizard makes it unique. The Weller die stamp would place it in their production period. Row 1, #4, may be termed "Modeled Matt"—no positive ID! There is no doubt in our minds that Rows 2 and 3 are simply "Roma" but these square vases with decorative panels are often referred to as "Atlantic." To support our belief, we have reprinted the catalogue pages that caused us to arrive at our conclusion. Study them, and make your own decision. (See catalogue reprint section.) Often an assortment was offered for sale, and "Atlantic" was the name of an assortment rather than a particular line . . . Selma was another. Atlantic included shapes from Melrose (or Arcola, or Malta, the page doesn't indicate the glaze—a common practice), Orris, and several of these Roma types. Parian was mentioned in a trade journal in 1924: "A most attractive decorated Graystone line of porch bowls . . . wall pockets, jardinieres, pedestals and other pieces too numerous to list are made in a variety of decorations, the most attractive being the effect of a colored tile set in the ware."

## Flemish

*Row 1:*
    *1. Ink well, 7" x 4½"; No mark; $350.00 – $425.00*
    *2. Covered Comport, 8½"; Marked Weller (die impressed); $150.00 – $175.00*

*Row 2:*
    *1. Tub, 4"; Marked Weller (die impressed); $75.00 – $95.00*
    *2. Tub 4"; No mark; $75.00 – $95.00*
    *3. Tub, 3½"; No mark; $65.00 – $85.00*

*Row 3:*
    *1. Tub, 4½"; Marked Weller (die impressed); $100.00 – $125.00*
    *2. Jardiniere, 6"; same mark; $80.00 – $110.00*
    *3. Tub, 4½"; No mark; $80.00 – $110.00*

*Row 4:*
    *1. Jardiniere, 7½"; No mark; $125.00 – $150.00*
    *2. Jardiniere, 8"; No mark; $100.00 – $125.00*
    *3. Jardiniere, 7½"; Marked Weller (die impressed); $100.00 – $125.00*

*In general, Flemish conforms to the description from an old florist sales pamphlet: "A mild pastel polychrome treatment with floral modeling brought out by tints in brighter colors." But occasionally, a piece with an ivory "Roma"-like background is identified as "Flemish."*

132

Top,
Left to Right;

    *1. BEDFORD MATT Umbrella Stand, 20"; Marked Weller (die impressed); $500.00 – $650.00*
    *2. IVORY Umbrella Stand, 19½"; No mark; $200.00 – $250.00*
    *3. IVORY Sand Jar, 16"; Marked with the half kiln ink stamp; $225.00 – $250.00*
    *4. CLAYWOOD Umbrella Stand, 19½" Marked WELLER (ink stamp); $200.00 – $250.00*

Bottom,
Left to Right:

    *1. FLEMISH Umbrella Stand, 21½"; Marked with the full kiln ink stamp; $325.00 – $400.00*
    *2. Light Glaze Umbrella Stand, 21½"; Weller (die impressed); $350.00 – $450.00*
    *3. ZONA Umbrella Stand, 20½"; Hi gloss, often shown in Flemish glaze also; No mark; $500.00 – $700.00*

*Courtesy Ohio Historical Society*

135

*Top,*
*Left to Right:*

1. *FLEMISH Jardiniere and Pedestal, 26½"; Marked Weller (die impressed); $550.00 – $650.00*
2. *IVORY Jardiniere and Pedestal, 27½"; No mark; $350.00 – $400.00*
3. *MALVERN Jardiniere and Pedestal, 34"; Marked Weller Pottery (by hand); $500.00 – $600.00*
4. *FLEMISH Jardiniere and Pedestal, 29½"; No mark; $450.00 – $550.00*

*Bottom,*
*Left to Right:*

1. *FOREST Jardiniere and Pedestal, 26"; No mark; $500.00 – $700.00*
2. *AURELIAN Jardiniere and Pedestal, 45½"; Artist signed: Ferrell; $3250.00 – $3750.00*
3. *ROSEMONT Jardiniere and Pedestal, 25½"; Marked Weller (die impressed); $450.00 – $550.00*

*Blue Drapery Jardiniere and Pedestal, 33½"; No mark; $750.00 – $1000.00*
*Zona Jardiniere and Pedestal, 28½"; Marked with the half kiln ink stamp; $350.00 – $450.00*

137

## Jardinieres

*Row 1:*
  1. IVORY Jardiniere, 7½"; Marked with the half kiln ink stamp; $125.00 – $150.00
  2. IVORY Jardiniere, 6½"; No mark; $75.00 – $100.00
  3. IVORY Jardiniere, 7½"; No mark; $125.00 – $150.00

*Row 2:*
  1. ZONA Jardiniere, 7"; No mark; $125.00 – $175.00
  2. ZONA Jardiniere, 6½;" Marked with the full kiln ink stamp; $125.00 – $175.00
  3. Brown Glaze Jardiniere, 7"; Weller (die impressed); $125.00 – $150.00

*Row 3:*
  1. Colored Glaze Jardiniere, 9"; No mark; $100.00 – $135.00
  2. ZONA Jardiniere, 7"; Weller (small die impressed); $125.00 – $150.00

*Row 4:*
  1. 1ST LINE DICKENS WARE Jardiniere, 9"; Marked with the Dickens Ware half circle seal; $275.00 – $325.00
  2. 1ST LINE DICKENS WARE Jardiniere, 9"; same mark; $300.00 – $400.00

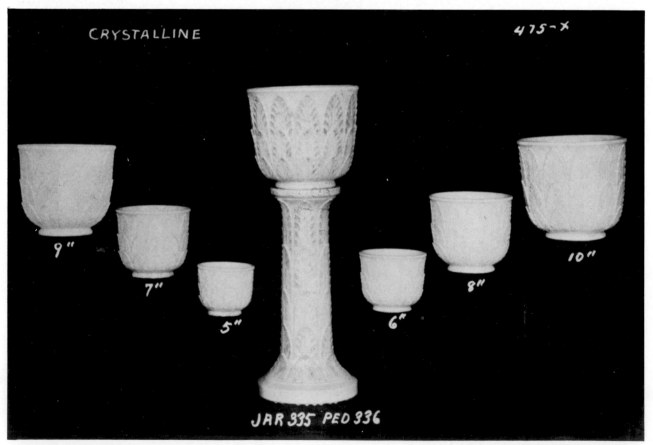

*Courtesy Ohio Historical Society*

# Jardinieres

*Row 1:*
    *1. Light Glaze Jardiniere, 7"; Marked Weller (die impressed); $200.00 – $250.00*
    *2. Colored Glaze Jardiniere, 9"; same mark; $125.00 – $175.00*

*Row 2:*
    *1. Light Glaze Jardiniere, 8"; Weller (small die impressed); $200.00 – $250.00*
    *2. Etna Jardiniere, 9½"; Weller (die impressed); $250.00 – $350.00*

*Row 3:*
    *2. Colored Glaze Jardiniere, 10"; No mark; $150.00 – $200.00*
    *2. Colored Glaze Jardiniere, 9½"; No mark; $175.00 – $225.00*

*Courtesy Ohio Historical Society*

# Jardinieres

Row 1:
   1. FLEMISH Jardiniere, 8"; Weller (die impressed); $250.00 – $350.00
   2. ZONA Jardiniere, 8½"; No mark; $200.00 – $250.00

Row 2:
   1. ROMA Jardiniere, 8½"; No mark; $175.00 – $225.00
   2. Shown as FLEMISH, 8½"; No mark; $175.00 – $225.00

Row 3:
   1. ROMA Jardiniere, 10½"; No mark; $225.00 – $275.00
   2. Decorated Graystone, shown as FLEMISH, 11"; No mark; $250.00 – $300.00

*Courtesy Ohio Historical Society*

# Jardiniere

Row 1:
1. Colored Glaze Jardiniere with Squirrels, 8"; No mark; $225.00 – $275.00
2. Colored Glaze Jardiniere, Pearl mold, 7"; No mark; $200.00 – $225.00

Row 2:
1. MARBLEIZED Jardiniere, 10"; Marked Weller (by hand); $250.00 – $350.00
2. Colored Glaze Jardiniere, 9"; Weller (die impressed); $250.00 – $300.00

Row 3:
1. CAMEO JEWEL Jardiniere, 11"; Weller (small die impressed); $300.00 – $375.00
2. CAMEO JEWEL Jardiniere, 8"; same mark; $325.00 – $375.00

# Jardinieres

*Row 1:*
    *FOREST Jardiniere, 8½"; No mark; $400.00 – $450.00*

*Row 2:*
    *1. Jardiniere, 8½"; Marked with the half kiln ink stamp; $250.00 – $300.00*
    *2. GREENAWAYS Jardiniere, 10"; Marked S.A. Weller ( in script by hand); $400.00  – $500.00*

*Row 3:*
    *1. COPRA\* Jardiniere, 10½"; No mark; $275.00 – $325.00*
    *2. ROSEMONT Jardiniere 8"; No mark; $175.00 – $200.00*

*Below:"Narona Ware" Jardinieres from Weller catalogue*

# Muskota

*Row 1:*
1. *Fence, 5"; Marked Weller (die impressed);  $150.00 – $175.00*
2. *Girl, 4"; No mark; $275.00 – $325.00*
3. *Gate with Pots and Cats, 7"; Weller (die impressed); $500.00  – $600.00*

*Row 2:*
1. *Fishing Boy, 6½"; No mark; $300.00 – $375.00*
2. *Fish and Stump, 5"; Weller (die impressed); $150.00 – $175.00*
3. *Boy, 3½"; Boat, 10½" x 2"; same mark as #2; $450.00 – $550.00*
4. *Foxy Grandpa Incense Burner, 4"; same mark; $475.00 – $575.00*

*Row 3:*
1. *Girl with Flowers and Hat, 9"; No mark; $350.00 – $450.00*
2. *Powder Jar, 7"; No mark; $225.00 – $325.00*
3. *Girl with Flowers and Hat, 8"; Weller (die impressed); $325.00 – $425.00*

*Row 4:*
1. *Bowl with Goose, 4½"; Weller (die impressed); $275.00 – $375.00*
2. *Nude on Rock, 8"; same mark; $275.00 – $325.00*
3. *Geese Flower Frog, 6"; No mark; $350.00 – $400.00*

*Courtesy Ohio Historical Society*

## Muskota

*Row 1:*
1. *Girl with Doll, 8"; No mark; $350.00 – $400.00*
2. *Girl on Stump, 8½"; Weller (die impressed); $350.00 – $400.00*

*Row 2:*
1. *Girl with Watering Can, 7"; No mark; $350.00 – $400.00*
2. *Two Boys Flower Frog, 7"; Weller (die impressed); $400.00 – $500.00*
3. *Boy on Flower Frog, 6"; Weller (die impressed); $350.00 – $450.00*

*Row 3:*
1. *Kneeling Nude, 3"; No mark; $225.00 – $275.00*
2. *Kneeling Woman, 7½"; Weller (die impressed); $300.00 – $350.00*

## Hobart Figures

3. *Girl, 4½"; No mark; $225.00 – $275.00*

*Row 4:*
1. *Girl with Flowers, 8½"; No mark; $250.00 – $350.00*
2. *Nude, Double Bud Vase, 10"; Weller (die impressed); $350.00 – $450.00*
3. *Nude, 8½"; No mark; $250.00 – $350.00*

*Courtesy Ohio Historical Society*

# Woodcraft

*Row 1:*
   *1. Bowl, 3"; No mark; $75.00 – $95.00*
   *2. Muskota Dogs, 7½"; No mark; $500.00 – $700.00*
   *3. Bowl, 3½"; Marked Weller (die impressed); $80.00 – $90.00*

*Row 2:*
   *1. Muskota Kingfisher Fish Bowl Base, 13½"; Marked Weller (die impressed); $600.00 – $900.00*
   *2. Bud Vase, with Muskota Fisher Boy, 11"; same mark; $450.00 – $650.00*
   *3. Muskota Fisher Boy on Fish Bowl Base, 12"; same mark; $600.00 – $900.00*

*Row 3:*
   *1. Lamp, 12½"; same mark; $275.00 – $300.00*
   *2. Owl Vase, 16"; same mark; $800.00 – $900.00*
   *3. Owl Lamp, 13½"; same mark; $350.00 – $450.00*

*Woodcraft is a popular line with collectors, especially those pieces decorated with Muskota figures . . . birds and animals. Identification of the line became a problem, to say the least! The squirrel pieces—wall pockets, lattice bowls, etc.—are often included in "Flemish." Some of the same twig or trunk–like shapes with the small flowers are identified as both Woodcraft and Flemish! If the glaze is a little glossy, it might be Alvin; and if the background is a pale yellow or mint green, it should be called "Voile." Confusing??*

*Courtesy of Ohio Historical Society*

# Woodcraft

*Row 1:*

    *1. Bowl, 3½"; No mark; $75.00 – $95.00*

    *2. Bud Vase, 6½"; No mark; $40.00 – $50.00*

    *3. Bowl, 3½"; Marked with Flemish paper label; $100.00 – $125.00*

    *4. Candleholder, 8½"; Weller (die impressed); $100.00 – $125.00*

    *5. Bowl, 3"; Weller (die impressed); $75.00 – $95.00*

*Row 2:*

    *1. Planter, 5½"; same mark; $275.00 – $350.00*

    *2. Fan vase, 8"; No mark; $70.00 – $80.00*

    *3. Double Bud Vase, 8"; No mark; $75.00 – $100.00*

    *4. Ash Tray, 3"; No mark ; $80.00 – $90.00*

*Row 3:*

    *1. Planter with Flower Frog, 6"; No mark; $275.00 – $325.00*

    *2. Muskota Crane on Fish Bowl Base, 11"; Weller (die impressed); $500.00 – $700.00*

    *3. Smoker Set with Butterfly, 5"; Weller (small die impressed); $250.00 – $300.00*

*Row 4:*

    *1. Vase, 13", No mark; $175.00 – $225.00*

    *2. Tankard, 12½" No mark; $550.00 – $650.00*

    *3. Mug, 6"; Weller (die impressed); $225.00 – $275.00*

    *4. Vase, 12"; Weller (small die impressed); $175.00 – $225.00*

## Woodcraft

*Row 1:*
1. Smoker Set, 5"; Marked Weller (die impressed); $175.00 – $225.00
2. Hanging Basket, 6"; No mark; $100.00 – $125.00
3. Jardiniere, 5½"; Weller (die impressed); $350.00 – $450.00

*Row 2:*
1. Fan Vase, 7"; No mark; $40.00 – $50.00
2. Fan Vase, 6"; No mark; $40.00 – $45.00
3. Owl Wall Pocket, 10"; Weller (small die impressed); $250.00 – $350.00
4. Fan Vase, 5"; No mark; $40.00 – $45.00
5. Bud Vase, 7"; (die impressed); $75.00 – $100.00

*Row 3:*
1. Bud Vase, 8½"; Weller (die impressed); $40.00 – $50.00
2. Vase, 8½"; No mark; $50.00 – $75.00
3. Vase, 9"; No mark; $125.00 – $150.00
4. Vase, 9"; No mark; $125.00 – $140.00
5. Bud Vase, 10"; Weller (die impressed); $75.00 – $90.00
6. Bud Base, 7½"; Marked with the full kiln ink stamp; $45.00 – $65.00

*Row 4:*
1. Console with Frog, 11"; Full kiln ink stamp mark; $150.00 – $200.00
2. Comport, 10"; No mark; $350.00 – $450.00
3. Basket, 9½"; Weller (die impressed); $200.00 – $250.00

## *Woodcraft*

*Row 1:*

*1. Hanging Basket with Owl, 5½" x10"; No mark; $250.00 – $300.00*
*2. Hanging Basket with Fox, 4½" x 9"; No mark; $250.00 – $300.00*

*Row 2.*

*1. Jardiniere with Woodpecker, 5"; Marked Weller (die impressed); $350.00 – $450.00*
*2. Jardiniere with Woodpecker and Squirrel, 9½"; same mark as #1; $450.00 – $550.00*

## *Mammy Line*

*Row 1:*

*1. Creamer, 3½"; Marked Weller (in-mold script); $300.00 – $400.00*
*2. Syrup Pitcher, 6"; same mark; $500.00 – $700.00*
*3. Sugar with Cover, 3½"; same mark; $325.00 – $425.00*

*Row 2:*

*1. Cookie Jar, 11"; Marked Weller Pottery Since 1872; $1500.00 – $2000.00*
*2. Teapot, 8"; same mark as #1; $750.00– $900.00*

*Mammy is a very popular line with collectors—in addition to the pieces shown here, a large batter bowl completes the set. Sold as set; $5000.00 – $7000.00 (with batter bowl).*

159

## Marbleized

*Row 1:*
1. Vase, 7½"; Marked Weller (by hand); $75.00 – $100.00
2. Vase, 4½"; same mark; $65.00 – $75.00
3. Comport, 8"; Weller (small die impressed); $90.00 – $110.00

*Row 2.*
1. Unusual matt glazed vase, 10½"; Weller (by hand); $165.00 – $195.00
2. Vase, 10½"; Weller (by hand); $125.00 – $150.00
3. Vase, 9½"; same mark as #2; $125.00 – $150.00
4. Vase, 9½"; same mark; $125.00 – $150.00

*Row 3:*
1. Bowl, 5½"; x 1½"; Weller (die impressed); $35.00 – $45.00
2. Vase, 4½"; Weller (by hand); $50.00 – $60.00
3. Vase, 8½"; same mark; $90.00 – $115.00
4. Vase, 5"; same mark; $50.00 – $70.00
5. Bowl, 7" x 1½"; Weller (die impressed); $40.00 – $50.00

*Row 4:*
1. Vase, 9"; Weller (by hand); $125.00 – $150.00
2. Vase, 10½"; same mark; $150.00 – $165.00
3. Vase, 10½"; same mark; $150.00 – $165.00
4. Vase, 10"; same mark; $150.00 – $175.00

# Zona

Row 1:
1. Rolled Edge Baby plate, 7½"; No mark; $100.00 – $135.00
2. Cream Pitcher, 3½"; Zona; No mark; $50.00 – $75.00
3. Rolled Edge Baby Plate, 7"; Zona; Marked with the Weller Pottery half kiln ink stamp; $75.00 – $90.00

Row 2:
1. Bowl, 5½"; Juvenile line; Marked Weller Pottery Since 1872 (in mold); $30.00 – $40.00
2. Plate, 7"; Same mark; $50.00 – $70.00
3. Milk Pitcher, 3½"; Marked Weller Pottery (in-mold script); $50.00 – $60.00
4. Mug, 3"; Marked Weller (in -mold script); $50.00 – $60.00
5. Mug, 3"; Zona; Marked with the half kiln ink stamp; $45.00 – $55.00

Row 3:
1. Pitcher, 6"; Zona; Marked Weller (die impressed); $50.00 – $60.00
2. Vase, 9"; Zona; Marked Weller (die impressed); $50.00 – $60.00
3. Pitcher, 7"; Zona; No mark; $125.00 – $150.00
4. Comport, 5½"; Zona; Marked Weller (die impressed); $60.00 – $70.00

Row 4:
1. Pitcher, 7½"; Zona; No mark; $150.00 – $200.00
2. Pitcher, 8"; Zona; Marked with the half kiln ink stamp; $200.00 – $300.00
3. Pitcher, 7½"; Zona; No mark; $100.00 – $150.00
4. Pitcher, 5½"; Zona; Marked Weller (die impressed); $120.00 – $150.00

Row 5:
1. Pitcher, 7"; Zona; Marked Weller (die impressed); $120.00 – $140.00
2. Pitcher, 8"; No mark; $120.00 – $135.00
3. Pitcher, 8"; No mark; $120.00 – $135.00
4. Pitcher, 7"; No mark; $110.00 – $125.00

The deluxe set in the fancy "circus" box of Zona baby dishes—including the plate, bowl, mug, and milk pitcher—sold for 95¢ in 1936…55¢ would buy the plate and mug. Both patterns—the "strutting" duck and the rabbit and bird in relief—were being produced in the early 30's, even though the "pouncing" technique used to decorate the duck line would seem to indicate an earlier origin.

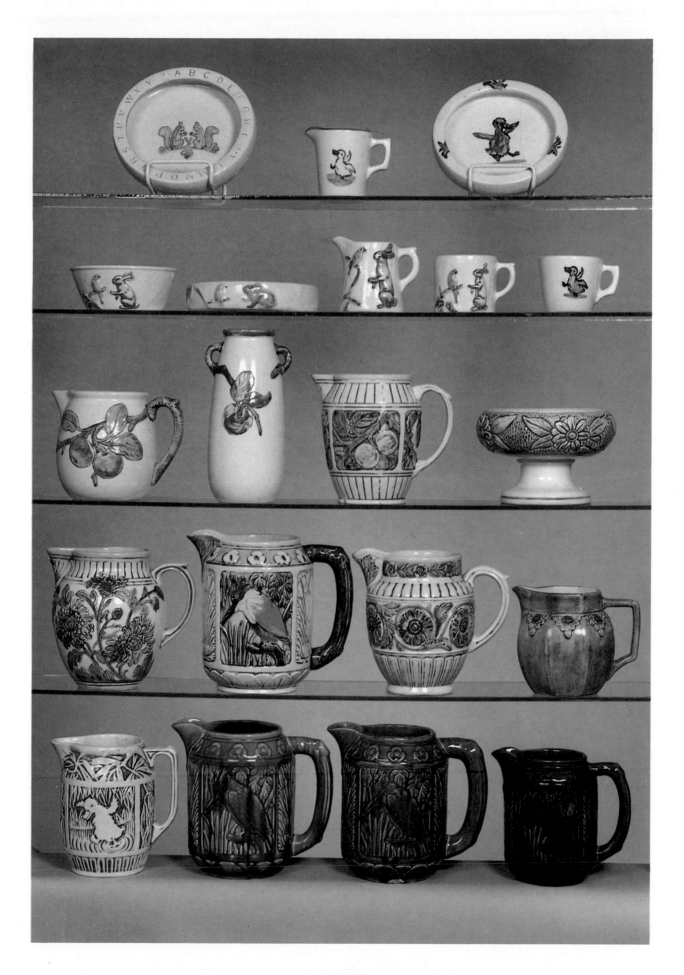

## Zona Dinnerware

*Row 1:*
    Pickle Dish, 11"; Marked Weller (die impressed); $45.00 – $65.00

*Row 2:*
    Tea Set; sugar 3", teapot 6", creamer 4"; each piece is marked Weller (die impressed); $200.00 – $250.00

*Row 3:*
    1,2,3. Tea Set; creamer 3½", teapot 6", both marked Weller (die impressed), sugar, 4½", Marked with the Weller Ware full kiln ink stamp; $200.00 – $250.00
    4. Matching Teapot, 5"; Marked Weller (die impressed); $70.00 – $90.00

*Row 4:*
    1. Dinner Plate, 10"; No mark; $25.00 – $30.00
    2. Salad plate, 7½"; No mark; $20.00 – $25.00
    3. Dinner Plate, 9½"; Marked Weller Ware (full kiln stamp); $25.00 – $30.00

*Row 5:*
    1. Bowl, 9½"; Marked Weller Ware (full kiln stamp);  $25.00 – $35.00
    2. Platter, 12"; No mark;  $50.00 – $80.00
    3. Bowl, 5½"; No mark;  $15.00 – $20.00

Zona dinnerware, modeled by Lorber, was a short-lived product; there were recurring problems in its manufacture, and eventually it was sold to Gladding McBean Company of California who used these molds to make their "Franciscan Apple" ware. The name "Zona" was also given to a colorful hi-glazed line of often intricately patterned jardinieres, vases, etc...as well as the two lines of baby dishes.

# Creamware

*Row 1:*

    *Hanging basket, 11½"; reticulated pattern; No mark; $150.00 – $200.00*

*Row 2:*

    *1. Bowl, 2½"; Cameo pattern\*, No mark; $30.00 – $40.00*
    *2. Vase, 7"; No mark; $50.00 – $65.00*
    *3. Planter with liner, 11½" wide; Marked Weller (by hand); $70.00 – $85.00*
    *4. Candleholder, 11", ; Marked Weller ( by hand); $75.00 – $90.00*
    *5. Match Holder, 6½"; Embossed pattern\*; No mark; $90.00 – $110.00*

*Row 3:*

    *1. Fan Vase, 6"; Ethel; Marked Weller (die impressed); $40.00 – $55.00*
    *2. Vase, 9½"; Ethel; Marked Weller (die impressed); $200.00 – $300.00*
    *3. Vase, 11½"; Ethel; Marked Weller (die impressed); $250.00 – $350.00*
    *4. Vase, 11"; Ethel; Marked Weller (die impressed); $250.00 – $350.00*
    *5. Fan Vase, 8½"; Ethel; Marked Weller (die impressed); $75.00 – $95.00*

*Row 4:*

    *1. Planter, 3"; No mark; $50.00 – $65.00*
    *2. Planter, 3½"; No mark; $85.00 – $100.00*
    *3. Planter, 3"; No mark ; $60.00 – $80.00*

*Row 5:*

    *1. Planter, 4"; Marked Weller (die impressed); $50.00 – $65.00*
    *2. Planter, 2"; No mark; $35.00 – $45.00*
    *3. Comport, 6"; No mark; $75.00 – $90.00*
    *4. Planter, 2"; No mark; $25.00 – $35.00*
    *5. Planter with liner, 3½"; Coat of Arms pattern\*, Marked Weller Ware (die impressed); $45.00 – $55.00*

*\*No official name, suggested for communication purposes only.*

## Forest

Row 1:
1. Pitcher, 5"; Hi-gloss; Marked Weller (die impressed); $150.00 – $200.00
2. Bowl, 2½"; Shape #3; No mark; $50.00 – $75.00
3. Hanging Basket, 8"; No mark; $150.00 – $200.00
4. Tub Planter, 3½"; Shape #3; Weller (die impressed); $75.00 – $90.00
5. Pitcher, 5½"; Hi-gloss; No mark; $150.00 – $200.00

Row 2:
1. Basket, 8½"; Weller (die impressed); $175.00 – $225.00
2. Vase, 8"; No mark; $125.00 – $175.00
3. Vase, 8"; No mark; $125.00 – $175.00
4. Teapot, 4½"; shown without lid; Hi-gloss; Weller (die impressed); $200.00 – $250.00

Row 3:
1. Jardiniere, 4½"; No mark; $100.00 – $125.00
2. Jardiniere, 7"; No mark; $300.00 – $400.00
3. Tub Planter, 6"; Weller (die impressed); $125.00 – $150.00
4. Tub Planter, 4"; No mark; $75.00 – $100.00

Row 4:
1. Vase, 13½"; No mark; $275.00 – $375.00
2. Window Box, 5½" x 14½"; Weller (die impressed); $350.00 – $400.00
3. Vase, 12"; No mark; $250.00 – $350.00

Mrs. Lucile Henzke relates that Forest was designed by Rudolph Lorber, inspired by the country side scenery he once observed from the window of a train. The matt glazing is typical; only rarely will you find an example done in a high gloss glaze.

## Blue Ware

Row 1:
  1. Comport, 5½"; Marked Weller (die impressed); $175.00 – $225.00

Row 2:
  1. Vase, 8½"; Marked Weller (small die impressed); $200.00 – $250.00
  2. Jardiniere, 6½"; Weller (die impressed); $150.00 – $225.00
  3. Vase, 8½"; Weller (die impressed); $200.00 – $250.00

Row 3:
  1. Jardiniere, 8½"; No mark; $200.00 – $275.00
  2. Vase, 10"; Weller (die impressed); $400.00 – $500.00
  3. Vase, 10"; Weller (die impressed); $200.00 – $250.00
  4. Lamp Base, 9"; Weller (die impressed); $150.00 – $200.00

Row 4:
  1. Jardiniere with Two Angels, 8½"; No mark; $200.00 – $300.00
  2. Lamp or Vase, 13"; Weller (die impressed); $300.00 – $400.00
  3. Jardiniere with Four Angels, 9"; same mark; $200.00 – $300.00

The process used in decorating Blue Ware was to brush a thin coating of paraffin over the embossing before the piece was dipped in the blue background color. During the firing, the wax melted away from the figures, and extra touches of color were added later.

## Flemish

Row 1:
   1. Vase, 6½"; No mark; $125.00 – $150.00
   2. Vase, 10"; Blue Flemish; Shape #8; Weller (die impressed); $200.00 – $250.00
   3. Vase, 6½"; Blue Flemish; same mark; $130.00 – $190.00

## Baldin

Row 2:
   1. Vase, 5½"; No mark; $150.00 – $175.00
   2. Vase, 7"; Weller (die impressed); $175.00 – $200.00
   3. Bowl, 4"; No mark; $100.00 – $150.00

Row 3:
   1. Vase, 7"; No mark; $40.00 – $50.00
   2. Vase, 8½"; No mark; $45.00 – $55.00
   3. Bowl, 4"; Blue Baldin, No mark; $175.00 – $225.00
   4. Vase, 8½"; No mark; $45.00 – $55.00
   5. Vase, 6"; No mark; $45.00 – $50.00

Row 4:
   1. Vase, 11"; Blue Baldin, No mark; $350.00 – $500.00
   2. Vase, 9½"; Marked Weller (die impressed); $200.00 – $300.00
   3. Vase, 9½"; No mark; $275.00 – $350.00

Row 1 was identified as Flemish from the old catalogues. The question here is in regard to the dark blue examples: are they "Flemish" and "Baldin" . . . or were they marketed under a separate, more definitive line name?? Nothing we could uncover gave us an answer. Since it is a natural reflex that collectors tend to identify shapes before glaze treatments, many prefer to call them simply "Blue Flemish" or "Blue Baldin."

# Rosemont

*Row 1:*
1. Jardiniere, 4½"; Marked Weller (die impressed); $125.00 – $150.00
2. Jardiniere, 7"; same mark; $175.00 – $200.00
4. Jardiniere, 5"; same mark; $110.00 – $125.00

*Row 2:*
1. Jardiniere, 6½"; same mark; $250.00 – $325.00
2. Jardinere, 7"; same mark; $250.00 – $325.00
3. Jardiniere, 7"; No mark; $250.00 – $325.00

*Row 3:*
1. Vase, 10½;" Marked Weller (die impressed); $350.00 – $400.00
2. Bowls, top two each 8"x 1½"; same mark; $40.00 – $50.00; second, $35.00 – $40.00
3. Bowls, bottom one has a thick rim and 4 feet, 12" x 21½"; $65.00 – $75.00
   No mark; the other has a rolled edge and 3 feet, and is marked Weller (die impressed); $50.00 – $65.00
4. Vase, 10"; same mark; $350.00 – $400.00

*Although the first recorded mention of the Rosemont line was dated 1930, it had evidently originated several years earlier, since the reference was to new additions to the line. The die stamp "Weller" would also place the origin of the line well before 1930. The stacked bowls were shown only with the Muskota line, even though their high gloss glaze is completely incompatible with the soft woodsy matt glaze of Muskota!*

# Pearl

Row 1:
1. Candleholders, pr, second one is turned to show pattern, 8½"; Marked Weller (die impressed); $150.00 – $225.00
2. Bowl, 3" Marked Weller (die impressed); $75.00 – $100.00

Row 2:
1, Basket, 6½"; No mark; $125.00 – $150.00
2. Vase, 6"; Marked Weller (die impressed); $75.00 – $100.00
3. Bowl, 3"; Marked Weller (die impressed); $55.00 – $75.00

Row 3:
1. Vase, 7"; No mark; $95.00 – $110.00
2. Vase, 9"; Marked Weller (die impressed); $150.00 – $200.00
3. Bud Vase, 7"; Marked Weller (die impressed); $40.00 – $50.00
4. Vase, 5"; Marked Weller (die impressed); $60.00 – $75.00

Row 4:
1. Wall Vase, 8"; Marked Weller (die impressed); $175.00 – $225.00
2. Wall Vase, 8½"; Marked Weller (die impressed); $175.00 – $225.00
3. Wall Vase, 7"; Marked Weller (die impressed); $175.00 – $225.00

Note Pearl, Orris, Claywood, and Flemish shapes in the Selma Assortment shown below.

*Courtesy Ohio Historical Society*

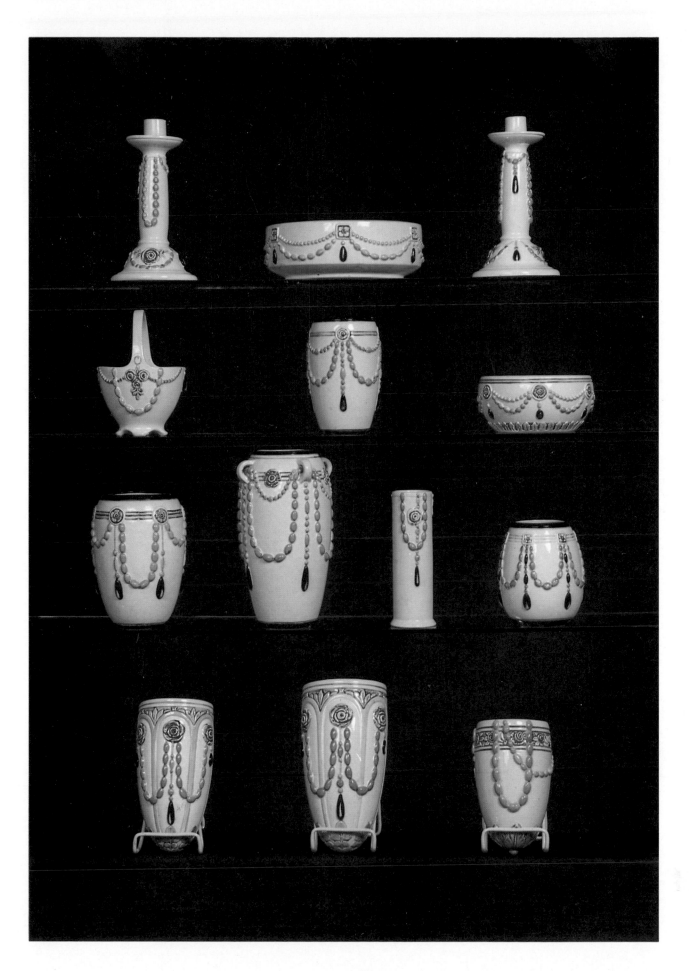

## Modeled Etched Matt

*Row 1:*
1. *Vase 6½"; Marked Weller (small die impressed); $300.00 – $350.00*
2. *Vase, 10"; Marked Weller (small die impressed); $350.00 – $450.00*

*Row 2:*
1. *Vase, 10"; Marked Weller (small die impressed); $350.00 – $450.00*
2. *Vase, 14"; Marked Weller (small die impressed); $500.00 – $700.00*
3. *Vase, 10½"; Marked Weller, 974 (by hand); $350.00 – $450.00*

# Dupont

*Row 3:*
1. *Bowl, 3"; Roma glaze; No mark; $40.00 – $50.00*
2. *Bowl, 2½"; No mark; $40.00 – $50.00*
3. *Square Planter, 3½"; No mark; $40.00 – $50.00*

*Row 4:*
1. *Square Planter, 5"; Marked Weller (die impressed); $45.00 – $60.00*
2. *Jardiniere, 7½"; No mark; $100.00 – $125.00*
3. *Vase, 10"; Marked Weller (die impressed); $100.00 – $125.00*

*Have you ever seen a piece of the type ware shown here marked Etched Matt?? There may be; we're not aware of any so marked except the ones decorated with the "Girls with the Flowing Hair"—so some collectors prefer to identify these as Modeled Etched Matt to distinguish between the two types. Although the bowl on Row 3, #1 is a DuPont mold, the glaze identifies it as Roma.*

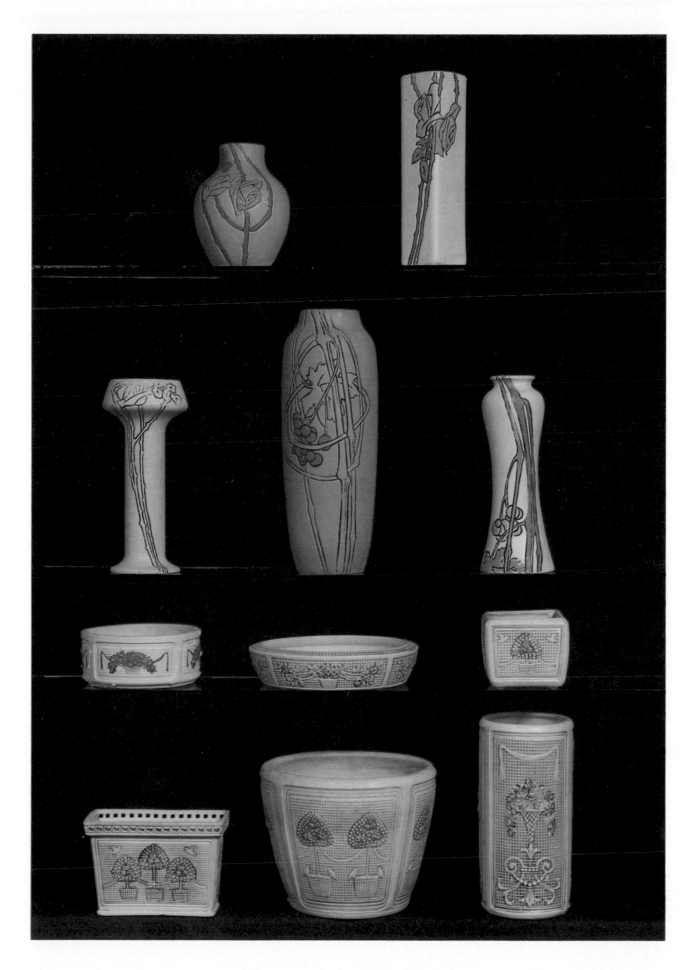

## Florala

*Row 1:*
  1. *Candleholders, 5"; Marked Weller (die impressed); $90.00 – $135.00*
  2. *Double Bud Vase, 5"; marked with Florala paper label; $40.00 – $65.00*

*Row 2:*
  1. *Wall Pocket, 10"; Marked Weller (die impressed); $125.00 – $175.00*
  2. *Console Bowl, 11"; No mark; $50.00 – $75.00*
  3. *Candlestick, 11"; No mark; $35.00 – $65.00*

## Mirror Black

*Row 3:*
  1. *Bud Vase, 5½"; No mark; $30.00 – $40.00*
  2. *Bowl, 11"; Marked Weller (small die impressed); $50.00 – $60.00*
  3. *Strawberry Jar, 6½"; No mark; $65.00 – $85.00*

*Row 4:*
  1. *Wall Pocket, 8"; No mark; $110.00 – $150.00*
  2. *Double Bud Vase, 9"; Marked Weller (die impressed); $50.00 – $70.00*
  3. *Vase, 12"; No mark; $150.00 – $200.00*
  4. *Vase, 8"; No mark; $60.00 – $80.00*
  5. *Wall Vase, 6"; No mark; $90.00 – $125.00*

*This enlightening article appeared in a January, 1924 trade paper…"The S.A. Weller Co., Zanesville, O, has a new line of mirror black vases—called their Euclid line—shows a hand painted decoration of red roses. There are also wall pockets, various shapes in bowls, and the shapes of these pieces are lovely enough to sell without the red rose decoration."*

*These Mirror Black examples shown here, with the exception of the bud vase in Row 1, do not appear on the Euclid catalogue page (which, by the way, is a good indication of their rather inaccurate presentations); and without the hand painted roses, this piece, too, may have been offered as simply Mirror Black. No doubt the most desirable Euclid pieces will be those with decoration…and we expect to see a trend develop among collectors toward using "Euclid" as a reference to those examples only.*

## Breton

Row 1:
1. Bowl, 4"; No mark; $75.00 – $90.00
2. Vase, 7"; No mark; $55.00 – $75.00
3. Vase, 6"; No mark; $45.00 – $55.00
4. Bowl, 4"; Marked Weller Pottery (by hand); $65.00 – $85.00

## Blue Drapery

Row 2:
1. Planter, 4"; Marked Weller (die impressed); $30.00 – $50.00
2. Vase, 4"; No mark; $25.00 – $35.00
3. Bowl, 3"; No mark; $35.00 – $40.00

Row 3:
1. Vase, 6"; No mark; $30.00 – $40.00
2. Planter, 4"; No mark; $50.00 – $75.00
3. Vase, 6½"; Marked Weller (die impressed); $30.00 – $40.00

Row 4:
1. Candlestick or Lamp Base, 9½"; No mark; $75.00 – $100.00
2. Jardiniere, 5½"; No mark; $40.00 – $50.00
3. Wall Pocket, 9"; No mark; $150.00 – $225.00
4. Jardiniere, 5"; No mark; $40.00 – $50.00
5. Vase, 8"; No mark; $30.00 – $50.00

*Row 1:*
  *1. FROSTED MATT Vase, 9½"; Marked Weller (die impressed); $30.00 – $40.00*
  *2. ECLAIR Comport Vase, 4½"; Weller (die impressed); $30.00 – $40.00*
  *3. Vase, 8½"; Weller (by hand); $150.00 – $200.00*

## Minerva

*Row 2:*
  *1. Vase, 8½"; Marked Weller (die impressed); $400.00 – $500.00*
  *2. Vase, 13½"; Weller (small die impressed); $700.00 – $900.00*
  *3. Vase, 8½"; same mark as #2; $450.00 – $550.00*

## Athens

*Row 3:*
  *1. Vase, 10"; No mark; $500.00 – $700.00*
  *2. Vase, 15"; No mark; $600.00 – $900.00*
  *3. Vase, 10½"; Marked Weller (die impressed); $500.00 – $600.00*

*Minerva Planter, 12" x 16"; Marked Weller (die impressed); $450.00 – $550.00*

## Candis*

*Row 1:*

Hanging Basket, 5½"; No mark; $75.00 – $100.00

*Row 2:*

1. Candleholder, 1½"; Marked Weller Pottery (in-mold script); $30.00 – $40.00
2. Console, 11" x 2½"; Weller (in-mold script); $40.00 – $50.00

*Row 3:*

1. Vase, 9"; Weller (in-mold script); $40.00 – $60.00
2. Vase, 9"; same mark; $70.00 – $90.00
3. Ewer, 11"; same mark; $50.00 – $70.00

## Tivoli

*Row 4:*

1. Vase, 9½"; No mark; $100.00 – $125.00
2. Bowl, 2½"; Weller (die impressed); $60.00 – $80.00
3. Vase, 6"; same mark as #2; $60.00 – $75.00
4. Vase, 8½"; No mark; $90.00 – $115.00

## Fairfield

*Row 5:*

1. Bowl, 4½"; No mark; $70.00 – $90.00
2. Vase, 9½"; No mark; $85.00 – $120.00
3. Vase, 8"; No mark; $85.00 – $115.00

*The simple, old-fashioned charm of the unknown line at the top of the opposite page seemed to call for a name to match—Candis is unofficial, and merely suggested for means of communication between collectors. Elegant Tivoli is rare in red, and Fairfield is very scarce—although its shapes are often found in the glaze of the Ivory line.*

187

## Montego*

Row 1:
1. Vase, 5"; marked with the half kiln ink stamp; $40.00 – $50.00
2. Vase, 8"; same mark; $200.00 – $300.00
3. Vase, 9½"; same mark; $250.00 – $350.00

## Dynasty*

4. Vase, 6"; No mark; $40.00 – $50.00
5. Vase, 4"; No mark; $30.00 – $40.00

## Underglaze Blue Ware

Row 2:
1. Bowl, 1½" x 6"; with Frog; Marked Weller (die impressed); $20.00 – $25.00
2. Bud Vase, 8"; No mark; $30.00 – $40.00
3. Bowl,  3" x 7"; with Frog; same mark; $25.00 – $35.00

## Monochrome*

Row 3:
1. Bowl, 3½" x 10"; No mark; $40.00 – $45.00
2. Double Bud, 7" Weller (die impressed); $45.00 – $50.00
3. Bowl, 8" x 1½"; same mark; $25.00 – $35.00


Row 4:
1. Comport, 8"; same mark; $50.00 – $65.00
2. Bowl, 11" x 2½"; No mark; $40.00 – $50.00
3. Comport, 10"; Weller (die impressed); $50.00 – $75.00

Both Montego and Dynasty are unofficial names—even though both had features similar to some lines in the catalogues, we couldn't definitely, or even probably connect them to our satisfaction! It is interesting to note that vases #1 and #3 are lined in the same blue glaze of the Dynasty pieces! Underglaze Blue Ware is recognized by the splotchy dark on medium blue high glaze. Although the flat bowls of "Monochrome" are shown in Muskota, the comports and the double bud are not—but the glaze is identical on all pieces shown. Monochrome was the name voted "most likely" by the several knowledgeable collectors present at the photography session; nothing in the catalogues would confirm or deny their opinion.

Row 1:
 1. ORRIS Bowl, 3" x 7"; No mark; $30.00 – $40.00
 2. JET BLACK Bowl; No mark; $30.00 – $40.00

Row 2:
 1. CAMELOT* Vase, 8"; No mark; $200.00 – $250.00
 2. CAMELOT* Vase, 6"; No mark; $110.00 – $135.00

Row 3:
 1. SOUEVO Vase, 8"; No mark; $125.00 – $150.00
 2. SOUEVO Bowl, 2½" x 6½"; No mark; $75.00 – $100.00
 3. SOUEVO Urn, 6½" x 8"; Marked Weller (die impressed); $140.00 – $165.00
 4. SOUEVO Tobacco Jar, 6"; (Mis-) Marked with the Dickens seal! $225.00 – $275.00

Row 4:
 1. RAGENDA Urn, 6½"; Marked Weller (in-mold script); $40.00 – $50.00
 2. RAGENDA Vase, 12"; Weller Pottery Since 1872; $65.00 – $90.00
 3. RAGENDA Vase, 9"; Weller (in-mold script); $50.00 – $75.00

   Souevo was probably made somewhere around 1910, and according to "legend" was primarily sold to the Indians who in turn sold this "Indian" pottery to unsuspecting tourists (probably from Ohio!). Whether the story is factual or not, Souevo is often unmarked. The Tobacco Jar is a fine example of Weller's flair for mismarking! A friend tells us she once saw a late floral line marked "Louwelsa"!

Souevo

Courtesy Ohio Historical Society

190

## Noval

*Row 1:*
1. *Comport, 5½"; No mark; $50.00 – $75.00*
2. *Candleholder, 9½"; Marked Weller (die impressed); $100.00 – $150.00*
3. *Comport, 9½"; No mark; $80.00 – $120.00*

*Row 2:*
1. *Bowl, 3½" x 9½"; No mark; $60.00 $75.00*
2. *Vase, 6"; No mark; $50.00 – $65.00*
3. *Bowl, 3½" x 8"; Weller (die impressed); $55.00 – $70.00*

## Velva

*Row 3:*
1. *Vase, 6"; Marked Weller (by hand); $35.00 – $50.00*
2. *Bowl, 3½" x 12½"; Weller Pottery (by hand); $50.00 – $65.00*
3. *Vase, 6"; same mark #2; $35.00 – $50.00*

*Row 4:*
1. *Vase, 9"; same mark; $55.00 – $70.00*
2. *Vase, 9½"; Marked with the Velvo paper label; same mark; $50.00 – $65.00*
3. *Vase, 9½"; Marked Weller Pottery (by hand); $55.00 – $70.00*
4. *Vase, 7½"; Weller (by hand); $45.00 – $50.00*

*Noval is always banded in black—without the bands it becomes Eclair. And Velva, as even company sales lists refer to it, is spelled Velvo on its paper label!*

*Courtesy Ohio Historical Society*

## Melrose

*Row 1:*
   1. Vase, 5"; No mark; $60.00 – $85.00
   2. Basket, 10"; Marked Weller (die impressed); $150.00 – $200.00
   3. Vase, 8½"; same mark; $100.00 – $125.00

*Row 2:*
   1. Console Bowl, 5" x 8½"; Weller (die impressed); $90.00 – $115.00
   2. Vase, 7"; same mark; $135.00 – $180.00
   3. Vase, 5" x 7"; same mark; $85.00 – $105.00

## Ivoris

*Row 3:*
   1. Covered Powder Box, 4"; Marked Weller Pottery (by hand); $40.00 – $50.00
   2. Vase, 6"; same mark; $25.00 – $40.00
   3. Vase, 7"; same mark; $30.00 – $45.00
   4. Vase, 6"; Weller (by hand); $25.00 – $40.00
   5. Vase, 5½"; Weller (in-mold script); $25.00 – $45.00

*Row 4:*
   1. Ginger Jar, 8½"; Weller Pottery (by hand); $65.00 – $90.00
   2. Covered Jar, 5"; same mark; $45.00 – $55.00
   3. Console, 3½" x 10"; Frog, 2½"; same mark; $55.00 – $75.00
   4. Basket, 5"; same mark; $35.00 – $65.00
   5. Pitcher, 6"; Weller Pottery Since 1872; $35.00 – $45.00

# Chase

*Row 1:*
  1. *Vase, 6½"; Marked Weller Pottery (by hand); $250.00 – $350.00*
  2. *Fan Vase, 8½"; same mark; $325.00 – $375.00*
  3. *Experimental Vase, 10"; No mark; $425.00 – $525.00*

*Row 2:*
  1. *Experimental Vase, 7½"; Marked with the half kiln ink stamp; COP.G. in red ink on base; Initialed: D.E.; $425.00 – $525.00*
  2. *Vase, 10½"; Weller Pottery (by hand); Unusual color; $325.00 – $425.00*
  3. *Vase, 7½"; No mark; Unusual black hi-gloss glaze; $425.00 – $525.00*

*Below,*
*Row 1:*
  1. *Vase with CHASE Scene in silver; 12" ,Weller Pottery (by hand); $450.00 – $500.00*
*Row 2:*
  1. *Vase, 7½"; same mark; $300.00 – $350.00*
  2. *Vase, 9"; Marked with the Chase paper label; same mark; $350.00 – $425.00*
  3. *Vase, 5½"; same mark; $225.00 – $250.00*

*Row 3: (Opposite page)*
  1. *LEBANON\* Vase, 9"; No mark; $400.00 – $450.00*
  2. *LEBANON\* Vase, 9"; No mark; $450.00 – $550.00*
  3. *LEBANON\* Vase, 6"; No mark; $350.00 – $400.00*
  4. *KNIFEWOOD Tobacco Box, 3½"; Marked Weller (die impressed); $350.00 – $400.00*
     *(Similer match holder; $100.00 – $125.00)*

*Row 4:*
  1. *KNIFEWOOD Vase, 7"; Weller (die impressed); $100.00 – $125.00*
  2. *KNIFEWOOD Urn, 8"; No mark; $125.00 – $175.00*
  3. *KNIFEWOOD Covered Jar, 8"; Weller (die impressed); $300.00 – $350.00*

## Paragon

*Row 1:*

1. Vase, 7½"; Marked Weller (in-mold script); $80.00 – $90.00
2. Vase, 7½"; same mark; $70.00 – $85.00

*Row 2:*

1. Vase, 6½"; same mark; $70.00 – $80.00
2. Candleholders, 2"; Weller Pottery Since 1872; $30.00 – $40.00
3. Bowl Vase, 4½"; Weller (in-mold script); $40.00 – $55.00
4. Same bowl, shown for color contrast; $40.00 – $55.00

## Knifewood

*Row 3:*

1. Bowl, 3"; Weller (die impressed); $75.00 – $100.00
2. Bowl, 4"; Hi-gloss; No mark; $125.00 – $150.00
3. Bowl, 2½"; Hi-gloss; No mark; $85.00 – $110.00
4. Vase, 4½"; Hi-gloss; Weller (die impressed); $75.00 – $100.00

*Row 4:*

1. Vase, 3"; No mark; $125.00 – $175.00
2. Bowl, 3"; Weller (die impressed); $125.00 – $150.00
3. Vase, 5"; same mark; $150.00 – $175.00

*Row 5:*

1. Vase, 9"; same mark; $175.00 – $250.00
2. Vase, 11"; No mark; $250.00 – $350.00
3. Tobacco Jar, 7"; No mark; $400.00 – $450.00

Knifewood, Zona, Forest, Ivory are a few among many lines modeled by Rudolph Lorber, but all of these demonstrate his keen skill at modeling in detail. The Knifewood line portrays animals and birds...flowers and trees, in both a high gloss and a matt finish. We make this statement with some trepidation, but with conviction. Although collectors often refer to the high gloss Knifewood as "Selma," if you will study the catalog page titled "Selma Asst." you will see just that...an assortment!...not a specific line. Orris, Pearl—even Zona and Claywood—and Knifewood, to be sure are all represented. In case you might encounter the tall vase in the middle of the bottom row with a smooth, rather than the typical bark-like background effect, be assured that it is Knifewood!

## Alvin

*Row 1:*

    *1. Vase, 8½"; No mark; $50.00 – $75.00*
    *2. Vase, 12"; Marked Weller (die impressed); $65.00 – $85.00*
    *3. Double Bud Vase, 6"; No mark; $45.00 – $55.00*

## Voile

*Row 2:*

    *1. Jardiniere, 6"; No mark; $50.00 – $85.00*
    *2. Fan Vase, 7"; No mark; $35.00 – $45.00*
    *3. Fan Vase, 8"; No mark; $60.00 – $75.00*
    *4. Fan Vase, 5½"; No mark; $25.00 – $35.00*
    *5. Vase, 9"; No mark; $85.00 – $95.00*

## Pumila

*Row 3:*

    *1. Bowl, 3½"; Marked with the half kiln ink stamp; $20.00 – $25.00*
    *2. Wall Pocket, 7"; No mark; $90.00 – $135.00*
    *3. Vase, 9"; Marked with the Weller Ware round ink stamp; $40.00 – $50.00*
    *4. Vase, 6½"; Weller (die impressed); $20.00 – $30.00*
    *5. Bowl, 4"; Marked with the round foil Weller Ware label; $25.00 – $35.00*

*Row 4:*

    *1. Vase, 9½"; Marked with the round Weller Ware ink stamp; $60.00 – $90.00*
    *2. Candleholder, 3"; marked with the full kiln ink stamp; $60.00 – $70.00*
    *3. Console Plate, 3" x 12"; No mark; $40.00 – $50.00*
    *4. Vase, 12"; Marked with the round Weller Ware ink stamp; $60.00 – $100.00*

*Theory: Row 1 has a definite shine to the glaze that is not typical of Woodcraft, so we feel that it is possibly Alvin. Voile is semi-matt, with pale solid color in the background. An occasional piece of Pumila was shown in the old catalogues in matt blue!*

## Glendale

*Row 1:*

    *1. Double Bud Vase, 7"; No mark; $250.00 – $300.00*

    *2. Vase, 6"; Marked with the Weller Ware round ink stamp; $300.00 – $400.00*

    *3. Vase, 6½"; No mark; $300.00 – $400.00*

    *4. Vase, 6"; No mark; $300.00 – $400.00*

    *5. Double Bud Wall Vase 7"; Marked with the large foil Weller Ware label, and the Glendale paper label; $250.00 – $350.00*

*Row 2:*

    *1. Vase, 12" ; Weller Ware round ink stamp, and Glendale paper label; $500.00 – $700.00*

    *2. Vase, 5"; Marked Weller (die impressed); $200.00 – $275.00*

    *3. Plate with Frog, 15½"; Marked WELLER (ink stamp); $350.00 – $500.00*

    *4. Vase, 4"; Marked with the Weller Ware round ink stamp; $175.00 – $250.00*

    *5. Vase, 8½"; No mark; $300.00 – $400.00*

*Row 3:*

    *1. Candleholders, 5½"; No mark*

    *2. Console Bowl with Frog, 16"; Marked WELLER (ink stamp); $500.00 – $625.00 four–piece set.*

*Glendale is a very popular line with middle period Weller collectors. It is beautifully modeled and meticulously decorated with birds of all types, often nesting. You may occasionally find a piece artist signed.*

203

# Experimentals

*Row 1:*

1. Experimental SILVERTONE vase, 7½"; No mark; $170.00 – $200.00
2. Experimental SILVERTONE Vase, 11½"; No mark; $225.00 – $250.00
3. ZONA Vase, 5½"; Marked Weller (die impressed); Crone D.35406 on base, experimental code ; $100.00 – $125.00
4. BALDIN Vase, 7"; Chromag N.Y. Old RKO N.D., experimental code; $125.00 – $150.00

*Row 2:*

1. GLENDALE Vase, 6"; Marked Weller (die impressed); $300.00 – $400.00
2. GLENDALE Vase, 6½"; same mark; unusual glaze; $200.00 – $250.00

# Arcola

3. Planter, 5" x 9"; No mark; $75.00 – $95.00
4. Lamp Base, 10"; No mark; $95.00 – $135.00
5. Vase, 5½"; No mark; $55.00 – $65.00

# Glendale

*Row 3:*

1. Vase, 9"; Marked with the Weller Ware round ink stamp; $500.00 – $700.00
2. Vase, 13"; same mark as #1; $700.00 – $900.00
3. Vase, 12"; Marked Weller (by hand); Artist signed: McLaughlin; $600.00 – $800.00
4. Vase, 10"; No mark; $550.00 – $750.00

# Ardsley

*Row 1:*

1. *Vase, 7"; Marked with the half kiln ink stamp; $125.00 – $175.00*
2. *Candleholders, 3"; Marked with the full kiln ink stamp; $75.00 – $110.00*
3. *Corner Vase, 7; Marked with the Ardsley Ware paper label, and the half kiln ink stamp; $100.00 – $150.00*
4. *Fan Vase, 8"; Marked with the round Weller Ware ink stamp; $125.00 – $175.00*

*Row 2:*

1. *Double Wall Pocket, 11½"; Full kiln ink stamp; $200.00 – $275.00*
2. *Candleholders, 3"; No mark; $90.00 – $125.00*
3. *Vase, 11½"; Full kiln ink stamp, and Weller (die impressed); $175.00 – $225.00*
4. *Double Vase, 9½"; Weller (die impressed); $150.00 – $200.00*

*Row 3:*

1. *Console Set; Bowl, 2"; Iris frog, 6"; Marked with the half kiln ink stamp; $165.00 – $225.00*
2. *Bulb Bowl, 5"; same mark; $100.00 – $125.00*
3. *Console Set; Bowl, 3½" x 12"; Fish Frog, 6½"; Marked with the full kiln ink stamp; $400.00 – $500.00*

*Row 4:*

1. *Bud Vase, 7½"; Marked with the full kiln ink stamp; $60.00 – $90.00*
2. *Console Set; Bowl, 3½" x 16½"; Kingfisher, 9½"; same mark; $500.00 – $700.00*
3. *Vase, 9"; Marked with the Weller Ware round ink stamp; $70.00 – $110.00*

*Ardsley is a most attractive line, probably introduced in the early-to-mid twenties. Cattails, iris and lily pads are its theme. The "lily pad line," Pumila, shares the candleholders on Row 1, and the bulb bowl on Row 3 quite compatibly!*

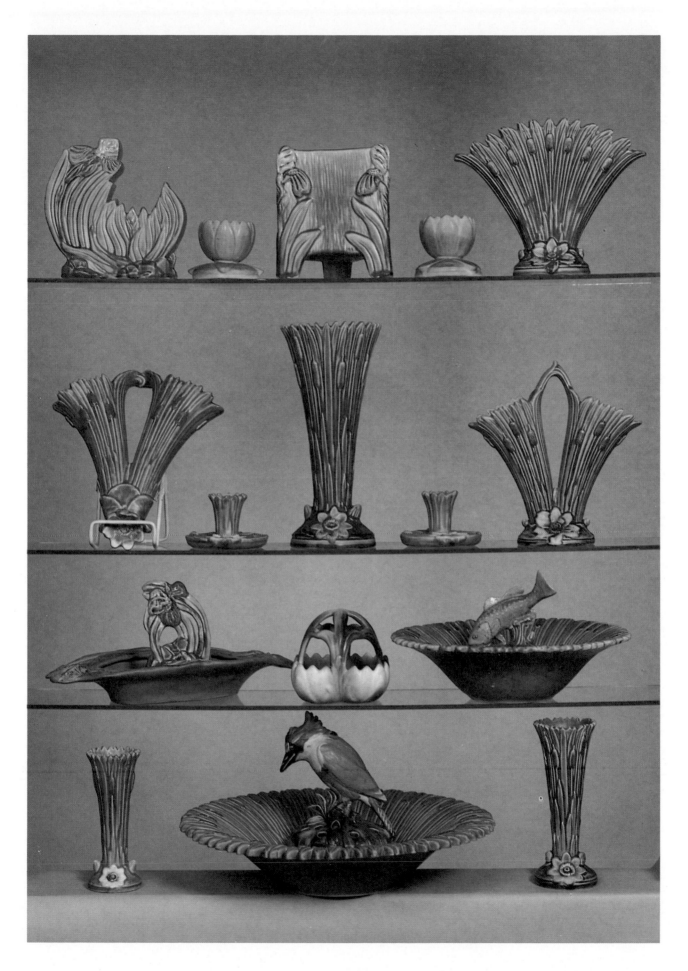

# Klyro

*Row 1:*
1. *Planter, 4"; Marked Weller (die impresssed);  $50.00 – $60.00*
2. *Candleholder, 9½"; same mark;  $50.00 – $65.00*
3. *Planter, 3½"; no mark;  $40.00 – $50.00*

*Row 2:*
1. *Bowl, 3½"; Weller (die impressed);  $55.00 – $60.00*
2. *Bud Vase, 8½"; same mark;  $35.00 – $45.00*
3. *Bud Vase, 7"; No mark;  $25.00 – $35.00*
4. *Planter, 3½" x 8"; same mark;  $40.00 – $55.00*

*Row 3:*
1. *Basket, 7"; No mark;  $75.00 – $100.00*
2. *Planter, 4"; Weller (die impressed);  $60.00 – $70.00*
3. *Fan Vase, 8"; Marked with the full kiln ink stamp;  $45.00 – $50.00*

*Row 4:*
1. *Wall Pocket, 7½"; Marked with the Klyro paper label;  $75.00 – $125.00*
2. *Circle Vase, 8"; Marked with the full kiln ink stamp;  $60.00 – $85.00*
3. *Vase, 8½"; Weller (die impressed);  $40.00 – $55.00*

## Evergreen

*Row 1:*

1. Vase, 4½"; Marked Weller Pottery (in-mold script); $30.00 – $40.00
2. Triple Candleholder, 7½"; same mark; $65.00 – $75.00
3. Vase, 4"; same mark; $20.00 – $25.00

## Fruitone

*Row 2:*

1. Vase, 6"; No mark; $60.00 – $85.00
2. Vase, 8"; Marked Weller (small die impressed); $100.00 – $150.00
3. Vase, 4½"; Weller (die impressed); $40.00 – $50.00
4. Wall Pocket, 5½"; same mark; $150.00 – $225.00

*Row 3:*

1. Fruitone Vase, 8½"; same mark; $140.00 – $160.00
2. Evergreen Vase, 10"; Weller Pottery (in-mold script); $90.00 – $100.00
3. Fruitone Bud Vase, 11½"; Weller (die impressed); $60.00 – $85.00

*Row 4:*

1. Fruitone Vase, 5½"; No mark; $40.00 – $50.00
2. Evergreen Candlestick, 1½"; Weller Pottery (in-mold script); $30.00 – $35.00
3. Evergreen Console Bowl, 5"; same mark; $50.00 – $70.00
4. Evergreen Vase, 5½"; Weller (die impressed); $50.00 – $70.00

Note the strong similarity between the glaze treatment of these two lines! Both are characterized by the tone-on-tone striations...but Fruitone was an early line—probably mid-to-late teens (indicated by the trademarks); and Evergreen was produced from the early-to-late thirties.

## Wall Vases

*Upper left:*
    1. WOODCRAFT, 9"; Marked Weller (die impressed); $110.00 – $140.00

*Row 2,*
*Center top, reading diagonally left:*
    1. WOODCRAFT, 14½" x 12½"; same mark; $1000.00 – $1250.00
    2. WOODCRAFT or FLEMISH, 9½"; No mark; $110.00 – $140.00
    3. WOODCRAFT, 8"; No mark; $110.00 – $140.00

*Row 3,*
*Top right, reading diagonally left:*
    1. ROMA, 8½"; Weller (die impressed); $125.00 – $150.00
    2. ROMA, 7"; No mark; $125.00 – $150.00
    3. WOODCRAFT or FLEMISH, 9"; No mark; $175.00 – $225.00
    4. SOUEVO, 6"; No mark; $125.00 – $175.00
    5. WARWICK, 11½"; Marked with the Warwick paper label, and the half kiln ink stamp; $175.00 – $225.00

*Row 4,*
*Far right, reading diagonally left:*
    1. ROMA, 7"; No mark; $100.00 – $135.00
    2. ROMA, 6"; Weller (small die impressed); $110.00 – $140.00
    3. Floral, 8½"; No mark; $100.00 – $150.00
    4. ROMA,10"; Dupont motif shown in Roma line; No mark; $150.00 – $200.00
    5. BLOSSOM, 7½"; Weller (die impressed); $110.00 – $140.00

*Row 5,*
*Bottom corner, far right:*
    1. KNIFEWOOD, 8"; Weller (die impressed); $175.00 – $225.00
    2. SABRINIAN, 8½"; Marked with the half kiln ink stamp; $400.00 – $500.00

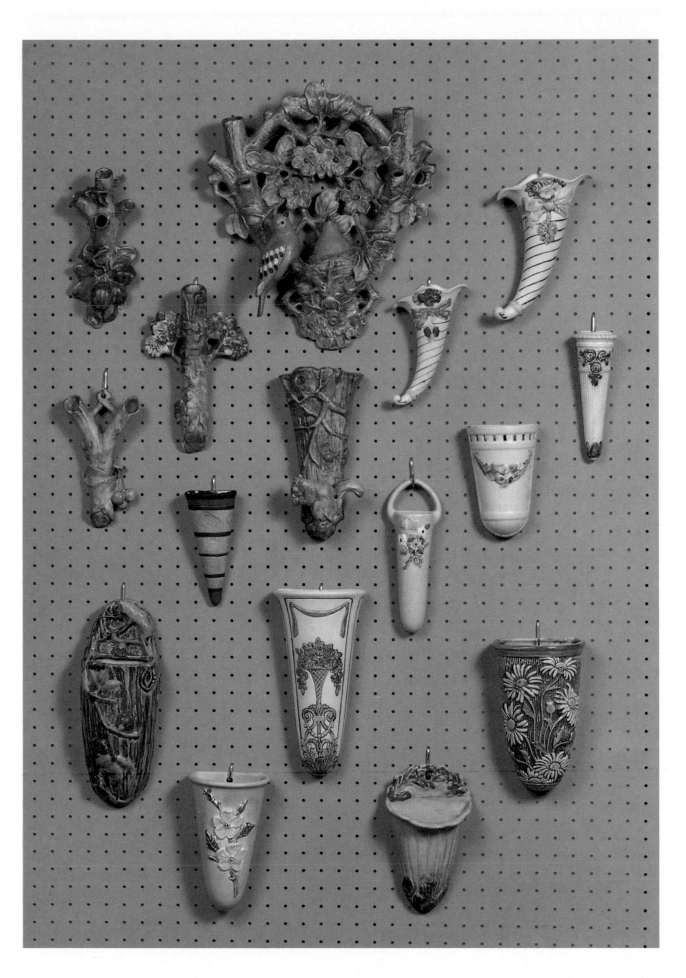

213

## Wall Vases

*Row 1:*

    *1. BRIGHTON Wall Vase, 9½"; Marked Weller (die impressed); $175.00 – $250.00*

    *2. NOVELTY Teapot, 9"; Weller Pottery; $90.00 – $125.00*

    *3. NOVELTY Pitcher, 7½"; same mark; $90.00 – $125.00*

    *4. NOVELTY Cup and Saucer, 3"; same mark; $60.00 – $90.00*

*Row 2,*
*Center:*

    *IVORY Ram Wall Pocket, 10½"; Marked Weller (by hand); $450.00 – $550.00*

*Row 3:*

    *1. EUCLID Wall Pocket, 10"; No mark; $125.00 – $175.00*

    *2. IVORY Eagle Letter Pocket, 9"; No mark; $300.00 – $350.00*

    *3. "U.S. Mail" Pocket, GOLDBROGREEN Glaze, 7½"; No mark; $200.00 – $225.00*

    *4. ARCOLA Wall Pocket, 11"; No mark; $175.00 – $250.00*

*Row 4:*

    *1. IVORY Stag Wall Pocket, 9"; Marked Weller (by hand); $400.00 – $500.00*

    *2. KNIFEWOOD Mold, unusual glaze, 5"; No mark; $125.00 – $175.00*

    *3. IVORY Wall Pocket, 9"; No mark; $125.00 – $175.00*

*Row 5:*

    *2. TRELLIS Wall Shelf, 10½"; No mark; $125.00 – $175.00*

    *2. IVORY Wall Shelf, 9½"; Weller (small die impressed); $110.00 – $150.00*

    *3. SYDONIA Wall Vase, 9½"; Weller Pottery (by hand); $150.00 – $200.00*

# Wall Vases

*Row 1:*
  1. *White and Decorated HUDSON Wall Pocket, 8"; Marked Weller (die impressed); $400.00 – $500.00*
  2. *ROMA Letter Pocket, 4½" x 7½"; No mark; $175.00 – $200.00*
  3. *ZONA Wall Pocket, 8"; No mark; $90.00 – $125.00*

*Row 2:*
  1. *Colored glaze Wall Pocket, 9"; No mark; $95.00 – $130.00*
  2. *PERFECTO (MATT LOUWELSA) Wall Pocket, 7"; Weller (die impressed); Artist signed: H.P.; $350.00 – $400.00*
  3. *ART NOUVEAU Wall Pocket, 6½"; No mark; $300.00 – $350.00*
  4. *PERFECTO (MATT LOUWELSA) Wall Pocket, 7"; Marked Weller (die impressed); $350.00 – $400.00*
  5. *SOUEVO Wall Pocket, 9½"; No mark; $175.00 – $225.00*

*Row 3:*
  1. *CLOUDBURST Wall Pocket, 5½"; No mark; $150.00 – $200.00*
  2. *Embossed Creamware Match Holder, 7"; Marked Weller (die impressed); $125.00 – $150.00*
  3. *LUSTRE Wall Vase, 5½"; No mark; $125.00 – $150.00*

*Row 4:*
  1. *KLYRO Wall Pocket, 6"; Weller (die impressed); $125.00 – $150.00*
  2. *PEARL Wall Pocket, Lustre glaze effect, 8½"; No mark; $150.00 – $200.00*
  3. *ZONA Wall Pocket, 8½"; No mark; $125.00 – $150.00*
  4. *ROMA Wall Pocket, 6"; Weller (die impressed); $125.00 – $150.00*

*Row 5:*
  1. *Floral Wall Pocket, 8½"; Weller (die impressed); $100.00 – $110.00*
  2. *GOLDENGLOW Wall Pocket, 11"; Weller Pottery (by hand); $125.00 – $175.00*
  3. *Wall Pocket, 8½"; No mark; $100.00 – $125.00*

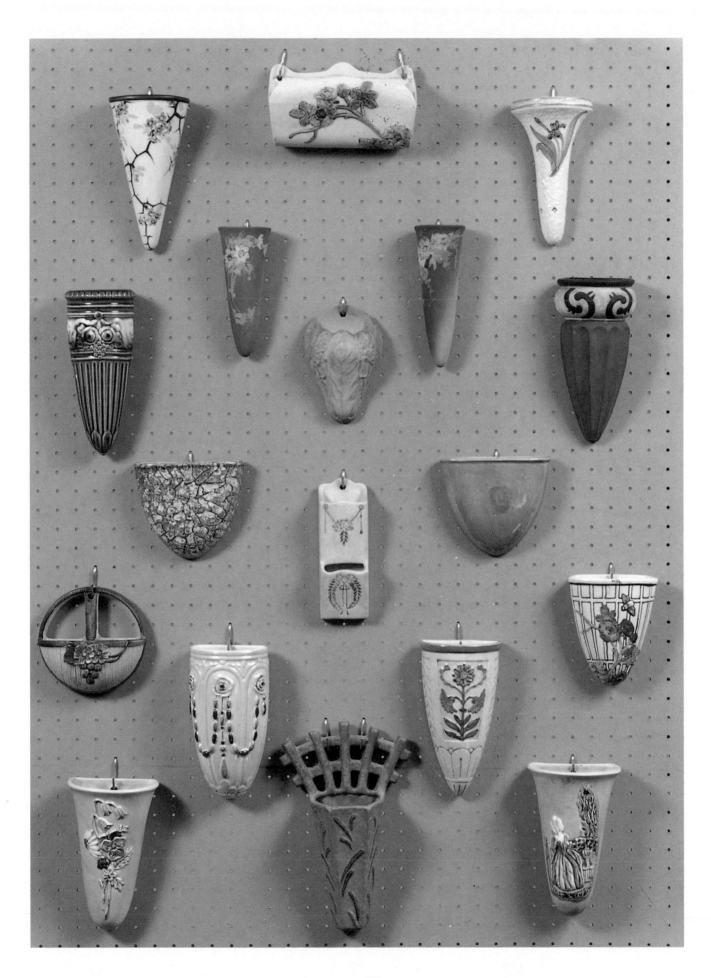

# Wall Vases

*Row 1*
*Left to Right:*
1. BRIGHTON Double Bud Vase, 12"; No mark; $900.00 – $1200.00
2. BRIGHTON Triple Bud Vase, 15"; Marked Weller (die impressed); $900.00 – $1200.00

*Row 2*
GLENDALE Wall Pocket, 7½"; Marked with the round Weller Ware ink stamp; $300.00 – $400.00

*Row 3*
*Left to Right:*
1. GLENDALE Wall Pocket, 12½"; Weller (die impressed); $250.00 – $350.00
2. GLENDALE Wall Pocket, 9"; marked with the full kiln ink stamp; $250.00 – $350.00
3. ARDSLEY Wall Pocket, 12"; No mark; $300.00 – $350.00
4. ARDSLEY Wall Pocket, 12"; same mark as #2 ; $200.00 – $275.00

*Row 4*
*Left to Right:*
1. ORRIS Wall Pocket, 9"; No mark; $100.00 – $125.00
2. SILVERTONE Wall Pocket, 11"; Marked with the half kiln ink stamp; $350.00 – $450.00
3. TUTONE Wall Pocket, 10½"; No mark; $150.00 – $175.00

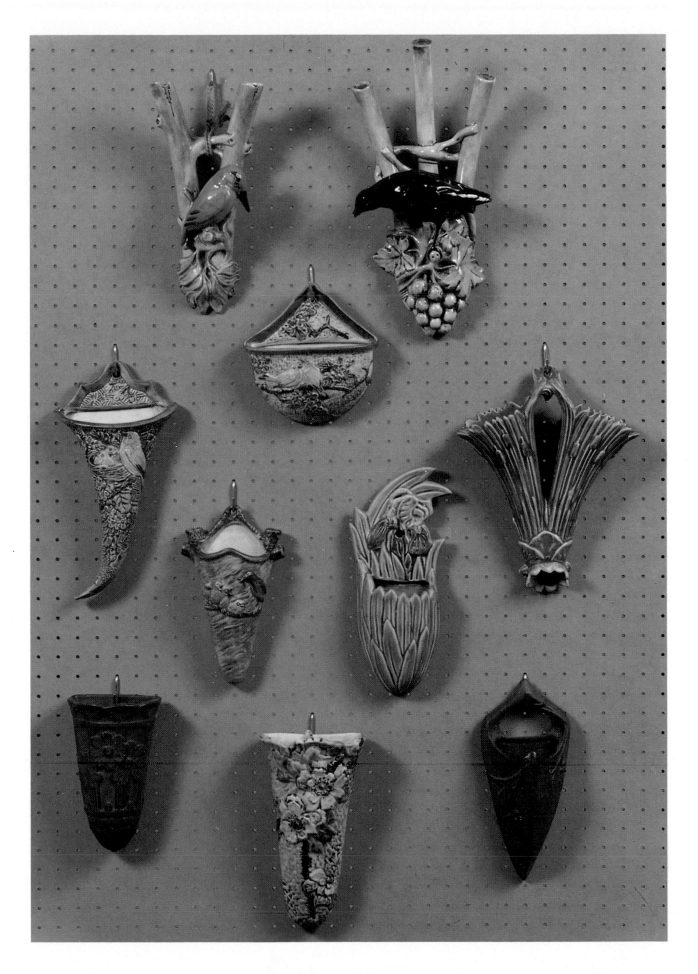

## Lustre

*Row 1:*

    *1. Candlestick, 8"; Marked Weller in small block letters with ink stamp; $50.00 – $75.00*
    *2. Cloudburst Vase, 4½"; No mark; $60.00 – $80.00*
    *3. Vase, 5"; Same as #1; $50.00 – $90.00*
    *4. Cloudburst Vase, 5"; No mark; $85.00 – $100.00*
    *5. Wall Pocket, 7½"; No mark; $70.00 – $100.00*

*Row 2:*

    *1. Basket, 6½"; No mark; $50.00 – $60.00*
    *2. Bowl, 2" x 4"; same mark as #1, Row 1; $20.00 – $25.00*
    *3. Cloudburst Bowl, 4"x 9"; No mark; $80.00 – $110.00*
    *4. Vase, 4½"; No mark; $40.00 – $50.00*
    *5. Comport, 4"; same mark as #1, Row 1; $40.00 – $50.00*

*Row 3:*

    *1. Vase, 8½"; No mark; $50.00 – $65.00*
    *2. Candleholder, 4½"; No mark; $40.00 – $45.00*
    *3. Comport, 7"; same mark as #1, Row 1; $55.00 – $70.00*
    *4. Candleholder, 3"; No mark; $35.00 – $40.00*
    *5. Candlestick, 9"; same mark as #1, Row 1; $35.00 – $45.00*

*Row 4:*

    *1. Besline Candlestick, 10½"; No mark; $125.00 – $150.00*
    *2. Bud Vase, 6"; No mark; $25.00 – $35.00*
    *3. Cloudburst Vase, 10½"; no mark; $200.00 – $250.00*
    *4. Bud Vase, 5½"; No mark; $25.00 – $35.00*
    *5. Vase, 9½"; same mark as #1, Row 1; $40.00 – $50.00*

*The vases with the crackle effect are "Cloudburst," identified from an article in an old trade paper...and an example of the rare acid-etched "Besline" was discovered with the name-label still intact.*

*Row 1:*
1. *Vase, 4½"; Marked Weller (by hand); "Ivory" on base; Artist signed D. E. (See paragraph below); $125.00 –*
*$150.00*
2. *Vase, 8"; Marked WELLER FAIENCE, D500 ½ 500/M ; $475.00 – $550.00*
3. *HUDSON-PERFECTO Vase, 6"; marked Weller Pottery (by hand); Artist signed: H.P.; $200.00 – $300.00*

## Besline

*Row 2:*
1. *Vase, 11"; Marked with the Besline paper label; $475.00 – $550.00*
2. *Vase, 12"; No mark; $475.00 – $550.00*
****
3. *SICARDO Vase, 2"; Signed Weller Sicard; $250.00 – $300.00*
4. *ROCHELLE Vase, 13"; Marked Weller (by hand); Artist signed: H.P.; $650.00 – $750.00*

## Sicardo

*Row 3:*
1. *Vase, 10½"; Signed Weller Sicard; $1250.00 – $1500.00*
2. *Lamp Base, 15½"; Signed Sicard Weller; (See paragraph below); $3000.00 – $4000.00*

****
3. *WELLER FAIENCE Vase, 13"; Marked Weller Faience, (by hand); 48 X F on base ; $500.00 – $600.00*

*This note was contained in the "Bonito" vase: "This piece was turned by Mr. Sam Weller himself, at Weller #1 Pottery...prior to WWI. It was done on a "kick wheel." It was then hand decorated by Dorothy England, one of Mr. Weller's favorite young artists at that time. Miss England decorated this with a stain. She stenciled "Weller Pottery" on the bottom and signed her initials "DE." It was later presented as a gift to one of the members of the Weller family." ...one can only speculate on the chain of events that eventually led from this original design to the decision to put "Bonito" into full production years later—not by Sam Weller, but by his nephew, Harry!*

*The Sicardo lamp has its bit of history to relate: "This Weller Sicardo lamp was originally in the possession of S.A. Weller, selected by him for his home. It was handed down to his brother-in-law Edward Pickens and eventually was passed on to Ed Pickens' sister-in-law Miss Ethel Hinnor, who has been deceased for several years." (Part of a letter, dated 1970, from Mrs. Ruth Moberg, foster sister of Mrs. Hermione K. Weber who was a niece of S.A. Weller and was saleslady in his salesroom for many years.) In 1905, the lamp cost $250.00. The two Besline pieces show two distinctly different methods of decorating this very rare line of the early 20's. On the left, acid etching over gold lustre; on the right, etched before the lustre was applied. (Thanks to Richard Schiller for pointing this out to us!)*

## Marengo

*Row 1:*
   1. Vase, 8"; No mark; $250.00 – $300.00
   2. Wall Pocket, 8½"; No mark; $175.00 – $225.00

## Lamar

*Row 2:*
   1. Vase, 6"; No mark; $100.00 – $150.00
   2. Vase, 7½"; Marked with the round Weller Ware paper label; $150.00 – $200.00
   3. Vase, 7½"; No mark; $150.00 – $200.00

*Row 3:*
   1. Vase, 8½"; No mark; $200.00 – $250.00
   2. Lamp, 16"; No mark; $375.00 – $475.00
   3. Vase, 11½"; No mark; $325.00 – $375.00

*Luster*

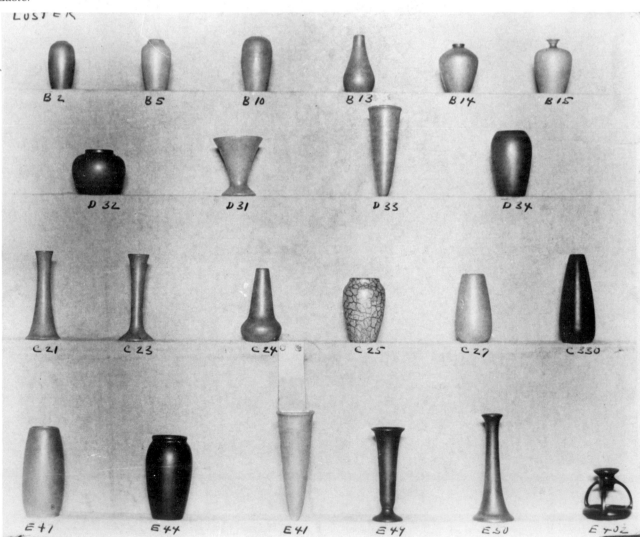

*Courtesy Ohio Historical Society*

## La Sa

*Row 1:*
1. *Vase, 6½"; Signed La Sa, Weller; $200.00 – $250.00*
2. *Vase, 3½"; Signed; $125.00 – $150.00*
3. *Vase, 6"; Signed; $200.00 – $225.00*

*Row 2:*
1. *Vase, 8"; No mark; $225.00 – $300.00*
2. *Vase, 6"; No mark; $200.00 – $250.00*
3. *Vase, 6½"; No mark; $175.00 – $200.00*
4. *Vase, 8"; Signed Weller, La Sa; $225.00 – $300.00*

*Row 3:*
1. *Vase or Lamp Base, 13½"; Signed; $500.00 – $700.00*
2. *Lamp, 8"; Signed; $200.00 – $230.00*
3. *Lamp, 14½"; Signed; $500.00 – $700.00*
4. *Vase, 6"; Signed; $150.00 – $175.00*
5. *Vase or Lamp Base, 12"; Signed; $350.00 – $450.00*

*Below: Two unmarked vases, 13"; Signed by Lessell  Black with stag; $2500.00 – $3000.00*
*White with camels; $2500.00 – $3250.00*

## Chengtu

*Row 1:*
1. Urn, 5½"; Marked with the half kiln ink stamp; $65.00 – $85.00
2. Urn, 3½"; marked with the Chengtu paper label; $45.00 – $55.00
3. Covered Jar, 8"; same mark as #1; $175.00 – $200.00
4. Urn, 3½"; same mark; $50.00 – $60.00
5. Vase, 6"; same mark; $40.00 – $60.00

*Row 2:*
1. Vase, 8"; Marked with the Chengtu paper label; $70.00 – $95.00
2. Vase, 11½"; Marked with the half kiln ink stamp; $125.00 – $150.00
3. Vase, 11"; same mark as #2; $125.00 – $150.00
4. Vase, 9"; same mark; $80.00 – $100.00

*Row 3:*
1. Ginger Jar, 12"; same mark; $200.00 – $225.00
2. Vase, 7½"; same mark; $60.00 – $75.00
4. Vase, 16"; same mark; $250.00 – $300.00
4. Vase, 6½"; same mark; $50.00 – $60.00
5. Vase, 12"; same mark; $150.00 – $175.00

Chengtu...Chinese Red...made in the middle-to-late twenties, was fired in a gold kiln. The temperature was crucial! Overfired, the red burned out; underfired, the glaze was not permanent. Just to be safe, never stick labels or tape to the glaze. We found this article from a Crockery & Glass Journal—mention is made of "Chinese Red."

"The new offerings in the novelty group of S.A. Weller Pottery Company, are many and varied. There are flower pots in a rope design...a hollowed tree trunk on two tricky twigs for legs...a new print glaze in a leafy design in a red crystalline effect...a Chinese red is also of interest. There are dogs and cats in a new idea of slip design...simple modern vases of trim and squared lines in black and white (?)...a finish that should be of sales interest is the gunmetal finish. A beer mug uses the face of Einstein and is labeled Ein Stein...clever no end!"

# Hudson

*Row 1,*
*Scenics:*

    1. Vase, 8"; Marked with the small Weller die; $1500.00 – $2250.00

    2. Vase, 9"; Marked with the half kiln ink stamp; Artist signed: Timberlake; $1500.00 – $2250.00

    3. Vase, 9½"same mark as #2; Artist signed: Pillsbury; $1750.00 – $2000.00

    4. Vase, 9"; same mark; Artist signed: Pillsbury; $1400.00 – $1700.00

    5. Vase, 8"; Marked with the small Weller die; $1500.00 – $2000.00

*Row 2:*

    1. Scenic Vase, 8"; Marked with the half kiln ink stamp; Artist signed: Pillsbury; $1800.00 – $2200.00

    2. HUDSON-PERFECTO Vase, 10"; No mark; Artist signed: Leffler; $400.00 – $450.00

    3. Scenic Vase, 8"; same mark as #1; Artist signed: Timberlake; $1800.00 – $2300.00

*Row 3:*

    1. Floral Vase, 13½"; Marked Weller Pottery (by hand); $1250.00 – $1750.00

    2. Scenic Vase, 14½"; same mark; Artist signed: Pillsbury; $2000.00 – $2500.00

    3. Floral Vase, 13½"; same mark; Artist signed: Pillsbury; $1250.00 – $1750.00

There are several variations within the Hudson artware line—a few of which the Weller Company provided with distinguishing "sub-titles"— and yet, there are others...obviously decorated with a different concept in mind than a "true" Hudson...for which no name is indicated. There are collectors who would prefer to use the broader term "Hudson" to apply to all types of the semi-matt artware, and basically they are right! But so that communication might be established between collectors...and buyers and dealers...on the pages to follow are some definitions that should be helpful.

# Hudson, Hudson Types

*Row 1:*
    *1. HUDSON-LIGHT Vase, 4½"; Marked Weller (die impressed); $125.00 – $175.00*
    *2. ROCHELLE Vase, 6"; same mark as #1; Artist signed: T.F.; $250.00 – $350.00*
    *3. HUDSON, Scenic Vase, 8½"; Weller Pottery (by hand); Artist signed: Timberlake; $700.00 – $800.00*
    *4. Vase, 7"; No mark; Artist signed: LBM; $200.00 – $225.00*
    *5. HUDSON-PERFECTO Vase, 4½"; No mark; Artist signed: H.P.; $125.00 – $175.00*

*Row 2:*
    *1. Vase, 9½"; No mark; Artist signed: Timberlake; $1250.00 – $1750.00*
    *2. Vase, 12"; Marked with the half kiln ink stamp; Artist signed: Pillsbury; $750.00 – $1250.00*
    *3. Vase, 9½"; same mark as #2; Artist signed: E. Roberts; $800.00 – $1200.00*

*Row 3:*
    *1. HUDSON-PERFECTO Vase, 13½"; Weller (die impressed) Artist signed: C. Leffler; $1100.00 – $1400.00*
    *2. HUDSON-PERFECTO Vase, 13½"; same mark; Artist signed: C. Leffler; $1150.00 – $1450.00*
    *3. HUDSON-PERFECTO Vase, 9½"; same mark; Artist signed: C. Leffler; $750.00 – $950.00*

*"True" Hudsons are characterized by a shaded background: blue to pink; buff to blue; pink to gray or soft green; or two values of blue; etc. They are decorated under a semi-matt glaze in heavy slip with a multi-color pastel palette. The artwork is usually artist signed; florals are most often found—but birds, animals, landscapes, and portraits are the most desirable: these are often referred to as "Scenics."*

*"Perfecto" (we use the hyphenated term Hudson-Perfecto to distinguish between this line and the earlier matt artware) is easily recognized by its smooth, "china painting" technique. Mineral colors, or stains, were used to execute the artwork (often signed) under the semi-matt glaze.*

*"Rochelle" is easily recognized from its shaded brown backgrounds. It is quite rare; only two examples are shown in the color plates. The catalogue reprint is on page 368.*

## Scenic Hudson

*Row 1:*
1. *Vase, 8"; Marked with the half kiln ink stamp; Artist signed: Pillsbury; $1400.00 – $1600.00*
2. *Vase, 12"; Marked Weller Pottery (by hand); Artist signed: McLaughlin; $2000.00 – $3000.00*
3. *Vase, 9"; no mark; Artist signed: Pillsbury; $1500.00 – $2000.00*

*Row 2:*
1. *Vase, 12"; Weller Pottery (by hand); Artist signed: Pillsbury; $2250.00 – $3250.00*
2. *Vase, 27½"; Marked with the half kiln ink stamp; Artist signed: McLaughlin; $12000.00 – $15000.00*
3. *Vase, 15"; same mark as #2; Artist signed: Pillsbury; $2500.00 – $3500.00*

WINDOW OF THE FARMER-CANNON JEWELRY CO:
BIRMINGHAM, ALABAMA

*Courtesy Ohio Historical Society*

234

# Hudson

*Row 1:*

    *1. Vase, 8½"; Marked with the half kiln ink stamp; Artist signed: Axline; $450.00 – $550.00*

    *2. DELTA Vase, 10"; marked with the full kiln ink stamp; Artist signed: Pillsbury, KKT on base; $450.00 – $600.00*

    *3. BLUE AND DECORATED Vase, 10"; Weller (die impressed); $250.00 – $300.00*

    *4. DELTA Vase, 7"; No mark; Artist signed: Pillsbury; $400.00 – $500.00*

    *5. Vase, 8"; No mark; Artist signed: Timberlake; $400.00 – $500.00*

*Row 2:*

    *1. Vase, 12"; Weller (die impressed) Artist signed: M. Timberlake ; $600.00 – $800.00*

    *2.WHITE AND DECORATED Vase, 11½"; same mark; $3000.00 – $4000.00*

    *3. WHITE AND DECORATED Vase, 10½"; Weller (small die impressed); $2750.00 – $3250.00*

    *4. Vase, 12½"; Weller (die impressed); Artist signed: McLaughlin; $600.00 – $800.00*

*Row 3:*

    *1. Vase, 12"; Marked with the round Weller Ware ink stamp; $1250.00 – $1750.00*

    *2. Vase, 15"; Marked with the half kiln ink stamp; Artist signed: Pillsbury; $1500.00 – $2000.00*

    *3. Vase, 12"; Marked Weller Pottery (by hand); Artist signed: McLaughlin; $1200.00 – $1500.00*

*"Delta" is simply a blue Hudson—the background may be two values blending together—with the artwork (often signed) done in blue tones of slip under semi-matt glaze.*

*Right: Original photograph from which "doughboy" was painted.*

## White And Decorated Hudson

*Row 1:*
1. *Bowl, 4"; No mark; $150.00 – $200.00*
2. *Vase, 7"; No mark; $150.00 – $200.00*
3. *Vase, 7"; Marked Weller (die impressed); $150.00 – $175.00*
4. *Vase, 6½"; same mark; $150.00 – $200.00*

*Row 2:*
1. *Vase, 9½"; same mark; $200.00 – $250.00*
2. *Vase, 10½"; Weller (small die impressed); $200.00 – $250.00*
3. *Vase, 11"; Weller (die impressed); $225.00 – $275.00*
4. *Vase, 11"; same mark; $200.00 – $250.00*
5. *Vase, 10"; same mark; $200.00 – $250.00*

## Blue And Decorated Hudson

*Row 3:*
1. *Vase, 7½"; same mark; $175.00 – $225.00*
2. *Vase, 8"; same mark; $175.00 – $225.00*
3. *Vase, 9½"; same mark; $200.00 – $250.00*
4. *Vase, 8½"; same mark; $175.00 – $225.00*
5. *Vase, 4½"; same mark; $125.00 – $150.00*

*Row 4:*
1. *Vase, 10"; No mark; $200.00 – $250.00*
2. *Vase, 10"; No mark; $225.00 – $275.00*
3. *Vase, 9"; No mark; $250.00 – $300.00*
4. *Bud Vase, 10"; No mark; $125.00 – $150.00*
5. *Vase, 9½"; Marked Weller (die impressed); $150.00 – $200.00*

*Both of these lines are characterized by a solid background of the color indicated. The slip work is often simple florals with horizontal bands incorporated into the designs, and the palette rather limited. But even when superior artwork is seen, such as in the examples on page 241, they are not artist signed!*

239

# Hudson

*Row 1:*
1. *HUDSON-LIGHT\* Vase, 9"; Marked Weller (die impressed); Artist signed: H.P.; $350.00 – $450.00*
2. *Scenic Vase, 9½"; Marked Weller Pottery (by hand); Artist signed: McLaughlin; $1250.00 – $1750.00*
3. *ROCHELLE Vase, 7"; same mark as #1; Artist signed: H.P.; $450.00 – $550.00*

*Row 2:*
1. *BLUE AND DECORATED Vase, 13½"; same mark; $950.00 – $1250.00*
2. *BLUE AND DECORATED Vase, 13½"; same mark; $1600.00 – $2000.00*
3. *Scenic Vase, 13½"; Weller (small die impressed); $1600.00 – $2000.00*
4. *HUDSON-LIGHT\* Vase, 13½"; Weller (die impressed); $1600.00 – $2000.00*
5. *BLUE AND DECORATED Vase, 13½"; same mark as #4; $1150.00 – $1500.00*

*Row 3:*
1. *WHITE AND DECORATED Vase, 15"; same mark; $1400.00 – $1800.00*
2. *SILHOUETTE\* Vase, 15"; No mark; Artist signed: Timberlake; $1500.00 – $2000.00*
3. *Floral Vase, 15½"; Marked Weller Pottery (by hand); Artist signed: Pillsbury; $900.00 – $1200.00*

*The beautiful girls on Row 2 may have been painted by Ed Pickens; they once stood in his home. The vase with the little fisherboy on a solid background with a black slip silhouette is an unusual piece, and "Silhouette" would seem an appropriate name. Note the 30's shape. "Hudson-Light" is our own term to indicate those with a very pale shaded background—gray, ivory, pale lavender, etc; and decorated in a limited palette of cool colors. This type was seldom artist signed.*

*Table top tiles, each 6" x 6"; Signed Timberlake; $2250.00 – $2750.00*

# Hudson

*Row 1:*
1. *Vase, 7"; Marked Weller Pottery (by hand); Artist signed: Timberlake; $300.00 – $350.00*
2. *Vase, 9½"; Marked with the half kiln ink stamp; Artist signed: L.B.M.; $350.00 – $400.00*
3. *Vase, 7"; Weller Pottery (by hand); Artist signed: Morris; $300.00 – $350.00*

*Row 2:*
1. *Vase, 15½"; no mark; Artist signed: M.T.; $1250.00 – $1600.00*
2. *Lamp, 14"; Weller (die impressed); (line unknown, Brighton glaze); $750.00 – $950.00*
3. *Vase, 15"; Marked with the full kiln ink stamp; Artist signed: McLaughlin; $1250.00 – $1600.00*

*Row 3:*
1. *Parrot, 7½" x 11"; Weller Pottery (by hand); $1400.00 – $1800.00*
2. *Vase with Parrot, 14"; same mark as #1; Artist signed: Timberlake; $2000.00 – $2500.00*
3. *Parrot, 7½" x 12"; No mark; $1400.00 – $1800.00*

*Hudsons are understandably very attractive to Weller collectors and even the value of the smaller floral pieces is rapidly increasing. The large florals by Mae Timberlake and Sarah McLaughlin on Row 2 are exquisite; and on the bottom—flanking a vividly beautiful parrot scenic—are two life size specimens...the only known examples in "captivity!"*

*Pair of decorative tiles, measuring 6" x 6", (frames, 8½" x 8½"); Signed: Pillsbury; $2000.00 – $2500.00. Bought at auction, $3200.00.*

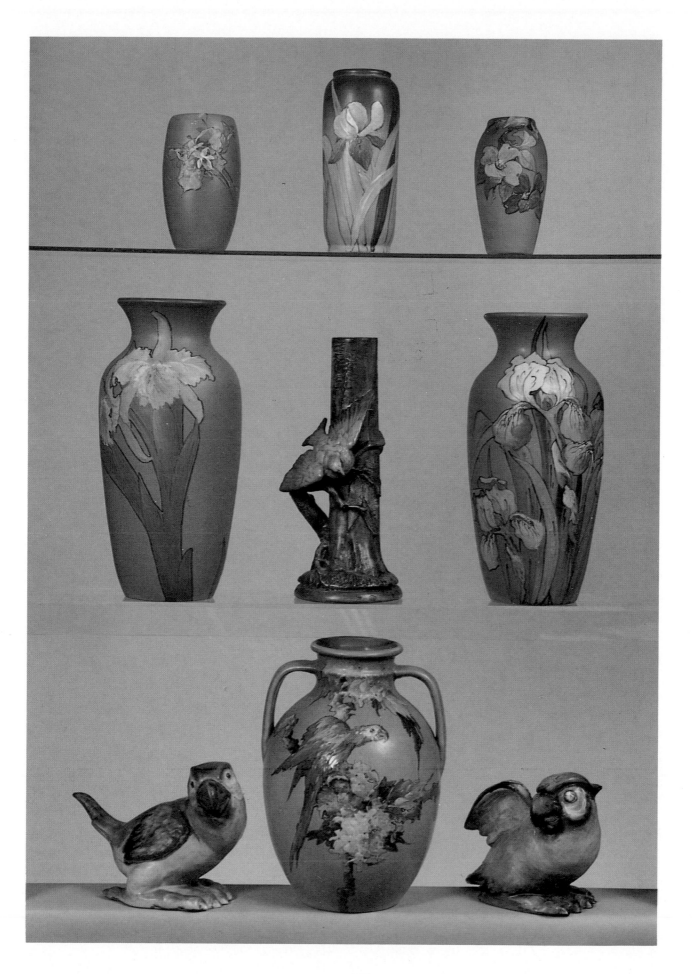

*Row 1:*
> *1. BONITO Vase, 8½"; Very unusual hi-gloss glaze; Marked Weller Pottery (by hand); Artist signed: F.DDTIS; $175.00 – $275.00*
> *2. XENIA\* Vase, 10½"; Weller (die impressed); $550.00 – $650.00*
> *3. XENIA\* Vase, 7"; same mark as #2; $350.00 – $450.00*

## Hudson

*Row 2:*
> *1. Vase, 6"; Marked with the half kiln ink stamp; Artist signed: Timberlake; $300.00 – $350.00*
> *2. Vase, 8"; Marked Weller Pottery (by hand); Artist signed: S.T. ; $350.00 – $400.00*
> *3. Vase, 5½"; Marked Weller (in-mold script), T-10 on base; Artist signed: H.P.; $200.00 – $250.00*

## Scenic Hudson

*Row 3:*
> *1. Vase, 8"; Marked with the half kiln ink stamp; Artist signed: McLaughlin; $900.00 – $1200.00*
> *2. Vase, 8½"; Weller (die impressed); $950.00 – $1250.00*
> *3. Vase, 7"; Weller Pottery (by hand); Artist signed: Pillsbury; $1000.00 – $1350.00*

## Hudson-Perfecto

*Row 4:*
> *1. Vase, 6½"; No mark; Artist signed: D.E.; $175.00 – $225.00*
> *2. Vase, 9"; Marked Weller (die impressed); $200.00 – $225.00*
> *3. Vase, 5½"; same mark as #2; $175.00 – $200.00*

*Many knowledgeable collectors believe these tiles are made by Weller..the one on the top is 10" x 5¾", the bottom one measures 13½" x 5½". Green, $350.00 – $500.00; Brown, $450.00 – $600.00*

*Row 1:*

    *1. PICTORIAL  Vase, 7"; Artist signed: Timberlake; Marked Weller Pottery (by hand ; $900.00 – $1200.00*

    *2. Vase, 9½"; Stylized Carnation design, "squeeze bag" application by artist Dorothy England; same mark; $400.00 – $500.00*

    *3. HUDSON-PERFECTO  Vase, 8½"; Marked Weller (in-mold script); $275.00 – $325.00*

    *4. HUDSON-PERFECTO Vase, 9"; same mark; FEW #2 on base; $300.00 – $325.00*

## Copra

*Row 2:*

    *1. Vase, 10"; Marked Weller (die impressed); $225.00 – $275.00*

    *2. Jardiniere, 8"; same mark; $150.00 – $200.00*

    *3. Basket, 11"; same mark; $225.00 – $275.00*

## Hudson

*Row 3:*

    *1. HUDSON-LIGHT* Vase, 15"; Marked Weller (small die impressed); $900.00 – $1200.00*

    *2. Floral Vase, 15"; Artist signed; Pillsbury; No mark; $1300.00 – $1600.00*

    *3. Floral Vase, 16"; Artist signed; M. T.; Weller (die impressed); $1350.00 – $1650.00*

*We'll be honest—the announcement of the Copra line in an old trade journal was a little vague, but we believe this is it! 1915 was the era of Louella (and don't those flowers look familiar!) and Flemish—this seems to be a mingling of the two.*

*Although from the photo the piece on Row 1, #1, may seem to be another "Silhouette," there is a difference in the depth of the work, which in this case has been applied with much more body to the slip than usual. Some advanced collectors feel this may be of the rare "Pictorial" line—nothing we can learn would either disprove nor authenticate their theory. In the photo of the Putnam plant decorating department taken in the early 20's, Ed Pickens is said to be holding a "Pictorial" vase. We cannot connect it with any familiar Weller lines—can you?? To add to the confusion, a 1910 catalogue mentions "Pictorial"—but the hand incised mark used here did not come into popular usage until the mid-to-late twenties!!*

# Bonito

*Row 1:*

    1. *Candleholders, 1½"; Marked Weller Pottery (by hand); $65.00 – $95.00*

    2. *Bowl, 3½"; Marked Weller Pottery (by hand); Artist initialed: C.F.; $100.00 – $135.00*

*Row 2:*

    1. *Vase, 5"; Marked Weller Pottery (by hand); $100.00 – $145.00*

    2. *Vase, 5"; Marked Weller Pottery (by hand); $100.00 – $135.00*

    3. *Bowl with frog, 3"; No mark; Artist initialed: D.E.; $100.00 – $145.00*

    4. *Vase, 4"; Marked Weller Pottery (by hand); $95.00 – $120.00*

    5. *Candleholder, 3½"; Marked Weller Pottery (by hand); $100.00 – $125.00*

*Row 3:*

    1. *Vase, 6"; Marked Weller Pottery (by hand); Artist signed: H.P.; $125.00 – $175.00*

    2. *Vase, 6½"; Marked Weller Pottery (by hand); Artist signed: H.P.; $125.00 – $175.00*

    3. *Vase, 7½"; Marked Weller Pottery (by hand); $150.00 – $200.00*

    4. *Vase, 7"; Marked Weller Pottery (by hand); Artist signed: N.W.; $150.00 – $200.00*

    5. *Vase, 7"; Marked Weller Pottery (by hand); Artist signed: R.A.; $150.00 – $200.00*

*Row 4:*

    1. *Vase, 10"; Marked with samll paper label; Artist signed: N.C.; $300.00 – $400.00*

    2. *Vase, 4"; Marked Weller Pottery (by hand); $65.00 – $95.00*

    3. *Vase, 10½"; Marked Weller Pottery (by hand); $350.00 – $450.00*

    4. *Vase, 6½"; Marked Weller Pottery (by hand); Artist signed: H P.; $100.00 – $125.00*

    5. *Vase, 11"; Marked Weller Pottery (by hand); Artist signed: H.P.; $300.00 – $400.00*

*Naomi Truitt Walch worked for Weller from 1927 to 1936. As one of the artists who decorated Bonito, she recalled that the freehand design was first drawn on the ware with India ink, and colored with a mineral stain. During the firing, the ink burned out and the stain was completely absorbed into the body. This was also the method used on the Hudson-Perfecto line, which she was able to identify.*

## Louella

*Row 1:*
1. Hair Receiver, 3"; Marked Weller (die impressed); $50.00 – $55.00
2. Vase, 9½"; same mark; $75.00 – $90.00
3. Bowl, 3"; same mark; $30.00 – $35.00
4. Powder Jar, 4"; same mark; $45.00 – $65.00

*Row 2:*
1. Basket, 6½"; same mark;  $85.00 – $100.00
2. Vase, 8"; same mark; $100.00 – $130.00
3. Vase, 6½"; same mark; $85.00 – $110.00
4. Vase, 4½"; same mark; $40.00 – $45.00

## Lorbeek

*Row 3:*
1. Wall Pocket, 8½"; Marked with full kiln ink stamp; $115.00 – $135.00
2. Candleholder, 2½"; same mark; $45.00 – $65.00
3. Bowl Vase, 5"; same mark;  $75.00 – $100.00
4. Frog, 2"; same mark

*Row 4:*
1. Vase, 7"; same mark; $95.00 – $115.00
2. Console set; Bowl, 3" x 14"; Frog, 5"; same mark; $150.00 – $200.00
3. Vase, 8"; same mark; $100.00 – $125.00

Louella and the similar Blue Drapery line were the early work of modeler Rudolph Lorber; the floral studies that somehow seem inappropriate to decorate Louella's shirred background were hand executed. Lorbeek, the futuristic line of the middle 1920's is most often found in this high gloss lavender pink glaze—but flat bowls in the line were done in matt glaze, and lined in contrasting colors.

251

# Marvo

Row 1:
1. Double Bud, 5"; No mark; $75.00 – $100.00
2. Hanging Basket, 5"; Marked with the full kiln ink stamp; $125.00 – $150.00
3. Double Bud, 4½"; No mark; $75.00 – $100.00

Row 2:
1. Vase, 8½"; Marked with the full kiln ink stamp; $60.00 – $95.00
2. Bowl, 5"; No mark; $50.00 – $85.00
3. Pitcher, 8"; Marked with the full kiln ink stamp; $100.00 – $125.00
4. Bowl, 4"; Marked with the Marvo paper label; and the round Weller Ware ink stamp; $30.00 – $40.00
5. Wall Vase, 8½"; No mark; $120.00 – $160.00

Row 3:
1. Vase, 6½"; Marked with the full kiln ink stamp; $40.00 – $50.00
2. Bud Vase, 9"; Marked with the half kiln ink stamp; $50.00 – $60.00
3. Vase, 11½" full kiln ink stamp; $90.00 – $110.00
4. Vase, 10"; No mark; $80.00 – $100.00
5. Vase, 9"; No mark; $60.00 – $90.00

Row 4:
1. Console Bowl, 2½" x 10"; No mark; $75.00 – $95.00
2. Frog, shown in bowl, 3"; No mark; $30.00 – $50.00
3. Candleholder, 2½"; Marked Weller (die impressed); $35.00 – $40.00
4. Frog, unusual in gray, 2"; No mark; $30.00 – $50.00
5. Console Bowl, 2½"; No mark; $75.00 – $95.00

253

## Silvertone

*Row 1:*
1. Double Bud Vase, 6"; Marked with the half kiln stamp; $125.00 – $175.00

*Row 2:*
1. Vase, 8½"; same mark; $250.00 – $350.00
2. Vase, 10"; Marked with the full kiln ink stamp; $225.00 – $275.00
3. Vase, 9"; same mark as #2; $300.00 – $375.00
4. Vase, 9"; Marked with the half kiln ink stamp; $275.00 – $350.00

*Row 3:*
1. Vase, 11½" same mark as #4; $300.00 – $400.00
2. Basket, 13"; same mark; $275.00 – $350.00
3. Vase, 11½"; same mark; $175.00 – $225.00

*Row 4:*
1. Candleholders, 3"; same mark; $100.00 – $125.00
2. Console Bowl, 3½" x 12"; Frog, 2½"; same mark; Bowl, $200.00 – $250.00; Frog, $75.00 – $100.00

Silvertone's delicate shading and exquisite floral modeling make this line a favorite of Weller collectors. Middle-to-late 20's would be its place in time, and we found no mention of it in the 1930's.

# Sabrinian

*Row 1:*
   1. Window Box, 3½ " x 9"; Marked with the half kiln stamp; $175.00 – $225.00
   2. Basket, 7"; same mark; $250.00 – $300.00
   3. Planter, 4½"; same mark; $150.00 – $175.00

*Row 2:*
   1. Candleholder, 6½"; same mark; $125.00 – $175.00
   2. Bud Vase, 7"; same; $90.00 – $120.00
   3. Ewer, 10½"; same mark; $225.00 – $275.00
   4. Ewer, 9"; same mark; $200.00 – $250.00
   5. Double Bud Vase, 6½"; same mark; $125.00 – $150.00

*Row 3:*
   1. Vase, 10½"; same mark; $200.00 – $225.00
   2. Candleholders, 2"; same mark; $100.00 – $125.00
   3. Bowl, 3½"; same mark; $135.00 – $180.00
   4. Vase, 9½"; same mark; $175.00 – $225.00

*Row 4:*
   1. Console Bowl, 3½" x 11½"; Frog, 4½"; same mark; $175.00 – $225.00
   2. Vase, 12"; same mark; $300.00 – $350.00
   3. Bowl, 2½" x 9"; Marked with the Sabrinian paper label, and the half kiln stamp; $150.00 – $190.00

Sabrinian was first made during the late 1920's; its unique shell and sea horse motif and its lovely glaze treatment make it a favorite of middle period collectors.

# Coppertone

*Row 1:*
1. *Vase, 6½"; No mark; $150.00 – $200.00*
2. *Basket, 8½"; No mark; $175.00 – $225.00*
3. *Vase, 6"; Marked Weller Hand Made (by hand); $175.00 – $225.00*

*Row 2:*
1. *Ashtray, 6½"; Weller Pottery (by hand); $175.00 – $225.00*
2. *Frog, 4"; same mark; $200.00 – $250.00*
3. *Flower Pot with Saucer, 5"; Weller Hand Made (by hand); $175.00 – $250.00*
4. *Frog, 2"; No mark; $175.00 – $200.00*
5. *Turtle Candleholder, 3"; Marked with the half kiln ink stamp; $225.00 – $275.00*

*Row 3:*
1. *Vase, 8½"; Weller Hand Made (by hand); $200.00 – $300.00*
2. *Candlestick, 3½"; same mark; $75.00 – $110.00*
3. *Pitcher, 7½"; Marked with the half kiln ink stamp; $550.00 – $750.00*
4. *Candleholder, 2"; Weller Pottery (by hand); $50.00 – $80.00*
5. *Vase, 8½"; No mark; $200.00 – $300.00*

*Row 4:*
1. *Fan Vase, 8"; No mark; $550.00 – $750.00*
2. *Vase, 15½"; Weller Hand Made (by hand); $600.00 – $700.00*
3. *Vase, 8"; Marked with the half kiln ink stamp; $650.00 – $850.00*

*The Coppertone glaze is described as having "the color of old bronze showing irregularly through a verdant green matt." Both its marks and the company it keeps (note Warwick, Silvertone and Pumila shapes on these two pages) place it in the period of the late 1920's into the 30's. The pieces with the frogs and fish are especially desirable.*

## Coppertone

*Row 1:*
1. *Vase, 6½"; No mark; $150.00 – $200.00*
2. *Frog with Banjo, 7½"; Weller Pottery (by hand); $1100.00 – $1500.00*
3. *Vase, 6½"; No mark; $150.00 – $200.00*

*Row 2:*
1. *Vase, 7"; Weller Hand Made (by hand); $200.00 – $250.00*
2. *Pillow Vase, 7"; No mark; $175.00 – $200.00*
3. *Vase, 8½"; Weller Hand Made (by hand); $185.00 – $235.00*

*Row 3:*
1. *Vase, 10½;" Weller Hand Made (by hand); $350.00 – $450.00*
2. *Vase with Frogs, 12"; Marked with the half kiln stamp; $900.00 – $1200.00*
3. *Vase, 8½"; No mark; $250.00 – $300.00*

*Row 4:*
1. *Console, 12" x 3"; Frog, 4½"; Half kiln ink stamp; $300.00 – $350.00*
2. *Frog, 4½"; No mark; $300.00 – $400.00*
3. *Console, 2" x 10½"; Frog, 2½"; Weller Pottery (by hand); $275.00 – $350.00*

# Barcelona

*Row 1:*
    *1. Vase, 6½"; Marked Weller (by hand); $175.00 – $225.00*
    *2. Vase, 7"; same mark; $125.00 – $175.00*
    *3. Vase, 6"; WELLER (ink stamp); $150.00 – $200.00*

*Row 2:*
    *1. Vase, 8"; No mark; $175.00 – $250.00*
    *2. Ewer, 9½"; Marked Weller (ink stamp, semi-script); $200.00 – $250.00*
    *3. Ewer, 8"; same mark as #2; $200.00 – $250.00*

*Row 3:*
    *1. Oil Jar, 25½"; No mark; $1000.00 – $1250.00*
    *2. Candleholder, 2" x 5"; WELLER (ink stamp); $75.00 – $100.00*
    *3. Vase, 14½"; same mark as candleholder; $450.00 – $600.00*

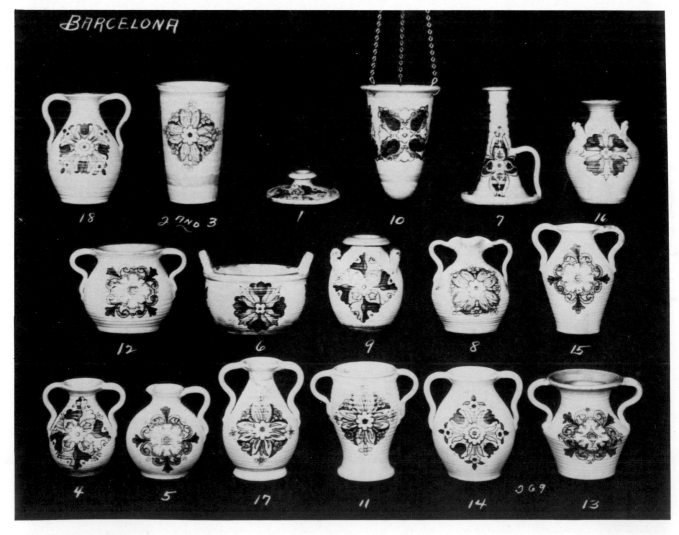

## Decorated Creamware

*Row 1:*
    1. Mug, 5"; No mark; Hand decorated; $100.00 – $125.00
    2. Mug, 5"; No mark; Decalcomania; $50.00 – $75.00
    3. Jug, 5"; No mark; Decalcomania; $50.00 – $75.00

*Row 2:*
    1. Vase, 11½"; Marked with the half kiln ink stamp; Hand decorated; $275.00 – $350.00
    2. Mug, 5"; No mark; Hand decorated; $100.00 – $125.00
    3. Vase, 11½"; Marked Weller (by hand); Hand decorated; $275.00 – $350.00

*Row 3:*
    1. Pitcher, 5"; No mark; Decalcomania; $100.00 – $150.00
    2. Teapot, 5½"; No mark; Decalcomania; $100.00 – $125.00
    3. Pitcher, 4"; No mark; Decalcomania; $100.00 – $150.00

The discovery of these marked pieces of creamware enabled a collector-friend of ours to finally identify other creamware in their extensive collection that they could never satisfactorily group with known examples from other potteries. These pieces have a distinct "orange peel" texture, most apparent when examined under strong light. If you collect creamware—better check closely. The vase on the right in the second row is marked by hand, nearly hidden under the glaze.

## Luxor

*Row 1:*
1. Bud Vase, 7½"; No mark; $30.00 – $60.00
2. Vase, 10½"; No mark; $55.00 – $85.00
3. Vase, 9"; No mark; $55.00 – $75.00

## Velvetone, Ansonia

*Row 2:*
1. Strawberry Pot, 10"; Ansonia; Marked Weller Pottery (by hand); $75.00 – $100.00
2. Pitcher, 10"; Velvetone; Marked Weller Ware Hand Made; $125.00 – $150.00
3. Vase, 9½"; same mark as pitcher; $100.00 – $150.00

*Row 3:*
1. Pitcher, 10"; Velvetone; No mark; $125.00 – $150.00
2. Batter Jug, 14½"; Ansonia; No mark; $175.00 – $250.00
3. Batter Jug, 10"; Marked Weller Hand Made; $125.00 – $175.00

*Velvetone shades are blended pastels; the matt clay finish is Ansonia; and the old catalogue page displaying the Ansonia line states simply in one corner: "In green, Fleron." These lines were all produced during the latter twenties.*

# Fleron

**Row 1:**
    *1. Bowl, 3"; #J-6; Marked Weller Ware Hand Made; $75.00 – $100.00*
    *2. Vase, 4½"; same mark; $90.00 – $125.00*
    *3. Bowl, 4"; same mark; $75.00 – $110.00*

**Row 2:**
    *1. Vase, 9"; same mark; $125.00 – $175.00*
    *2. Vase, 9"; same mark; $125.00 – $175.00*
    *3. Vase, 8½"; same mark; $125.00 – $175.00*
    *4. Vase, 8"; Marked with the half kiln ink stamp; $125.00 – $175.00*

**Row 3:**
    *1. Vase, 14½"; Marked Weller Ware Hand Made; $325.00 – $375.00*
    *2. Vase, 19½"; same mark ; $500.00 – $750.00*
    *3. Batter Pitcher, 11½"; Marked with the half kiln ink stamp; $200.00 – $250.00*

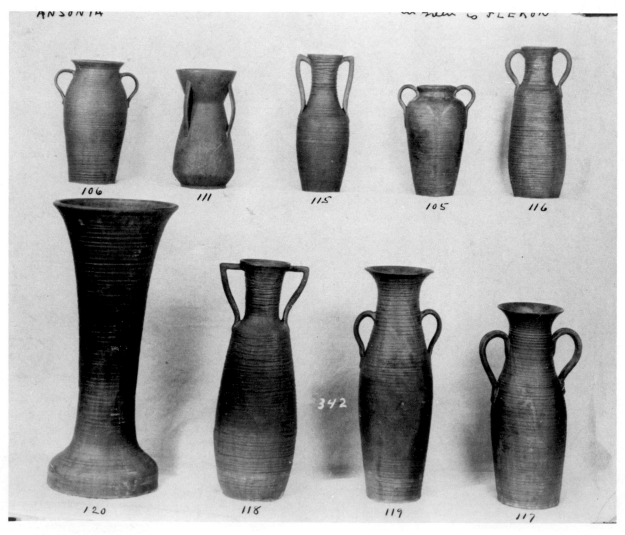

*Courtesy Ohio Historical Society*

# Malverne

*Row 1:*
    1. *Vase, 5½"; Marked Weller Pottery (in script, by hand); $40.00 – $50.00*
    2. *Circle Vase, 8"; Marked with the half kiln ink stamp; $75.00 – $95.00*
    3. *Vase, same as #1, shown for color; $40.00 – $50.00*

*Row 2:*
    1. *Pillow Vase, 8½"; No mark; $85.00 – $115.00*
    2. *Bud Vase, 8½"; Weller Pottery (in script–by hand); $50.00 – $75.00*
    3. *Pillow Vase, 6½"; same mark; $80.00 – $110.00*

*Row 3:*
    1. *Wall Pocket, 11"; No mark; $150.00 – $200.00*
    2. *Boat Bowl, 5½" x 11"; same mark; $60.00 – $80.00*
    3. *Candleholder, 2"; Marked with the Malverne paper label; same mark; $40.00 – $50.00*
    4. *Vase, 9"; No mark; $100.00 – $150.00*

*Row 4:*
    1. *Console Bowl, 14½" x 2"; Frog, 6"; No mark ; $125.00 – $175.00*
    2. *Console Bowl, 2½" x 11"; Frog, 2½"; No mark; $125.00 – $150.00*

# Warwick

Row 1:
1. Planter, 3½"; Marked with the Weller Pottery half kiln silver and black foil label, and the Warwick paper label; $60.00 – $75.00
2. Vase, 4½"; Marked with the half kiln ink stamp; $50.00 – $60.00
3. Pillow Vase, 7"; No mark; $50.00 – $75.00
4. Double Vase, 4½'"; Marked with the half kiln ink stamp; $45.00 – $60.00
5. Frog, 3½"; same mark; $25.00 – $35.00

Row 2:
1. Planter and frog cover, 5"; Half kiln ink stamp; $100.00 – $125.00
2. Vase, 4½"; same mark; $55.00 – $65.00
3. Basket, 9"; same mark; $150.00 – $200.00
4. Bud Vase, 7"; same mark; $30.00 – $40.00
5. Circle Vase, 7"; same mark; $50.00 – $65.00

Row 3:
1. Double Bud, 8½"; same mark; $60.00 – $75.00
2. Vase, 9½"; same mark; $100.00 – $135.00
3. Vase, 12"; same mark; $125.00 – $150.00
4. Vase, 6½"; same mark; $70.00 – $95.00
5. Basket, 7"; same mark; $125.00 – $150.00

Row 4:
1. Vase, 10"; same mark; $175.00 – $225.00
2. Console Bowl, 10½"; same mark; $125.00 – $175.00
3. Frog, 5½"; same mark (frog shown in console bowl); $100.00 – $150.00
4. Jardiniere, 7"; same mark; $125.00 – $150.00

# Tutone

*Row 1:*

    *1. Vase, 4"; Marked with the half kiln ink stamp; $30.00 – $45.00*

    *2. Vase, 6"; No mark; $30.00 – $45.00*

    *3. Vase, 6½"; same mark as #1; $45.00 – $55.00*

    *4. Vase, 6"; same mark; $35.00 – $45.00*

*Row 2:*

    *1. Vase, 7½"; No mark; $50.00 – $75.00*

    *2. Vase, 7½"; same mark; $100.00 – $125.00*

    *3. Vase with Candleholder, 7"; same mark; $50.00 – $60.00*

*Row 3:*

    *1. Basket, 7½"; same mark; $95.00 – $120.00*

    *2. Wall Pocket, 10½"; No mark; $150.00 – $225.00*

    *3. Planter 5½"; same mark; $55.00 – $65.00*

*Row 4:*

    *1. Vase, 12½"; same mark; $125.00 – $150.00*

    *2. Candleholders, 2½"; same mark; $100.00 – $125.00*

    *3. Console Bowl, 3½"; with Frog, 1½"; same mark; $100.00 – $110.00*

    *4. Vase, 11"; same mark; $120.00 – $150.00*

*Arrowhead leaves, berries and flowers are not always prerequisites of the Tutone line—study the catalogue page!*

# Classic

*Row 1:*

    *1. Window Box, 4"; Marked with the Classic Ware paper label, and Weller Pottery (in-mold script);  $60.00 – $70.00*

    *2. Fan Vase, 5"; same mark;   $50.00 – $55.00*

*Row 2:*

    *1. Vase, 6½"; same mark; $40.00 – $50.00*

    *2. Plate, 11½"; same mark; $40.00 – $45.00*

    *3. Wall Pocket, 7½"; same mark; $65.00 – $95.00*

*Row 3:*

    *1. Bowl, 8"; same mark; $30.00 – $40.00*

    *2. Wall Pocket, 6"; same mark; $100.00 – $125.00*

    *3. Bowl, 11"; same mark; $40.00 – $50.00*

*Row 4:*

    *1. Bowl with Goose Boy Frog; Bowl, 14½"; Figure, 9"; no mark; $350.00 – $400.00*

    *Boy, $300.00 – $350.00*

## Hobart

*Row 1:*

    1. Candleholder, 6"; No mark; $250.00 – $300.00

    2. Bowl, 9½" x 3"; No mark; $75.00 – $100.00

    3. Same as #1

*Row 2:*

    1. Nudes Flower Frog, 7½"; Console Bowl, 2½" x 12"; No mark; $350.00 – $450.00

    2. Nude with Duck Flower Frog, 4½"; Console Bowl, 2½" x 9"; Marked Weller (die impressed); $300.00 – $400.00

## Lavonia

*Row 3:*

    1. Hobart girl, 7½"; Bowl, 11" x 2½"; Marked with the Weller Ware round ink stamp; Girl, $150.00 – $225.00; Bowl, $75.00 – $100.00

    2. Vase, 10"; Marked with the Weller Ware foil paper label; $125.00 – $175.00

    3. Vase, 9"; No mark; $125.00 – $150.00

*Row 4:*

    1. Candleholders, 4"; Marked with the Weller Ware round ink stamp; Console Bowl, 3" x 15"; Marked with the full kiln ink stamp; $125.00 – $150.00

    2. Girl Figurine, 11"; Marked with the full kiln ink stamp; $225.00 – $275.00

Hobart was a line comprised principally of figures and low bowls. It was offered in matt glazes and used in conjunction with other lines—as it is here with Lavonia.

Row 1:
  1. Vase, 9"; Marked Weller (die impressed); $60.00 – $80.00
  2. CAMELOT* Lamp, 11½"; No mark; $250.00 – $350.00
  3. Lamp, 12½"; Forest blank; No mark; $250.00 – $350.00

Row 2:
  1. Vase with Nude, 8½"; Weller Pottery (by hand); $200.00 – $250.00
  2. Vase with Horse, 11"; same mark; $200.00 – $250.00
  3. Vase with Bird, 9"; No mark; Artist signed: D.E.; $175.00 – $225.00

Row 3:
  1. Vase, 11½"; Marked Hand Made Weller Ware; $300.00 – $350.00
  2. Vase, 10"; A Timberlake original restored by Art Wagner; $2500.00 – $3500.00
  3. Vase, 10"; Marked Weller Pottery (by hand); Initialed: D E.; $175.00 – $200.00

Below: CAMELOT* Catalogue page

Courtesy Ohio Historical Society

*Row 1:*

    *1. Orange Lustre Vase on Glendale shape, 8½"; Experimental; 06KF on base; $250.00 – $300.00*

    *2. Vase, 8½"; Hand painted decoration over molded piece; marked with the full kiln  ink stamp; $300.00 – $350.00*

    *3.  BLUE WARE Shape, 9½"; unusual color; No mark; $350.00 – $400.00*

*Row 2:*

    *1. Vase, 12½"; decorated with mineral colored stain rather than slip; Weller Pottery (by hand); $1250.00 – $1500.00*

    *2. SOUEVO Vase, 10"; No mark; $300.00 – $350.00*

*Row 3:*

    *1. LORBER\* Vase 13"; Marked R. Lorber in the mold; Weller (die impressed); $900.00 – $1200.00*

    *2. LORBER\* Jardiniere, 10"; marked in the same manner; $700.00 – $900.00*

    *3. LORBER\* Vase, 13"; Hi-gloss; Artist signed: D.E.; $900.00 – $1200.00*

*These Burntwood-type pieces depict the lecherous satyr cavorting through the vineyard with fiendish glee. They are signed in the mold by modeler Rudolph Lorber, and are very rare.*

*Row 1:*
1. *MUSKOTA Elephant, 7½" x 12½"; Marked Weller (die stamp); $900.00 – $1200.00*
2. *Cat, 14½" x 6½"; Weller Pottery (by hand); $1250.00 – $1500.00*

*Row 2:*
1. *"Pop-eye" Dog, 4"; Weller Pottery (by hand); $400.00 – $500.00*
2. *Scottie Pup, 5" x 8"; same mark; $550.00 – $750.00*
3. *Scottie Pup, 4½"; same mark; $450.00 – $500.00*
4. *"Pop-eye" Dog, 4"; same mark; $350.00 – $400.00*

*Row 3:*
1. *"Pop-eye" Dog, 9½"; same mark; $1000.00 – $1250.00*
2. *"Pop-eye" Dog, 4"; same mark; $325.00 – $375.00*
3. *"Pop-eye" Dog, 8½"; No mark; $950.00 – $1200.00*

*Row 4:*
1. *Scottie Dog, 12" x 15"; same mark; $1250.00 – $1750.00*
2. *Terrier Dog, 10½" x 16"; Marked with the half kiln ink stamp; $1250.00 – $1750.00*

*Imagine that mother Scottie dog with her brood around her—one sniffing at a bug, the other attacking an irritating flea! All of these darling creatures (with the exception of the elephant which was produced much earlier) went into production in the late 20's, and ran well into the 1930's. There are five sizes of those Muskota elephants; four are known: 6" x 9", 6¾" x 10½", 7½" x 12", 8¾" x 13¼".*

## Graystone Garden Ware

Top,
Row 1:
   1. REGAL Birdbath, 21½"; No mark; $250.00 – $300.00
   2. Jardiniere and Pedestal, 28"; No mark; $300.00 – $400.00

Bottom,
Row 1:
   1. COPPERTONE Floor Vase, 26½"; No mark; $800.00 – $1100.00
   2. COPPERTONE Frog, 11½" x 15"; No mark; $2000.00 – $2500.00
   3. SUNRAY Birdbath with Fountain, overall height, 33½" ; $500.00 – $700.00

These Graystone pieces from the Regal line are from the estate of Paul Phillips, senior salesman for the Weller Company from 1898 to 1948. The large Coppertone floor vase was rescued from the basement under the old Weller Showrooms, and is one of a pair hand turned especially to decorate the rooms early in the 1930's.

GARDEN WARE; Goose, 12½" x 13"; No mark; This goose does have a mate—his neck is stretched to its full length while he looks straight ahead...his bill is parted and you can almost hear his call!! $1500.00 – $2000.00; Pelican, 19½" x 17"; No mark; $2000.00 – $2500.00

287

*Row 1:*
    *1. Squirrel on Bowl, 5½" x 7"; No mark; $100.00 – $150.00*
    *2. Squirrel Lawn Ornament, 12"; No mark; $1250.00 – $1750.00*
    *3. Squirrel, 4"; Marked Weller (die impressed); $150.00 – $200.00*

*Row 2:*
    *1. Monkey, 7½"; Marked Weller Pottery (by hand); Initialed C.W.; $800.00 – $1200.00*
    *2. Rabbit, 7½" x 13"; Marked with the half kiln ink stamp; $1200.00 – $1500.00*

*Row 3:*
    *1. Crow, 14" x 15" tall; Marked Pat. Applied For ; $1250.00 – $1750.00*

*There is also a "tree" squirrel, 13" long and shaped to hug the curve of a tree—and the 1930's trade journals show a standing rabbit. Many of these animals were modeled by Dorothy England. (We asked her about the rabbit with its ear down—she couldn't remember that Weller ever made one, but she cautioned us not to rule it out completely.) The majestic crow is one of a quartet—each in a different pose—designed on pegs to stick into the ground.*

*Two more lovely GARDEN WARE creatures, a pair of Swans; the one on the left measures 14½" x 20"; the other 18½" x 10". Neither are marked.  $2000.00 – $2750.00 each*

## Garden Ornaments

*Top,*
*Row 1:*

1. *"Gnome," 14"; Marked Weller Pottery (by hand); $1250.00 – $1750.00*
2. *Fisher Boy, 21"; Marked with the half kiln ink stamp; $3000.00 – $4000.00*
3. *"Banjo Frog," 13½"; Marked Weller Pottery (by hand); $1200.00 – $1500.00*

*Bottom,*
*Row 1:*

1. *"Pan with Fife," 16½"; Marked Weller Pottery (by hand); $1400.00 – $1800.00*
2. *"Gnome on Boulder," 18"; Marked with the half kiln ink stamp; $2000.00 – $2450.00*
3. *"Gnomes on Toadstool," 17"; Weller Pottery (by hand); $3000.00 – $4250.00*

*The catalogue indicates there were four sizes of the Banjo Frog, but lists no dimensions. Look for at least one other "Garden Ornament"—Pan with Rabbit, 14" x 11".*

No. 111—CHICKEN "HEN"
Two sizes, 7½ and 10 inches

No. 112—ROOSTER
Two sizes,
9 x 10½ and 10 x 12½

No. 115—THE ANGRY DUCK
Height 10 inches

PELICAN
Height 19½ inches

No. 104—CAT ON ROOF
11 x 13 inches

No. 109—DOG
10 inches

No. 110—PUP
3½ inches

*All these pieces are decorated in underglaze colors to give the animal a natural appearance.*

Courtesy Ohio Historical Society

Row 1:
    *Weller Sign, 3" x 8½"; $350.00 – $400.00*

Row 2:
    *1. MUSKOTA Turtle Bowl, 4½" x 9½"; Weller (die impressed); $325.00 – $375.00*
    *2. Pagoda Flower Frog, 6"; Weller (die impressed); $200.00 – $250.00*
    *3. MUSKOTA Swan, 5"; No mark; $200.00 – $300.00*

Row 3:
    *1. Starfish Flower Frog, 1½" x 5"; Weller (die impressed); $125.00 – $150.00*
    *2. Lobster Flower Frog, 1" x 6"; same mark as #1; $125.00 – $150.00*
    *3. Duck on Flower Frog Base, 11½"; Weller Pottery (by hand); $850.00 – $1250.00*
    *4. Crab Flower Frog, 1½" x 5"; No mark; $125.00 – $150.00*
    *5. MUSKOTA Swan Flower Frog, 2½" x 6"; No mark; $125.00 – $150.00*

Row 4:
    *1. Cat, 8½" x 15½"; marked with the half kiln ink stamp; $1250.00 – $1750.00*
    *2. Cat on Roof, 14" x 11½"; Weller Pottery (by hand); $1500.00 – $1900.00*

*GRAYSTONE GARDEN WARE Catalogue page*

Courtesy Ohio Historical Society

292

293

*Top,*
*Row 1:*

    *1. Duck, 2" x 4"; No mark; $175.00 – $225.00*

    *2. Weller Ware sign, 5½" x 2½"; Marked with the half kiln ink stamp, in use during the mid-1920's; $350.00 – $450.00*

    *3. Duck, 3" x 3"; No mark; $175.00 – $225.00*

    *4. Duck, 2" x 2½"; No mark; $175.00 – $225.00*

*Row 2:*

    *1. Chicken "Hen"; 11½"; Marked Weller Pottery (by hand); $1400.00 – $1750.00*

    *2. Chicken "Hen"; 7½"; same mark; $1200.00 – $1550.00*

*Bottom, Row 1:*

    *1. COPPERTONE Frog, 4"; Marked Weller Pottery (by hand); $250.00 – $300.00*

    *2. COPPERTONE OWL", 9"; unusual mottled effect, green with blue; No mark; $500.00 – $700.00*

    *3. ART NOUVEAU Sunflower Bank, 2" x 4"; Weller (die impressed); $150.00 – $175.00*

*Row 2.*

    *1.Vase, with Morning-glories and Butterflies, 12"; Marked Weller (by hand); $150.00 – $200.00*

    *2. "Drunken Ducks," 13½" ; Marked with the half kiln ink stamp; $1500.00 – $2000.00*

    *3. SILVERTONE Vase, 12" ; same mark as #2; $350.00 – $500.00*

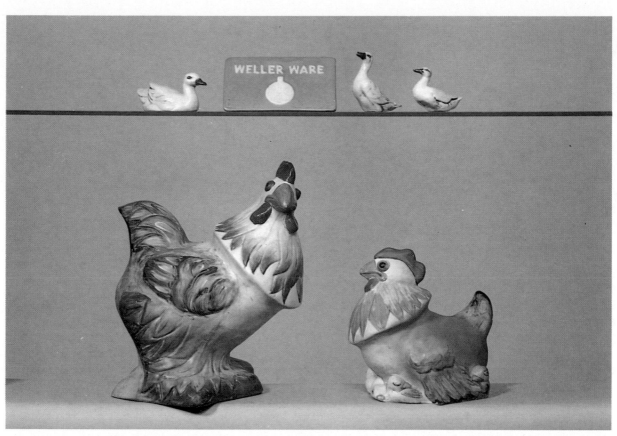

## Cactus

*Row 1:*
   1. Camel, 4"; Marked Weller Pottery (by hand); $75.00 – $100.00
   2. Cat, 5½"; same mark; $75.00 – $100.00
   3. Pan with Lily, 5"; same mark; $75.00 – $100.00

*Row 2:*
   1. Duck, 4½"; same mark; $85.00 – $110.00
   2. Boy with Bag, 5"; same mark; $85.00 – $110.00
   3. Horse, 5"; same mark; $85.00 – $110.00
   4. Snail, 3½"; same mark; $85.00 – $110.00

*Row 3:*
   1. Frog, 4"; same mark; $70.00 – $85.00
   2. Monkey, 4"; same mark; $80.00 – $110.00
   3. Camel, 3½"; same mark; $70.00 – $85.00
   4. Elephant, 4"; same mark; $90.00 – $110.00

*Row 4:*
   1. GLOUSTER WOMAN, 11½"; Marked Weller (in-mold script); C.B.M. on base; $500.00 – $750.00
   2. SILVA, THE DANCER, 8"; same mark; $375.00 – $575.00
   3. CHANTICLEER ROOSTER, 7"; same mark; $250.00 – $350.00
   4. PESCA, OLD MAN WITH FISH, 12½"; same mark; $400.00 – $600.00

Look for three more figures to complete the Cactus line: a boy standing erect holding a basin, and looking over his left shoulder; a fish with open mouth; and a boy holding a basket, bent at the waist.

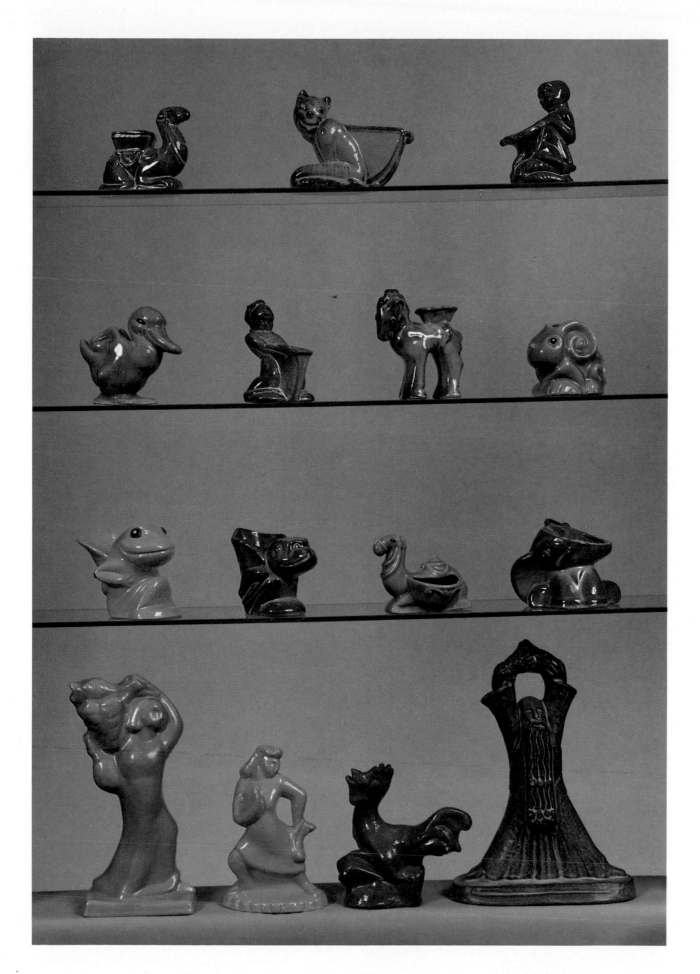

*Row 1:*
  *1. Dachshund, 4½" x 8½"; Marked Weller (in-mold script); $65.00 – $95.00*
  *2. Dachshund, 3" x 6"; same mark; $40.00 – $70.00*

## Novelty Line

*Row 2:*
  *1. Three Pigs Ashtray, 4"; No mark; $125.00 – $150.00*
  *2. Frog and Lotus, 4"; No mark; $50.00 – $90.00*
  *3. Dog with Bone Ashtray, 4½"; Marked Weller (by hand); $90.00 – $120.00*

*Row 3:*
  *1. Sitting Dog Ashtray, 5"; Weller (by hand); $75.00 – $110.00*
  *2. Monkey on Peanut, 5" x 8"; Weller Pottery (by hand); $70.00 – $90.00*
  *3. Kangaroo and Pouch, 5½"; No mark; $80.00 – $95.00*

*Row 4:*
  *1. Fox Tray, 3" x 7"; Weller Pottery (by hand); $115.00 – $135.00*
  *2. Fish Flower Frog, 1½" x 7"; Weller Pottery (by hand); $30.00 – $50.00*
  *3. LORBEEK Gazelle Flower Frog, 7"; Weller (die impressed); $75.00 – $85.00*
  *4. PATRICIAN Duck, 2½" x 4½"; Weller Pottery (by hand); $50.00 – $60.00*
  *5. Seal Tray, 3" x 5½"; Weller (in-mold script); $40.00 – $50.00*

*Row 5:*
  *1. Pot, 2½"; No mark; $50.00 – $60.00*
  *2. Wall Pocket, 10"; Weller Pottery (by hand); $200.00 – $300.00*
  *3. Jar, 6"; No mark; $75.00 – $95.00*

*The Novelty line animal pieces are complete on lines 2, 3, and 4. The small pot in Row 5 is "Woman"—here is also a matching "Man"; and the "Man" (item #3) is shown on the Novelty line catalogue page with his "Woman." A teapot, pitcher, cup and saucer wall ornament set; a tall pedestal vase with vertical ribbing; and a bottle with stopper complete the line.*

## Blo'Red

Row 1:
1. Vase, 7"; Marked with half kiln ink stamp; $70.00 – $90.00
2. Vase, 9½"; Marked with Blo'Red paper label; $125.00 – $140.00
3. Vase, 9"; Marked with half kiln ink stamp; $110.00 – $130.00
4. Vase, 3½"; same mark; $40.00 – $50.00

## Turkis

Row 2:
1. Vase, 5"; Marked Weller Pottery (by hand); $40.00 – $60.00
2. Vase, 5"; same mark; $45.00 – $65.00
3. Vase, 4"; same mark; $35.00 – $45.00
4. Vase, 5"; same mark; $50.00 – $60.00

Row 3:
1. Vase, 8"; same mark; $125.00 – $150.00
2. Vase, 8½"; Initialed D.E.; same mark; $150.00 – $175.00
3. Vase, 7½"; same mark; $125.00 – $150.00

Row 4:
1. Vase, 5½"; same mark; $75.00 – $100.00
2. Vase, 14"; Marked Weller Ware (by hand); $275.00 – $350.00
3. Vase, 7"; Marked Weller Pottery (by hand); $125.00 – $150.00

Blo'Red...Turkis...Elberta...Nile...Juneau...Greenbriar—all have shapes typical of the early years of the 30's. Occasional pieces which may have never belonged to any particular line, can at least be attributed to this era, by learning to recognize these distinctive shapes.

## Scandia*

Row 1:
  1. Vase, 9"; No mark; $90.00 – $120.00
  2. Bowl, 3"; No mark; $50.00 – $60.00
  3. Vase, 6"; No mark; $60.00 – $90.00

## Greenbriar

Row 2:
  1. Vase, 6"; No mark; $50.00 – $75.00
  2. Vase, 7½"; No mark; $100.00 – $150.00
  3. Vase, 6½"; No mark; $100.00 – $135.00

Row 3:
  1. Vase, 8½"; No mark; $150.00 – $200.00
  2. Vase, 7½"; No mark; $150.00 – $200.00
  3. Vase, 8"; No mark; $150.00 – $200.00

Row 4:
  1. Pitcher, 10"; No mark; $175.00 – $225.00
  2. Vase, 9½"; Marked with the Greenbriar paper label; $165.00 – $215.00
  3. Ewer, 11½"; No mark; $165.00 – $225.00

## Scandia*

303

# Patra

## Row 1:
1. Basket, 5½"; Marked Weller Pottery (by hand); $100.00 – $125.00
2. Vase, 5"; same mark; $50.00 – $90.00

## Row 2:
1. Vase, 4½"; Shape #6; same mark; $50.00 – $70.00
2. Bowl, 3"; #13; same mark; $50.00 – $80.00
3. Vase, 4½"; same mark; $50.00 – $70.00

## Row 3:
1. Nut Dish, 3"; Shape #2, same mark; $45.00 – $65.00
2. Vase, 7"; same mark; $75.00 – $100.00
3. Jardiniere, 6"; same mark; $80.00 – $125.00
4. Vase, 8"; #15; same mark; $100.00 – $150.00
5. Vase, 3½"; #1; same mark; $45.00 – $65.00

# Woodrose

## Row 4:
1. Wall Pocket, 6"; No mark; $95.00 – $120.00
2. Bowl, 2½" x 8½"; No mark; $45.00 – $60.00
3. Jardiniere, 3½"; Marked Weller (die impressed); $50.00 – $60.00

## Row 5:
1. Vase, 4"; Marked Weller (die impressed); $35.00 – $40.00
2. Vase, 7"; same mark; $50.00 – $70.00
3. Jardiniere, 7"; No mark; $125.00 – $175.00
4. Wall Vase, 6½"; Marked Weller (die impressed); $75.00 – $100.00
5. Wall Vase, 5½ "; Shape #348; same mark; $75.00 – $90.00

305

## Teapots

*Row 1:*
    1. Teapot, 6"; Weller full kiln stamp in gold; $60.00 – $75.00
    2. Teapot, 7½"; same mark; $60.00 – $75.00
    3. Teapot, 4"; Gold-Green; Marked with the Weller Ware round ink stamp; $40.00 – $50.00

*Row 2:*
    1. Teapot, 5"; Gold-Green; Weller Ware round ink stamp; $50.00 – $75.00
    2. Teapot, 7"; Gold-Green; Full kiln stamp in gold; $75.00 – $90.00
    3. Teapot, 4"; Gold-Green; same mark; $40.00 – $50.00

## Greora

*Row 3:*
    1. Frog, 4½"; Marked Weller Pottery (in-mold script); $35.00 – $45.00
    2. Vase, 4½"; No mark; $40.00 – $50.00
    3. Vase, 9"; Weller Pottery (in-mold script); $125.00 – $150.00
    4. Vase, 5"; No mark; $35.00 – $45.00
    5. Vase, 4½"; Weller Pottery (in-mold script); $30.00 – $40.00

*Row 4:*
    1. Strawberry Pot, 8½"; Weller Pottery (in-mold script); $150.00 – $175.00
    2. Vase, 5"; No mark; $30.00 – $40.00
    3. Vase, 11½"; Weller Pottery (in-mold script); $125.00 – $150.00
    4. Strawberry vase, 5"; No mark; $60.00 – $70.00
    5. Vase, 8½"; Weller Pottery (in-mold script); $80.00 – $110.00

*Dorothy England recalls that toward the end of the Weller history, often only she and Carl Weigelt would be working in the decorating room. He decorated these teapots with their gold transfers.*

## Stellar

    1. *Vase, 5"; Marked Weller Pottery (in-mold script; $400.00 – $500.00*
    2. *Vase, 5½"; same mark; $400.00 – $500.00*
    3. *Vase, 6"; same mark; $400.00 – $500.00*

## Geode

    4. *Vase, 5½"; same mark; $400.00 – $500.00*
    5. *Vase, 3½"; same mark; $250.00 – $300.00*

## Atlas

*Row 2:*

    1. *Star Dish, 2"; #C-2; Marked Weller (in-mold script); $20.00 – $25.00*
    2. *Candleholders, #C-12; No mark; $40.00 – $45.00*
    3. *Star Dish, 2½"; #C-6; Marked Weller (in-mold script); $25.00 – $35.00*
    4. *Vase, 5½"; same mark; $25.00 – $35.00*

*Row 3:*

    1. *Bowl, 4"; #C-3; same mark; $35.00 – $45.00*
    2. *Vase, 7"; Weller Pottery Since 1872; $60.00 – $70.00*
    3. *Covered Dish, 3½"; #C-2; Marked Weller (in-mold script); $60.00 – $80.00*

*Row 4:*

    1. *Vase, 10½"; Weller (in-mold script); $50.00 – $65.00*
    2. *Vase, 13"; #C-10; Weller Pottery Since 1872; $70.00 – $85.00*
    3. *Vase, 6"; Weller (in-mold script); $50.00 – $60.00*

309

*Row 1:*
     *1. XENIA\* Vase, 9½"; Marked Weller (die impressed); $400.00 – $450.00*
     *2. RACEME Vase, 9"; Marked Weller Pottery (by hand); $225.00 – $275.00*
     *3. Vase, 6½"; Weller (die impressed); matt glaze with very heavy slip decoration; $200.00 – $250.00*

## Cretone

*Row 2:*
     *1. Vase, 8"; Weller Pottery (by hand); $275.00 – $350.00*
     *2. Vase, 3½'; Marked "New Yellow, exp."; $325.00 – $375.00*
     *3. Vase, 7"; same mark as #1; Artist signed: H.P.; $325.00 – $375.00*

*Row 3:*
     *1. ROMA Window Box, 5½" x 13½"; Weller Pottery (by hand); $100.00 – $125.00*
     *2. ZONA Vase, 8"; No mark; $225.00 – $300.00*

*Row 4:*
     *1. IVORY Window Box, 8" x 20½"; Weller (die impressed); $350.00 – $400.00*


*Xenia is only a reference name. There were several examples of bi-color matt glaze ware whose slip decoration was incorporated into the background englobe—also an unnamed catalogue page of similar ware. Raceme was identified from an old trade journal, Cretone by the process of elimination (a catalogue page showing four lines, —three of which were familiar to us). Perhaps Webster's definition of "cretonne" gives a reason for their choice of the name: " a heavy cotton or linen cloth with printed patterns." The soft matt Roma glaze identifies the window box, which would become Zona if in a glossy glaze!*

# Elberta

*Row 1:*

    *1. Vase, 5"; Marked Weller Pottery (by hand); $20.00 – $30.00*
    *2. Vase, 6"; same mark; $22.00 – $30.00*
    *3. Vase, 5"; same mark; $20.00 – $25.00*
    *4. Vase, 4"; same mark; $22.00 – $30.00*

*Row 2:*

    *1. 3-part Bowl, 3½"; same mark; $40.00 – $50.00*
    *2. Jardiniere, 5½"; same mark; $40.00 – $50.00*
    *3. Bowl Vase, 3½"; same mark; $22.00 – $30.00*

*Row 3:*

    *1. Nut Dish, 3"; same mark; $20.00 – $25.00*
    *2. Console Bowl, 6" x 11½"; same mark; $30.00 – $40.00*
    *3. Candlestick, 3"; same mark; $40.00 – $50.00*

*Row 4:*

    *1. Vase, 8"; same mark; $35.00 – $45.00*
    *2. Bowl with Frog, 10" across; same mark; $80.00 – $90.00*
    *3. Cornucopia, 8"; same mark; $35.00 – $45.00*

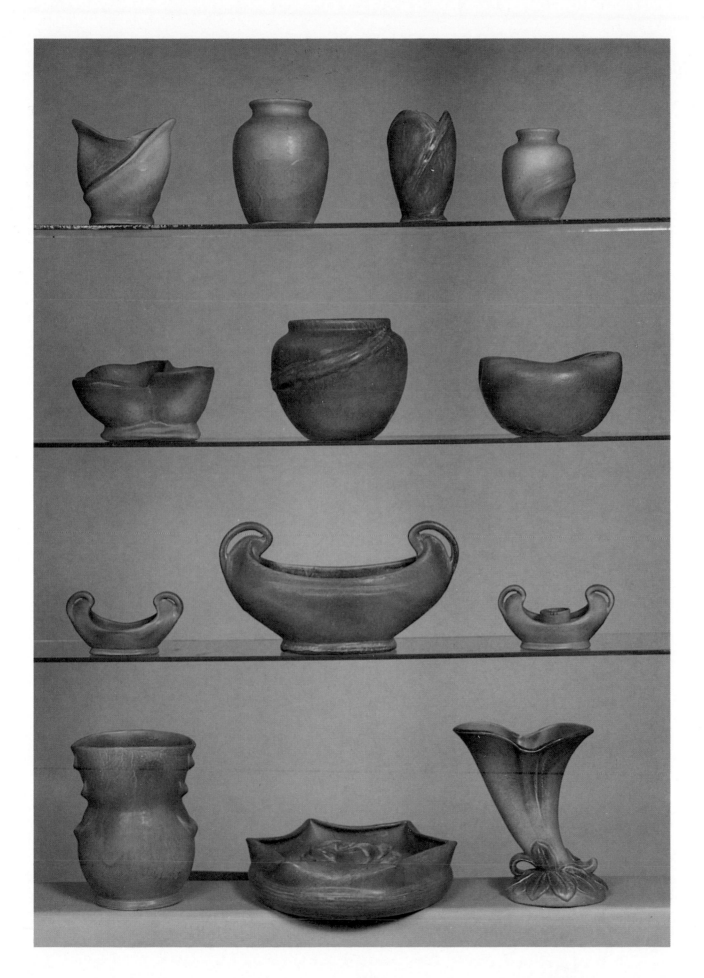

# Goldenglow

*Row 1:*
    1. Bowl, 16" x 3½"; No mark; $60.00 – $70.00

*Row 2:*
    1. Triple candleholder, 3½"; Marked Weller Pottery (in-mold script); $50.00 – $75.00
    2. Triple candleholder, 7½"; No mark; $100.00 – $150.00
    3. Bowl, 3"; Weller Pottery (in-mold script); $45.00 – $65.00

*Row 3:*
    1. Bud vase, 8½"; Marked Weller (in-mold script); $60.00 – $80.00
    2. Bowl vase, 5½"; same mark; $60.00 – $80.00
    3. Ginger jar, 8"; Weller Pottery (in-mold script); $125.00 – $175.00
    4. Vase, 6"; No mark; $55.00 – $75.00
    5. Vase, 8½"; Weller Pottery (in-mold script); $60.00 – $80.00

# Golbrogreen

*Row 4:*
    1. Candleholder, 4½"; No mark; $45.00 – $65.00
    2. Bowl, 3½"; No mark; $125.00 – $135.00
    3. Wall Vase, 8½"; No mark; $150.00 – $200.00

*Row 5:*
    1. Bowl, 4½"; No mark; $100.00 – $125.00
    2. Lamp Base, 12"; No mark; $175.00 – $225.00
    3. Bowl, 4½"; No mark; $120.00 – $140.00

# Sydonia

*Row 1:*
1. *Planter, 4"; Marked Weller Pottery (by hand); $35.00 – $50.00*
2. *Candleholder, 7"; same mark; $75.00 – $100.00*
3. *Planter, 3½"; same mark; $30.00 – $40.00*

*Row 2:*
1. *Double Vase, 7½"; Weller (by hand); $60.00 – $80.00*
2. *Double Vase, 9½"; Weller Pottery (by hand); $90.00 – $110.00*
3. *Double Vase, 10½"; same mark; $80.00 – $100.00*

*Row 3:*
1. *Fan Vase, 6½"; same mark; $60.00 – $80.00*
2. *Double Candleholder with Bud Vase, 11½"; same mark; $100.00 – $135.00*
3. *Triple Bud Vase, 8½"; same mark; $70.00 – $90.00*

*Row 4:*
1. *Cornucopia, 8"; same mark; $50.00 – $60.00*
2. *Console, 17" x 6"; same mark; $70.00 – $80.00*
3. *Cornucopia, 8½"; No mark; $60.00 – $70.00*

## Softone

Row 1:

1. Double Bud Vase, 9"; Marked Weller (in-mold script); $22.00 – $28.00
2. Vase, 5½"; same mark; $15.00 – $20.00
3. Hanging Basket, 10"; same mark; $55.00 – $65.00
4. Candleholder, 2½"; Weller (by hand); $20.00 – $25.00
5. Planter, 4" x 8"; Weller (in-mold script); $20.00 – $35.00

Row 2:

1. Vase, 5"; same mark as #4; $15.00 – $20.00
2. Ewer, 9½"; same mark; $30.00 – $35.00
3. Vase, 10"; same mark; $40.00 – $50.00
4. Vase, 11"; same mark; $40.00 – $45.00
5. Cornucopia, 8½"; Marked with the Softone paper label; and same mark; $22.00 – $30.00

## Raydance

Row 3:

1. Vase, 7½"; Weller Since 1872; $25.00 – $35.00
2. Vase, 9"; same mark; $50.00 – $60.00
3. Vase, 8"; same mark; $25.00 – $35.00

## Pastel

Row 4:

1. Planter, 4" x 8"; #P-5; Weller (in-mold script); $22.00 – $30.00
2. Planter, 6"; #P-10; Weller Pottery Since 1872; $30.00 – $40.00
3. Planter, 4" x 7"; #P-3; same mark as #2; $25.00 – $35.00

Row 1:

    *1. Jardiniere with Flower Frog Cover, 7"; Metallic glaze; marked Weller (in ovoid die stamp); $80.00 – $90.00*

    *2. Covered Jar, 4"; Metallic glaze; same mark; $35.00 – $45.00*

    *3. Mug, 6"; Biscuit fired, undercorated WOODCRAFT; $100.00 – $125.00*

    *4. Vase, 8"; Weller (in-mold script); $30.00 – $40.00*

Row 2:

    *1. Vase, 7"; #46; Weller (by hand); $200.00 – $250.00*

    *2. ROSEMONT, 2ND LINE Bowl, 3½"; Weller Pottery (by hand); $45.00 – $55.00*

    *3. Vase Sabrinian shape, 7"; no mark; $45.00 – $55.00*

Row 3:

    *1. JUNEAU Bud Vase, 6"; Marked with the half kiln ink stamp; $30.00 – $40.00*

    *2. JUNEAU Vase, 8"; same mark; $70.00 – $85.00*

    *3. JUNEAU Vase, 6½"; same mark; $60.00 – $65.00*

    *4. Vase, 9"; Weller Pottery (by hand); $40.00 – $45.00*

    *5. ROSEMONT, 2ND LINE Jar, shown without lid, 7"; same mark as #4; $60.00 – $80.00*

Row 4:

    *1. ZENIA* Vase, 7½"; Marked Weller (small die impressed); $375.00 – $475.00*

    *2. Vase, Flemish type glaze, 11½"; No mark; $200.00 – $250.00*

    *3. Vase, 9½"; Weller Pottery Since 1872; $40.00 – $50.00*

    *4. Lamp Base, 10"; Weller Pottery (by hand); $125.00 – $175.00*

*Row 1:*

    *1. Candleholders, 4½"; Lavonia shape; Marked Weller (die impressed); $30.00 – $35.00*

    *2. Double Vase, 10"; Ardsley shape; No mark; $40.00 – $50.00*

*Row 2:*

    *1. Powder Box, 3½"; Marked with the half kiln ink stamp; $50.00 – $60.00*

    *2. Bowl with Frog, 2" x 7½"; Marked S.A. Weller, Zanesville, Ohio, round ink stamp; $40.00 – $50.00*

    *3. Vase, 5"; Weller (die impressed); $30.00 – $35.00*

    *4. ZONA Pitcher, 3"; No mark; $40.00 – $45.00*

*Row 3:*

    *1. CRYSTALLINE Vase, 10"; No mark; $70.00 – $85.00*

    *2. Nude, 11"; No mark; $400.00 – $550.00*

    *3. Ashtray, "The Falls Evergreen Tube, Manufactured by The Falls Rubber, Co., Cuyahoga Falls, Ohio"; Marked with the half kiln ink stamp; $30.00 – $35.00*

    *4. IVORY Vase, Ardsley shape, 10"; No mark  $40.00 – $50.00*

*Row 4:*

    *2. LORBEEK Bowl, 2½" x 10½"; Marked with the Lorbeek paper label, and the half kiln ink stamp; $50.00 – $55.00*

    *2. EVERGREEN Turtle, 5½"; Weller Pottery Since 1872; $20.00 – $25.00*

    *3. EVERGREEN Console Bowl, 7½" x 14"; Weller Pottery (in-mold script); $25.00 – $35.00*

*Strange as it may seem, this conventional, matt-glazed console bowl carries the Lorbeek paper label, and is shown in the old Weller catalogues! The nude was probably not a production run piece, but she belonged originally to someone who verified that her origin was the Weller Pottery.*

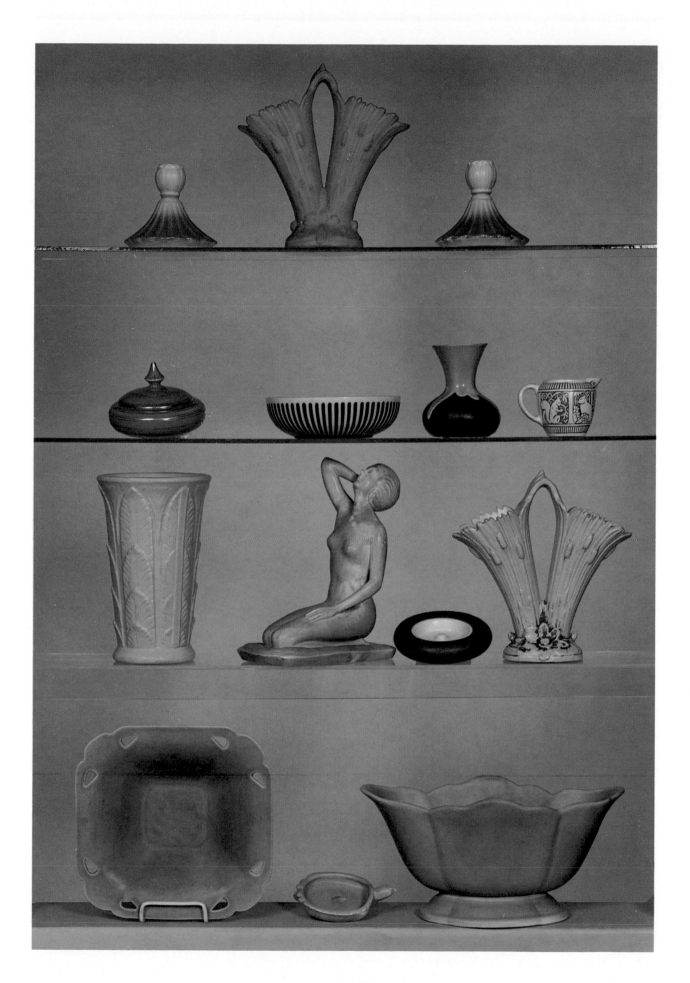

*Row 1:*

    *1. Vase, 6"; Marked Weller (die impressed); $75.00 – $100.00*

    *2. ROSELLA Double Vase, 5"; same mark; $50.00 – $75.00*

    *3. Footed Bowl, 3½" x 7"; Weller (in-mold script); $22.00 – $30.00*

*Row 2:*

    *1. MONOCHROME Triple bud, 7"; Weller (die impressed); $40.00 – $50.00*

    *2. MONOCHROME Candlestick, 7"; same mark; $25.00 – $35.00*

    *3. MONOCHROME five-finger Bud Vase, 10½"; same mark; $80.00 – $95.00*

    *4. Vase, 7"; Tutone shape, line unknown; No mark; $40.00 – $50.00*

*Row 3:*

    *1. KENOVA Vase, 6½"; Weller (die impressed); $250.00 – $300.00*

    *2. Vase, 11½"; Decorated with silver applique; same mark; $350.00 – $400.00*

    *3. Comport, 4"; Lustre shape, IVORIS Glaze; No mark; $25.00 – $35.00*

    *4. Vase, 9"; Weller Pottery (by hand); $75.00 – $90.00*

    *5. Vase, 7"; Weller (die impressed); $220.00 – $300.00*

*Row 4:*

    *1. Glossy HUDSON-PERFECTO\* Vase, 6"; Weller Pottery; $250.00 – $300.00*

    *2. Lamp, 11"; this is the type usually marked WELLER MATT WARE but this piece is marked only Weller (die impressed); $300.00 – $350.00*

    *3. Vase, 6"; Hand tooled; Weller (by hand); $400.00 – $500.00*

*There are several "mis-fits" here that defy identification. The double vase is a Florenzo shape—but the color is wrong...Rosella is a possibility. The colors of the first vase suggest "Fleron" glazing—but its obviously not Fleron. There's Tutone in a yellow high gloss, and even the wide variations of Tutone do not include this glaze treatment.*

# Patricia

**Row 1:**
1. Vase, 4"; Marked Weller (in-mold script); $22.00 – $30.00
2. Vase, 5"; No mark; $20.00 – $30.00
3. Pelican Planter, 5"; Marked Weller Pottery (in-mold script); $80.00 – $90.00
4. Swan Planter, 3½"; same mark; $30.00 – $40.00
5. Duck Planter, 2¼"; same mark; $20.00 – $30.00

**Row 2:**
1. Bowl, 3"; same mark as above; $35.00 – $40.00
2. Duck Planter, 6½"; same mark; $90.00 – $110.00
3. Urn, 4½"; same mark; $40.00 – $50.00

**Row 3:**
1. Vase, 8½"; No mark ; $80.00 – $90.00
2. Vase with Geese, 8"; Marked Weller Pottery (in-mold script); $200.00 – $215.00
3. Vase, 6"; same mark; $50.00 – $60.00

**Row 4:**
1. Bowl, 7"; same mark as above; $150.00 – $165.00
2. Bowl, 13" across; same mark; $120.00 – $135.00
3. Vase, 7"; same mark; $55.00 – $65.00

*Patricia—graceful geese with long pliable necks (some form handles), ducks and pelicans make her a captivating line! Her colors were listed on an old price list as white, beige and green—the latter two with a crystalline overglaze effect. Her shapes are often found in the deep-sea green of the Evergreen line.*

*PATRICIA Vase, 18"; Marked Weller Pottery; $200.00 – $225.00 and ROSEMONT, 2nd line experimental, 9½"; Bisq. Tq Gr LEAV, marked on base; Weller Pottery; Signed: D.E. ; $120.00 – $140.00*

327

*Row 1:*
    *Hanging Basket or Bird Feeder, 5" x 9½"; No mark; $275.00 – $350.00*

*Row 2:*
    *1. Owl on Book, 6½"; No mark; $175.00 – $225.00*
    *2. Frog, Flower Frog, 3½"; Marked Weller (die impressed); $125.00 – $175.00*
    *3. WOODCRAFT Vase with Owl, 7"; same mark as #2; $500.00 – $750.00*

*Row 3:*
    *1. EVERGREEN Pelican, 5½"; Weller (by hand); $50.00 – $75.00*
    *2. HOBART Kingfisher Flower Frog, 6½"; No mark; $125.00 – $175.00*
    *3. EVERGREEN Goose, 6½"; Weller (by hand); $50.00 – $75.00*

*Row 4:*
    *1. EVERGREEN Pelican, 7½"; Weller (by hand); $90.00 – $115.00*
    *2. Pelican Lamp, GOLDENGLOW, 5"; WELLER (by hand); $145.00 – $165.00*
    *3. PATRICIA Goose, 10"; Weller Pottery (by hand); $75.00 – $85.00*

*Evergreen was made not only in green, but black and gray—and not named for the green shade at all, but for a small Ohio town! (A quick scan through your zip code book will surprise you. You'll find many Weller line names. The story is told how often they were chosen from names on the boxcars of the trains passing by the pottery windows.)*

*Courtesy Ohio Historical Society*

328

329

## Darsie

*Row 1:*

1. *Vase, 5½"; Marked Weller (in-mold script); $20.00 – $25.00*
2. *Vase, 7½"; same mark; $20.00 – $30.00*
3. *Pot, 3"; same mark; $20.00 – $25.00*
4. *Vase, 5½"; same mark; $15.00 – $20.00*

*Row 2:*

1. *Vase, 5½" same mark; $20.00 – $35.00*
2. *Vase, 9½"; Marked Weller Pottery (in-mold script); $50.00 – $65.00*
3. *Vase, 7½"; same as #2 ; $30.00 – $35.00*
4. *Flower Pot, 5½"; same as #2 ; $20.00 – $30.00*

## Cornish

*Row 3:*

1. *Bowl, 4"; Marked Weller (in-mold script); $25.00 – $35.00*
2. *Candleholder, 3½"; Marked with the Cornish Ware paper label, and Weller Pottery (in-mold script); $30.00 – $40.00*
3. *Bowl, 7½" across, same mark; $20.00 – $25.00*
4. *Vase, 3½"; Marked Weller (in-mold script); $15.00 – $20.00*
5. *Vase, 7"; Weller Pottery (in-mold script); $25.00 – $30.00*

*Row 4:*

1. *Vase, 6"; No mark; $25.00 – $30.00*
2. *Vase, 10"; Weller Pottery (in-mold script); $30.00 – $40.00*
3. *Jardiniere, 7"; same mark; $70.00 – $80.00*
4. *Jardiniere, 5"; same mark; $25.00 – $30.00*

## Florenzo

*Row 1:*

     1. *Planter, 3½"; Marked Weller Ware (full kiln ink stamp); $45.00 – $65.00*
     2. *Planter 4"; marked with half kiln ink stamp; $40.00 – $50.00*
     3. *Vase, 7"; Marked with full kiln ink stamp; $65.00 – $85.00*
     4. *Window Box, 3"; Marked with full kiln ink stamp; $45.00 – $55.00*

*Row 2:*

     1. *Basket, 5½"; Marked Weller (die impressed) and full kiln ink stamp; $85.00 – $110.00*
     2. *Pillow Vase, 4"; marked with full kiln ink stamp; $40.00 – $50.00*
     3. *Vase with Frog Cover, 7"; same mark; $100.00 – $120.00*
     4. *Fan Vase, 5½"; same mark; $40.00 – $50.00*
     5. *Double Bud Vase, 5½"; same mark; $40.00 – $50.00*

## Gloria

*Row 3:*

     1. *Double Vase, 4½"; Weller Pottery Since 1872 (in-old script); $35.00 – $45.00*
     2. *Bowl, 3½"; Shape #G-15; same type mark as above piece; $35.00 – $45.00*
     3. *Vase, 6½"; #G-14; same mark; $40.00 – $50.00*

*Row 4:*

     1. *Ewer, 9"; Shape #G-12; same mark as above; $40.00 – $50.00*
     2. *Vase, 5"; #G-13; same mark; $30.00 – $40.00*
     3. *Vase, 12½"; same mark; $75.00 – $85.00*
     4. *Vase, 5½"; #G-5; same mark; $20.00 – $30.00*
     5. *Vase, 8"; #G-22; same mark; $25.00 – $35.00*

# Clarmont

**Row 1:**
1. Candleholder, 8"; Marked Weller (die impressed); $150.00 – $175.00
2. Vase, 8"; Marked with the Clarmont paper label; same mark; $140.00 – $160.00
3. Candlestick, 10"; same mark; $100.00 – $150.00
4. Bowl, 3"; same mark; $35.00 – $45.00

# Lido

**Row 2:**
1. Vase, 7"; Weller (in-mold script); $22.00 – $30.00
2. Planter, 2" X9"; Weller Pottery Since 1872; $20.00 – $25.00
3. Candleholder, 2½"; #15; same mark as #2; $40.00 – $45.00

**Row 3:**
1. Vase, 6"; same mark; $22.00 – $30.00
2. Cornucopia, 5"; Weller Pottery (in-mold script); $15.00 – $20.00
3. Basket, 8½"; Weller Pottery Since 1872; $35.00 – $45.00
4. Triangle Planter, 4½"; Weller Pottery Since 1872; $35.00 – $45.00

**Row 4:**
1. Vase, 12"; Weller Pottery Since 1872; $50.00 – $55.00
2. Ewer, 10½"; same mark; $45.00 – $50.00
3. Vase, 8"; #11; same mark; $30.00 – $40.00
4. Vase, 10½"; same mark;   $80.00 – $95.00

Clarmont

335

## Arcadia

Row 1:
1. Vase, 5½"; Shape #A-4; Weller Since 1872; $22.00 – $30.00
2. Fan Vase, 8" x 15"; Marked Weller (in-mold script); $50.00 – $60.00
3. Bud Vase, 7½"; Weller Pottery Since 1872; $15.00 – $20.00

Row 2:
1. Vase, 8"; #A-6; Weller Pottery Since 1872; $50.00 – $75.00
2. Covered Dish, 4½"; #A-8; same mark; $40.00 – $50.00
3. Vase, 8½"; #A-11; same mark; $40.00 – $50.00

## Manhattan

Row 3:
1. Vase, 5½"; Weller (by hand); $25.00 – $35.00
2. Vase, 8"; same mark; $60.00 – $70.00
3. Vase, 8"; same mark; $50.00 – $55.00
4. Vase, 6½"; Marked with the Manhattan paper label; same mark; $45.00 – $55.00

Row 4:
1. Vase, 7½"; Weller Pottery (by hand); $70.00 – $75.00
2. Vase, 9"; same mark; $80.00 – $85.00
3. Pitcher, 10"; same mark; $90.00 – $100.00
4. Vase,  8½"; No mark;  $60.00 – $65.00

Arcadia

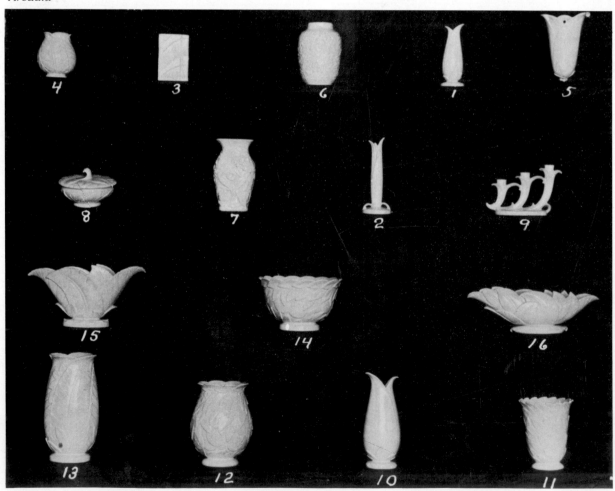

*Courtesy Ohio Historical Society*

336

# Cameo

*Row 1:*
1. *Vase, 5"; No mark; $25.00 – $35.00*
2. *Hanging Basket, 5"; No mark; $70.00 – $90.00*
3. *Footed Bowl, 4"; No mark; $25.00 – $35.00*

*Row 2:*
1. *Basket, 7½"; Marked Weller (in-mold script); $30.00 – $50.00*
2. *Planter, 4"; Weller Pottery Since 1872; $30.00 – $40.00*
3. *Basket, 7½"; Weller (in-mold script); $35.00 – $45.00*

*Row 3:*
1. *Vase, 7"; Weller (in-mold script); $25.00 – $35.00*
2. *Flower arranger, 3"; Weller Since 1872; $25.00 – $40.00*
3. *Ewer, 10"; Weller (in-mold script); $40.00 – $50.00*

*Row 4:*
1. *Square Vase, 8½"; Weller Pottery (in-mold script); $25.00 – $35.00*
2. *Vase, 6½"; same mark; $20.00 – $30.00*
3. *Vase, 13"; Weller Pottery Since 1872; $55.00 – $85.00*
4. *Vase, 7"; Weller (in-mold script); $25.00 – $35.00*
5. *Vase, 10"; Weller Pottery Since 1872; $40.00 – $50.00*

## Mi-Flo

*Row 1:*
1. *Vase, 7"; #M-8: Marked Weller (in-mold script); $45.00 – $65.00*
2. *Vase, 9½"; #M-12; Weller Pottery Since 1872; $60.00 – $80.00*
3. *Bowl, 4"; No mark; $22.00 – $30.00*

## Floral

*Row 2:*
1. *Candleholders, 2"; Weller Pottery Since 1872; $40.00 – $50.00*
2. *Console, 4½" x 10"; #F-9; same mark*

*Row 3.*
1. *Vase, 6½"; Marked Weller Pottery (in-mold script); $30.00 – $40.00*
2. *Double Vase, 5½"; Weller Pottery Since 1872 ; $20.00 – $35.00*
3. *Vase, 6½"; Weller Pottery (in-mold script); $30.00 – $50.00*
4. *Vase, 4½"; #F-2: Weller (in-mold script); $20.00 – $30.00*

## Bouquet

*Row 4:*
1. *Vase, 5½"; #B-5; Weller Pottery Since 1872; $25.00 – $35.00*
2. *Console Bowl, 5" x 12½"; #B-12; same mark; $35.00 – $45.00*
3. *Urn Vase, 5"; #B-6; same mark; $22.00 – $30.00*

*To all of you who collect floral lines: we've tried, we really have, to properly sort these lines out for you! But because one shape may appear in Blossom, Floral, and Bouquet, too...it's almost an impossible task! Bouquet seems to be a medium blue, or dull light green, or a soft gold—with a slightly paneled effect in the mold, and sometimes even a diagonal line or two. Shape numbers help—and "B" numbers are more likely Bouquet than Blossom. But Bouquet and Floral shapes are almost the same, and the two pieces with "F" shape numbers are the same blue as the Bouquet line. Blossom comes in light blue or a light gray-green; and, for whatever help it is, seems to have more intricately molded handles. Gloria is at least done in a rich caramel, but evidently comes in light green also, judging by the "G" shapes. Does any of this help? We thought not!*

# Wild Rose

Row 1:

    *1. Triple Candleholder, 6"; Marked Weller (in-mold script); $75.00 – $100.00*
    *2. Basket, 5½"; same mark; $20.00 – $25.00*
    *3. Double Vase, 6"; same mark; $20.00 – $25.00*

Row 2:

    *1. Vase, 6½"; same mark; $20.00 – $25.00*
    *2. Vase, 8½"; same mark; $25.00 – $30.00*
    *3. Vase, 6½"; same mark; $15.00 – $20.00*

Row 3:

    *1. Vase, 6½"; same mark; $15.00 – $20.00*
    *2. Console Bowl, 6" x 18"; No mark; $50.00 – $65.00*
    *3. Vase, 8"; same mark; $15.00 – $20.00*

Row 4:

    *1. Vase, 7½"; same mark; $22.00 – $30.00*
    *2. Vase, 10½"; same mark; $25.00 – $35.00*
    *3. Vase, 9½" same mark; $25.00 – $35.00*

*Unidentified line from the Weller catalogues*
Courtesy Ohio Historical Society

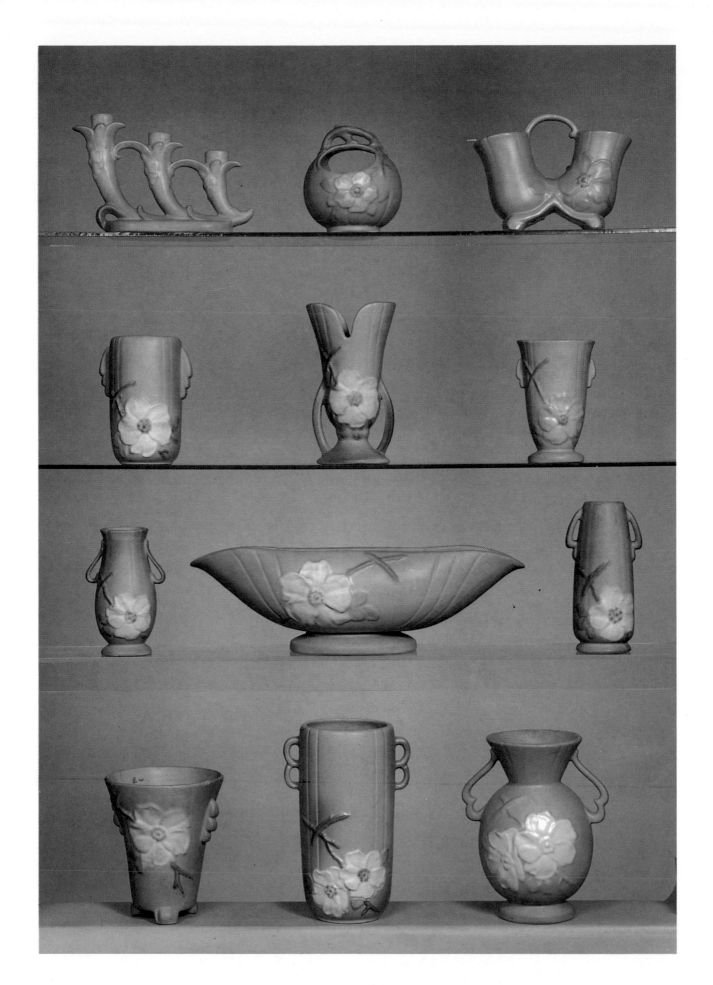

## Rudlor

*Row 1:*

1. *Vase, 6"; Marked Weller (in-mold script); $20.00 – $25.00*
2. *Vase, 6½"; same mark; $22.00 – $30.00*
3. *Vase, 6"; same mark; $20.00 – $25.00*

*Row 2:*

1. *Vase, 9"; same mark; $35.00 – $45.00*
2. *Console Bowl, 4½" x 17½"; Weller Pottery Since 1872; $40.00 – $50.00*
3. *Vase, 8"; Weller (in-mold script); $20.00 – $25.00*

## Senic

*Row 3:*

1. *Vase, 5½"; Shape #S-4; Weller (in-mold script); $65.00 – $75.00*
2. *Planter, 5½"; #S-17;' Weller Since 1872; $65.00 – $75.00*
3. *Pillow Vase, 7½"; #S-11; same mark; $70.00 – $80.00*
4. *Vase, 5"; #S-1; Weller (in-mold script); $50.00 – $60.00*

*Row 4:*

1. *Vase, 6½"; #S-2; Weller (in-mold script); $35.00 – $40.00*
2. *Vase, 10"; #S-14; Weller Pottery Since 1872; $100.00 – $125.00*
3. *Vase, 12½"; #S-16; same mark as #2; $150.00 – $200.00*
4. *Vase, 9½"; #S-8; Weller Since 1872; $70.00 – $90.00*
5. *Vase, 8"; #S-9; Weller Pottery Since 1872; $90.00 – $100.00*

*Perhaps the most interesting thing about Rudlor is that it shares a page in the Weller catalogues with the blended brown Hudsons "Rochelle." Rudlor's in-mold script trademark places its production in the early-to-middle 30's, so evidently Rochelle was still marketed at this time, even though one piece of this hard-to-find Hudson-type carries the much earlier "Weller" die stamp.*

## Neiska

Row 1:
1. Footed Bowl, 4"; Marked Weller Pottery (in-mold script); $22.00 – $30.00
2. Vase, 6"; same mark; $22.00 – $30.00
3. Vase, 6"; same mark; $15.00 – $20.00

## Bouquet

Row 2:
1. Bowl Vase, 4½"; Shape #B-3; Marked Weller (in-mold script); $20.00 – $30.00
2. Pitcher, 9½"; Shape #B-18; Weller Since 1872 (in mold); $60.00 – $80.00
3. Bowl, 4"; #B-8; same mark as above; $30.00 – $40.00
4. Vase, 5"; #B-15; Weller (in-mold script); $20.00 – $30.00

Row 3:
1. Vase, 9"; #B-7; Weller Pottery Since 1872 (in mold); $35.00 – $55.00
2. Vase, 15"; same mark; $90.00 – $120.00
3. Vase, 12"; same mark; $60.00 – $80.00
4. Vase, 8"; #B-5; Marked Weller (in-mold script); $40.00 – $60.00

Neiska colors were listed in a 1933 trade journal as yellow or blue stippled, lined with ivory. Since we had two nearly identical catalogue pages—one Neiska and the other called Seneca—and neither clear enough to show the glazing (obviously the only difference between the two) this information helped us to determine the proper identification for these three pieces.

Courtesy Ohio Historical Society

## Pastel

*Row 1:*

 *1. Vase, 6½"; Shape #P-14; Marked Weller (in-mold script); $15.00 – $20.00*

 *2. Vase, 6"; #P-17; Weller Pottery Since 1872; $25.00 – $35.00*

 *3. Circle Vase, 6"; Weller (in-mold script); $40.00 – $45.00*

*Row 2:*

 *1. Candleholder, 1½"; No mark; $15.00 – $20.00*

 *2. Vase, 6"; Weller (in-mold script); $15.00 – $20.00*

 *3. Ewer, 10"; same mark; $40.00 – $50.00*

 *4. Vase, 6"; same mark; $18.00 – $22.00*

## Panella

*Row 3:*

 *1. Footed Bowl, 3½"; Marked Weller (in-mold script); $20.00 – $25.00*

 *2. Wall Pocket, 8"; Weller Pottery Since 1872; $75.00 – $110.00*

 *3. Ginger Jar, 6½"; Weller (in-mold script); $50.00 – $60.00*

 *4. Vase, 5½"; same mark; $20.00 – $30.00*

 *5. Vase, 4"; No mark; Gloria; $12.00 – $15.00*

*Row 4:*

 *1. Vase, 6½"; Weller (in-mold script); $15.00 – $20.00*

 *2. Cornucopia, 5½"; Weller Pottery Since 1872; $15.00 – $20.00*

 *3. Vase, 8"; Weller (in-mold script); $20.00 – $25.00*

 *4. Vase, 9"; same mark; $22.00 – $30.00*

 *5. Basket, 7"; same mark; $35.00 – $50.00*

 *6. Vase, 6½"; same mark; $20.00 – $25.00*

# Delsa

*Row 1:*

    *1. Vase, 6"; Marked Weller (in-mold script); $15.00 – $20.00*
    *2. Vase, 6"; Weller Since 1872; $25.00 – $30.00*
    *3. Vase, 6"; Weller (in-mold script); $20.00 – $25.00*

*Row 2:*

    *1. Ewer, 7"; #10; Weller Pottery Since 1872; $22.00 – $30.00*
    *2. Basket, 7"; Weller (in-mold script); $35.00 – $50.00*
    *3. Vase, 6"; #2; same mark as #2; $15.00 – $20.00*
    *4. Vase, 7"; same mark; $15.00 – $20.00*

*Row 3:*

    *GOLDENGLOW Flower arranger, 4" x 16½"; same mark; $40.00 – $50.00*

*Row 4:*

    *1. LIDO Vase, 4"; Weller Since 1872; $20.00 – $25.00*
    *2. LIDO Console Bowl, 3½" x 12"; Weller Pottery Since 1872; $30.00 – $35.00*
    *3. PASTEL Candlestick, 3½"; #P-12; No mark; $20.00 – $25.00*

*Row 5:*

    *1. LIDO Vase, 7½"; same mark; $20.00 – $25.00*
    *2. DORLAND Vase, 7½"; same mark; #D-14; $25.00 – $35.00*
    *3. DORLAND Vase, 6"; same mark; #D-3; $15.00 – $20.00*

# Roba

**Row 1:**

    1. Ewer, 6"; Marked Weller (in-mold script); $60.00 – $75.00

    2. Planter, 4½"; same mark; $40.00 – $50.00

    3. Vase, 6½"; same mark; $35.00 – $45.00

**Row 2:**

    1. Cornucopia, 5½"; same mark; $25.00 – $35.00

    2. Wall Pocket, 10"; Weller Pottery Since 1872; $90.00 – $125.00

    3. Vase, 6"; Weller (in-mold script); $30.00 – $40.00

**Row 3:**

    1. Vase, 9"; Shape #R-2; Weller Pottery Since 1872; $75.00 – $95.00

    2. Ewer, 11"; Weller (in-mold script); $100.00 – $135.00

    3. Vase, 8"; Weller Pottery Since 1872; $75.00 – $80.00

**Row 4:**

    1. Vase, 12½"; same mark; $135.00 – $185.00

    2. Vase, 11"; same mark; $140.00 – $190.00

    3. Vase, 13"; #R-20; same mark; $150.00 – $200.00

*Utility Ware Catalogue Page*
Courtesy Ohio Historical Society

353

## Oak Leaf

*Row 1:*
    *1. Basket, 7½"; Shape #G-1; Weller (in-mold script); $80.00 – $100.00*
    *2. Bowl, 3½"; Weller Pottery (in-mold script); $30.00 – $45.00*
    *3. Wall Pocket, 8½"; same mark; $90.00 – $120.00*

*Row 2:*
    *1. Basket Vase, 9½"; same mark; $50.00 – $75.00*
    *2. Planter, 6"; same mark; $35.00 – $75.00*
    *3. Vase, 9"; Marked Weller (in-mold script); $30.00 – $40.00*

*Row 3:*
    *1. Vase, 6"; Weller (in-mold script); $20.00 – $30.00*
    *2. Vase, 8"; same mark; $30.00 – $40.00*
    *3. Ewer, 14"; Marked Weller Pottery (in-mold script); $100.00 – $125.00*
    *4. Ewer, 8½"; Weller (in-mold script); $40.00 – $60.00*
    *5. Vase, 8½"; same mark; $35.00 – $55.00*

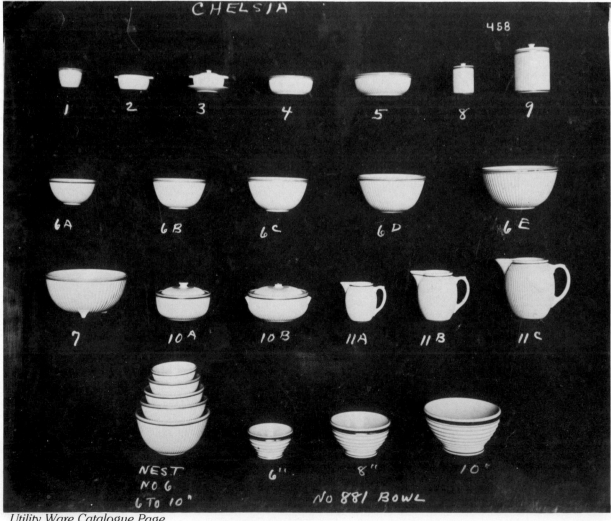

*Utility Ware Catalogue Page*
Courtesy Ohio Historical Society

354

# Blossom

Row 1:
1. Cornucopia, 6"; Marked Weller (in-mold script); $35.00 – $45.00
2. Planter, 4"; same mark; $40.00 – $60.00
3. Vase, 6"; same mark; $20.00 – $35.00

Row 2:
1. Basket, 6"; same mark; $50.00 – $60.00
2. Double Cornucopia, 6½"; same mark; $30.00 – $40.00
3. Vase, 5½"; #G-1; Weller Pottery Since 1872; $35.00 – $45.00

Row 3:
1. Cornucopia, 8½"; Marked Weller (in-mold script); $35.00 – $45.00
2. Vase, 9½"; same mark; $30.00 – $50.00
3. Vase, 9½"; same mark; $30.00 – $50.00
4. Ewer, 7"; same mark; $30.00 – $40.00

Row 4:
1. Double Vase, 12½"; #G-24; same mark; $125.00 – $150.00
2. Vase, 14"; Marked Weller (in-mold script); $150.00 – $200.00
3. Vase, 9½"; same mark; $75.00 – $100.00

*Utility Ware Catalogue Page*

Courtesy Ohio Historical Society

# Loru

**Row 1:**

1. Cornucopia, 4"; Marked Weller (in-mold script); $20.00 – $30.00
2. Bowl, 2½" x 8"; Weller Pottery Since 1872; $25.00 – $35.00
3. Same as #1, shown for color; $20.00 – 30.00

**Row 2:**

1. Bowl, 4"; Marked Weller (in-mold script); $30.00 – $40.00
2. Vase, 8½"; same mark; $25.00 – $35.00
3. Vase, 5"; same mark; $25.00 – $35.00

**Row 3:**

1. Vase, 8"; same mark; $30.00 – $40.00
2. Vase, 8"; No mark; $50.00 – $60.00
3. Vase, 10"; same mark; $40.00 – $45.00

**Row 4:**

1. Vase, 9½"; Weller Pottery Since 1872; $40.00 – $50.00
2. Vase, 11½"; No mark; $65.00 – $75.00
3. Vase, 11"; No mark; $60.00 – $70.00

*Utility Ware Catalogue Page*

Courtesy Ohio Historical Society

# Reno And Utility Ware

Row 1:
 1. Reno Custard, 2"; Marked Weller (die impressed); $8.00 – $15.00
 2. Reno Bowl, 3"; No mark; $8.00 – $15.00
 3. Custard, 2"; No mark; $8.00 – $15.00

Row 2:
 1. Mustard Pot with Metal Holder, 2½"; Marked Weller in relief (block letters); $30.00 – $40.00
 2. Bean Pot, 5½"; Weller (die impressed); $35.00 – $45.00
 3. Cup, 2"; Weller (die impressed); $15.00 – $20.00

Row 3:
 1. Tumbler, 4"; Weller (die impressed); $12.00 – $15.00
 2. Casserole, 5"; Weller (in-mold block letters); $35.00 – $55.00
 3. Mug, 4"; Weller (die impressed); $30.00 – $35.00

Row 4:
 1. Teapot, 4"; No mark; $30.00 – $40.00
 2. Casserole with Metal Holder, 5" x 7½"; Marked Weller in relief; $50.00 – $60.00
 3. Pitcher, 4"; Weller (in-mold block letters); $20.00 – $30.00

Row 5:
 1. Pitcher, 5½"; No mark; $30.00 – $35.00
 2. Casserole with Holder, 6" x 9½"; Weller (in-mold block letters); $50.00 – $60.00
 3. Pitcher, 6"; same mark; $35.00 – $45.00

## Utility Ware

*Row 1:*

1. *Pineapple Teapot, 6½"; Marked Weller (in-mold script); $160.00 – $170.00*
2. *Ollas Water Bottle, 11"; Underplate, 8½"; same mark; $65.00 – $75.00*
3. *Pumpkin Teapot, 6"; Weller Pottery (by hand); $110.00 – $135.00*

*Row 2:*

1. *Color Banded Covered Jar, 4½"; Marked with the half kiln ink stamp; $15.00 – $20.00*
2. *Flower Pot or Jar, 3½"; same mark as jar; $15.00 – $20.00*
3. *Kitchengem Pitcher, 5½"; same mark; $25.00 – $35.00*

*Row 3:*

1. *Cream Light Blue Banded Pitcher, 7"; No mark; $40.00 – $45.00*
2. *Pitcher, 5½"; Weller (die impressed); $25.00 – $35.00*
3. *Pitcher, 4½"; No mark; $25.00 – $30.00*
4. *Pitcher, 4"; No mark; $20.00 – $25.00*

## Pierre

*Row 4:*

1. *Sugar, 2"; Weller (in-mold script); $10.00 – $15.00*
2. *Creamer, 2"; same mark; $10.00 – $15.00*
3. *Pitcher, 5"; same mark; $22.00 – $30.00*
4. *Casserole with Plate; 5½", 3"; same mark; $15.00 – $20.00*

*Row 5:*

1. *Pitcher, 7½"; Weller Pottery Since 1872; $40.00 – $45.00*
2. *Cookie Jar, 10"; same mark as pitcher; $100.00 – $150.00*
3. *Teapot, 8½"; Weller (in-mold script); $60.00 – $70.00*

*We were delighted while in Zanesville to have lunch with Mr. William Curphey, Sam Weller's son-in-law and a vice president of the company. Over lunch he recalled many amusing anecdotes and bits of information pertaining to the Weller history. One subject he enlightened us on was the Ollas Water Bottle, modeled by Dorothy England in the late 1930's. The bottle was ordered by a customer who had bought a similar one in Paris. This type of water bottle had been made for years in North Africa—the gourd was unglazed, so that the water was absorbed, and as the moisture was evaporated from the surface of the ware, the contents were cooled. Although unattractive and not especially efficient, the idea was so novel to the public, that when they were introduced in Pittsburgh the store was sold out by 10:00 A.M. The order was quadrupled, and in five years, 200,000 Ollas Water Bottles had been sold. (The first ones were styled with a straighter neck.)*

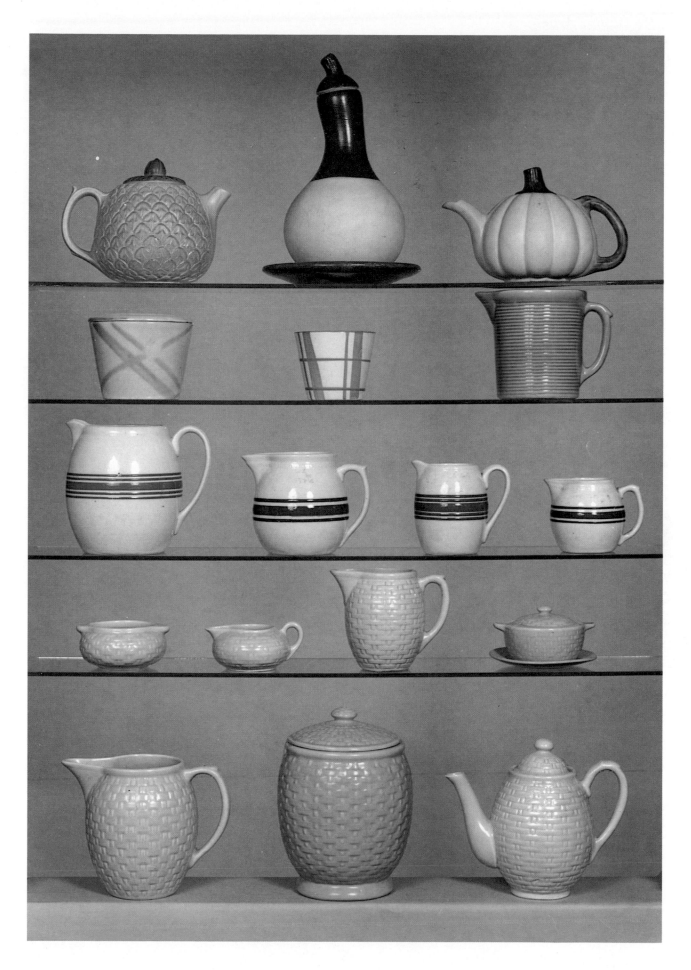

# Oils By Weller Artists

14" x 7",  Anthony Dunlavy; $500.00 – $700.00

16" x – 20",  K. Kappes; $1750.00 – $2250.00

12"x 8 ",  Minnie Mitchell; $650.00 – $850.00
1902

18" x 24", K. Kappes; $1800.00 – $2400.00

Tin  Basin – Hester Pillsbury; $450.00 – $600.00
1901

# Original Oils By Karl Kappes

*15" x 18", K. Kappes; $1400.00 – $1700.00*

*16" x 20", K. Kappes; $1400.00 – $1700.00*

*Fireplace Screen, 30" x 30"; $1400.00 – $1700.00*

*by C. Leffler*

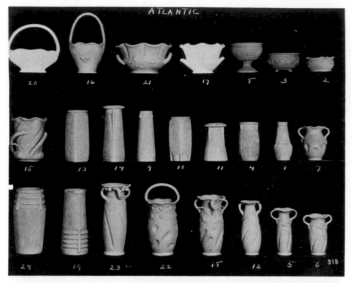

*Atlantic*

*Bronze Ware*

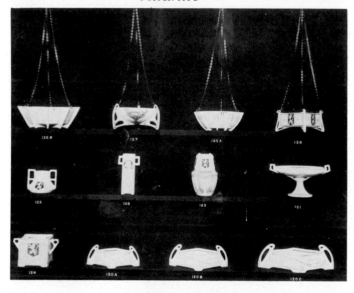

*Creamware*

*Creamware*

*Euclid*

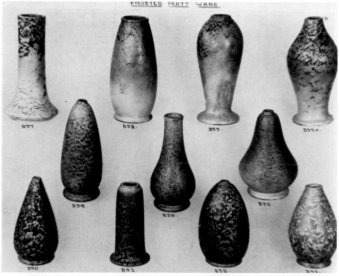

*Frosted Matt Ware*

*Fruitone*

*Ivory*

*Kenova*

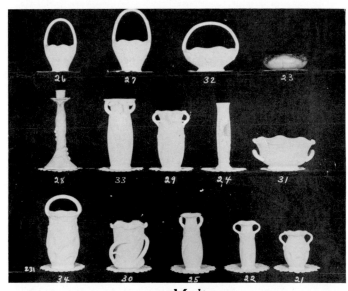

*Malta*

*Neiska*

*Nile*

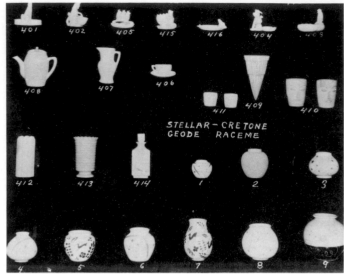

*Novelty*

*Orris Ware*

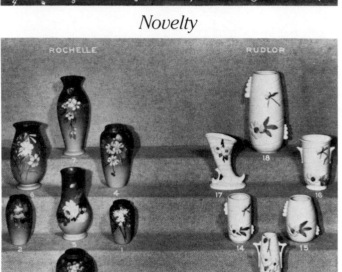

*Rochelle, Rudlor*

*Roma*

*Selma*

*Ting*

*Old Catalogue Sheets, Courtesy Ohio Historical Society*

Tupelo

Xenia

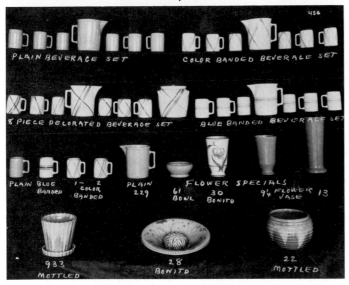

Tearose

*Old Catalogue Sheets,* Courtesy Ohio Historical Society

## The Walter M. Hughes Scholarship Fund

*Walter M. Hughes was born in Zanesville, Ohio, on March 23, 1902, the son of William C. and Grace McKinnie Hughes. He attended public school in Zanesville, graduated from Lash High School in 1920. He graduated from Ohio State University 1924 with a Ceramic Engineering Degree. Later, he received his Masters Degree. He was registered as a Professional Engineer by the Ohio State Board of Registration for Professional Engineers in 1946; and joined the American Encaustic Tiling Company, becoming its vice president. In 1933, he associated himself with the S.A. Weller Pottery firm where his father was a traveling representative for 42 years. Three years later, he was elected president of that company.*

*He was a modest and unassuming man who chose a splendid way of passing the fruits of his efforts and good fortune on to others. Recognizing and anticipating the mounting opportunities in ceramic engineering he made provision in his will to assist worthy young people of Muskingum County to obtain an education in this field.[28]*

# BIBLIOGRAPHY

1. Crooks, Guy E; "Brief History of the Pottery Industry of Crooksville"; Official Souvenir Program, Bi-Centennial Pottery Festival Issue; 1976.
2. Cox, Lucille T; *Successful Potters For 66 Years*; The Pottery, Glass, and Brass Salesman; Nov., 1938.
3. Zanesville and Muskingum Co. History; Samuel A. Weller
4. Crockery and Glass Journal, "Samuel A. Weller Dies"; Oct. 8, 1925.
5. Crockery and Glass Journal, "Three Score Years of Achievement"; Oct., 1931.
6. Evans, Paul; *Art Pottery of the United States;* Scribners, 1974,
7. Schneider, Norris; "Louwelsa Ware Skyrocketed Weller To National Prominence"; *Sunday Times Recorder*, Feb. 7, 1971.
8. Zanesville and Muskingum Co. History; "Weller Plant In Flames"; From the *Daily Signal.*
9. Personal Conversation with William Curphey.
10. Peck, Herbert; *The Book of Rookwood Pottery*; Bonanza Books. 1968.
11. Henzke, Lucile; *American Art Pottery;* Thomas Nelson, Inc. 1970.
12. Weller Art Pottery; Company Letter to Buyers and Clerks in China Departments of Retail Stores, unpublished.
13. Purviance and Schneider; *Weller Art Pottery in Color*; Wallace Homestead, 1971.
14. Fred Radford; *A Radford Pottery, His Life and Works*; Published by the Author, 1973.
15. Gitter, Josephine; "Pottery Industry in Muskingum Co., Ohio"; Bulletin of the American Ceramic Society.
16. Barber, Edwin A.; *Marks of American Potters*; Patterson and White, 1904.
17. Cook, May E.; *Our American Potteries*; Sketch Book; May 1906.
18. Schneider, Norris; "Sentimental Frenchman Left Mark on Pottery Here"; *Sunday Times Signal*, Jan., 1969.
19. Cobb, Laura M.; *A Visit to Some Zanesville Potteries*; Southwestern Book, Dec., 1905.
20. Crockery and Glass Journal; July 29, 1913; Aug. 14, 1913; July 3, 1916; July 20, 1916; Dec. 17, 1925.
21. Personal Conversation with Dorothy England Laughead.
22. Henzke, Lucile; Camark Pottery; unpublished.
23. Tiles and Tile Work, June 1930.
24. Henzke, Lucile; "A Visit With Naomi Walch, A Weller Artist"; Pottery Collectors Newsletter
25. Henzke, Lucile;"Clewell"; Pottery Collectors Newsletter.
26. Family of Merrill Weller, Genealogical Research.
27. Personal Correspondence with Charles Staley.
28. Pamphlet, Walter M. Hughes Scholarship Fund; provided by Mrs. Hughes.
    Zanesville and Muskingum Co. History, Local Potters Stood At the Wheel As Early As the Year 1808.
    Zanesville and Muskingum Co. History; The Weller Theatre.
    The Weller File, Original Catalogues, Records, on Deposit at the Ohio Historical Society Archives.
    Kovel, Ralph and Terry; *The Kovel's Collectors Guide to American Art Pottery;* Crown, 1974.

# INDEX TO COLOR PLATES BY LINES OF MANUFACTURE
## With Approximate Dates

The dates of manufacture listed below are shown either by a specific year (in which case that year was mentioned in an acceptable source of information); or by a period of time (i.e., early 20's, late teens, etc.), indicating an approximation suggested by trademark, by a style or decorative technique that could be related to a particular era, by lines obviously competitive with Roseville's production, or any other pertinent clues we could discover. In the absence of more accurate information, these sources gave us an indication within a few years, at least, of the production periods of some of the more obscure lines.

For your convenience, the numbers correspond to pages in the color plates where examples of each line are shown. Page numbers in parenthesis indicate a catalogue reprint (reproduced courtesy of the Ohio Historical Society Archives).

Lines marked with an asterisk are *not* official names, but are only suggested reference terms.

# INDEX

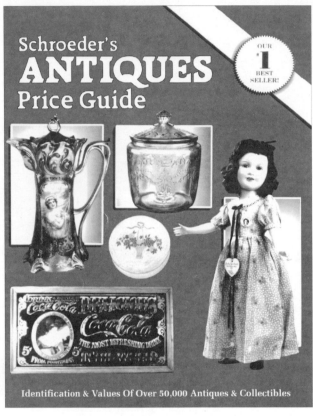